ANGOLA

ANGOLA

Louisiana State Penitentiary
A Half-Century of
Rage and Reform

by
Anne Butler
and
C. Murray Henderson

University of Louisiana at Lafayette Press

Other Books by Anne Butler (Hamilton)

James M. Imahara: Son of Immigrants

Little Chase and Big Fat Aunt May

Little Chase and Big Fat Aunt May Ride Again

The Little Chase and Big Fat Aunt May Recipe Book: A Cook's Tour of Hog Heaven

A Tourist's Guide to West Feliciana Parish: A Little Bit of Heaven Right Here on Earth

The Herman and Little Leon Stories

The Travels of Baby Stewart

More Than a Cookbook: An Eclectic Collection

Library of Congress Catalog Number: 90-82517
ISBN Number: 978-1-935754-55-8

University of Louisiana at Lafayette Press
P.O. Box 40831
Lafayette, LA 70504-0831
http://ulpress.org

Contents

Foreword

What's wrong with corrections in Louisiana today, or in America for that matter? We spend more to warehouse offenders than it would cost to restructure their lives and rehabilitate them into productive members of society. We seem to be getting nowhere fast, yet we keep trying the same old solutions. They never worked particularly well in the past, and they sure aren't going to work now.

What can we do? For one thing, we can start early, with childhood education programs designed to provide lifelong alternatives for potential lawbreakers. For another thing, we can learn from a provocative book like this one, thoroughly researched and written by a widely respected professional penologist and a Louisiana writer whose work I have long admired. The stories they have chosen to delve into in such great detail are ones from which we can gain great insight into the field of corrections, both its successes and its failures.

Besides having much to teach us, these stories entertain as well, for they are absolutely fascinating accounts moving from the commission of the crime through our court system into the very heart of Louisiana's prison system. By the end of each story, the reader has formed an intimate relationship with those involved, both victims and offenders, and not only knows but *cares* about them all. These are, remember, all people, after all.

Perhaps that's the main thing we must never forget in our quest for solutions to the problem of crime and correction. We are ultimately dealing not with caged animals, nor with inhuman robots far removed from our own experience, but with warm flesh-and-blood people. People with the right to be treated as human beings. At least some of them can be helped, if only we will learn how. While we may not agree with every solution suggested in this book, at least it makes us think, and that's the most important first step of all.

Governor John J. McKeithen
Columbia, Louisiana

Acknowledgments

Photos Furnished By: Anne W. Shoemake, retired Captain C. C. Dixon, Hazel Walters, JoAn Spillman Oubre, Russell Sonnier, Jack Favor family, Wilbert Rideau, Ron Wikberg, former Louisiana Governor Edwin W. Edwards, former Angola Warden Frank Blackburn, Nola Faye Cole.

We are grateful for the assistance of those listed here, as well as others who permitted us to interview them and so generously shared their experiences and perceptions, rummaging through memories and family photo albums, resurrecting painful feelings long buried, re-examining moments by choice forgotten and forever folded away in the attic closets of the mind.

We are grateful to Jeanne and Jerry Henderson for editorial and legal advice. We are also grateful for the courtesies extended by the present and former wardens and staff of the Louisiana State Penitentiary at Angola, Wade Correctional Center at Homer, and the Louisiana Department of Corrections.

Especially are we grateful to the inmates and victims and family members featured here for being so candid in sharing their very personal stories so that we might all learn something from them.

Introduction

One tried to swim his way out, masquerading in woman's finery which eventually dragged him beneath the raging waters of the encircling Mississippi River. Others tried to learn their ways out, educating themselves, improving themselves, rehabilitating themselves even into the national spotlight, only to find themselves after all still mired inescapably in the turbulent murky quagmire of Louisiana politics. Yet others tried merciless self-mutilation to rivet the attention of the press and an uncaring public upon brutalities of the system, and this worked, but only briefly.

Louisiana's immense and infamous penitentiary called Angola held them all. The more they struck out in despair and desperation and yes, violence, in protest against the system and the place, the more tightly it clutched them to its bloody breast, like a time-worn and ultimately irresistible tar baby. And so the ones who are not dead are still in there, but this book is not just about them, though their stories are fascinating enough.

The stories in this book provide intimate and heart-rending glimpses into what it was like to grow up black and deprived in South Louisiana and awaken to the dichotomy of what life promised and what it actually delivered—what it was like to grow up the privileged princess-daughter of the captain of the prison guard in a free enclave surrounded by inmate-slaves—what it was like to fight stubbornly to preserve life and limb and maybe even a modicum of dignity and manhood in the face of beatings and unspeakable savageries from free captains and armed inmate guards and fellow prisoners—what it was like to pay a debt to society and be so close to freedom it could be tasted and then get vindictively kicked back behind bars—what it was like to try to fight a suffocating system smothering the life out of an innocent inmate yearning for the wide-open wilds of West Texas—what it was like when certain officials sworn to uphold the law and protect the innocent instead seemed to try to protect the guilty for reasons still not entirely clear to this day.

And yet these stories are also as universal as they are unique, for in every penal system in the country may be found similar inmate case histories. Each case featured here has been carefully chosen to represent certain facets and failings in the American criminal justice system. Presented now for the first time in depth and detail, the stories represent months of meticulous research in archives, in exhaustive personal interviews, in historic materials as well as contemporary records, and in photographic evidence—combining facts and viewpoints never before put together. But besides being intriguing and moving case histories, these stories also provide a forum for one of the country's foremost professionals in the field to comment on what we need to do in this country and more specifically in this state to make our criminal justice system work.

At a time in the late sixties when the Louisiana State Penitentiary was at the height of what prison journalists call its "knock 'em down and drag 'em out" days, Angola, as the prison is familiarly known, was considered one of the nation's worst, a brutal world of violence and intrigue, political abuse and racial turmoil, where a staggering one in ten inmates would suffer stab wounds annually and others slept with thick mail-order catalogues taped to the chest to deflect knives in the night. Louisiana Governor John J. McKeithen requested advice on handling the situation from Dr. Preston Sharp, executive director of the American Correctional Association, and was given a single name, that of respected professional penologist C. Murray Henderson, a man unusually qualified to clean up the country's largest maximum-security penitentiary.

A Tennessee native, Henderson graduated from Carson-Newman College with a major in Sociology and obtained his law degree from John R. Neal College of Law in Knoxville. He would also receive a Masters degree in Psychiatric Social Work from the University of Tennessee, where his thesis was on state penitentiary inmates previously incarcerated in juvenile institutions. He completed additional work toward a Ph. D. in Sociology at Vanderbilt University, as well as further studies at Yale's School of Alcohol Studies, the University of Wisconsin in Correctional Administration, and the FBI Training Academy. This rare combination of legal training with sociological and psychiatric social work would provide a background eminently suited to a career in corrections.

After serving in the military for three and one-half years during World War II, Henderson was selected from a small group of recent college graduates for intensified internee training as military government experts on Germany, studying in great depth the different departments of military and civilian government--public health, legal, economic, export-import, welfare. His position also involved participation in meetings of the Allied four-power committee governing Berlin before the split, as well as working closely with the German judicial system in regards to both internal restitutions and criminal justice.

After three months in Wiesbaden in the state capital of Hesse and another three in county government in Giessen, a stint at the European Command Intelligence School at Oberammergau followed. Henderson led a military government detachment, first at Alsfeld in Hesse, then in Schwabisch Hall, where he had responsibilities for prisoners sentenced by American courts to the prison there and where he also became a Foreign Service officer with the State Department, functioning as the resident officer handling liaison between the German government and the military. From there he transferred to Karlsruhe as liaison between the French and American armies and German government, and was also responsible for intelligence in that area.

After four years in Germany, Henderson returned to the States for graduate school before accepting a position at the Tennessee Forensic Facility of Central State Hospital as director of adjunctive therapy, followed by a stint as associate warden of the Men's

Reformatory in Anamosa, Iowa. In 1965 he was appointed warden of the Tennessee State Penitentiary in Nashville and continued in that position until he was appointed warden of the huge Louisiana State Penitentiary at Angola, where he would leave a lasting mark.

Award-winning prison journalist Wilbert Rideau of *The Angolite* says Henderson, who won the respect of both inmates and prison officials alike, was "a popular warden, a corrections professional, but never so professional that he forgot the humanity of those he managed, both free and imprisoned. He was outspoken in his criticism of the justice system and penal practices, calling for a fairer, more rational and effective system, for shorter sentences, more humane treatment of prisoners, and for the state to mount a genuine effort to rehabilitate its offenders."

When Henderson arrived at Angola in March 1968, the sprawling institution had an unsavory reputation as one of the worst in the country, 18,000 isolated acres where since 1901 the state of Louisiana had held thousands of inmates, working them in farm fields under the supervision of unpaid and untrained but well-armed convict-guards. Henderson is credited with stablizing the volatile situation there, reducing official brutality and making substantial progress in the face of budget inadequacies and opposition from conservative traditionalists. Revitalizing neglected educational and vocational programs, Henderson encouraged self-help activities and rehabilitative programs, and it was also he who finally integrated the prison, hiring the first black correctional officers and the first women too. Says Rideau, an articulate spokesman knowledgeable about the Louisiana

C. Murray Henderson

correctional system's history, C. Murray Henderson was "the administrator Angola needed during those harsh years, a much better penal administrator than Louisiana deserved."

Henderson did not think the situation at Angola could possibly go anywhere but up and considered the appointment an outstanding opportunity to make a contribution in the field of corrections. The first year, however, his budget, only about $3.5 million for around 3500 inmates to begin with, was cut drastically, though afterward progress was fairly steady, if slow. With assistance from politicians like Secretary of Education Bill Dodd, a good vocational program was established at the prison, and the Louisiana State Library helped start an excellent inmate facility. Because trained salaried staff was in short supply, a lot of professional organizations were called upon to fill the gaps—the Jaycees, Dale Carnegie, Great Books clubs, Mensa and various religious groups with outside sponsors. "We improvised and did what we could with the meager resources we had," the former warden recalls.

Ordered by the courts to do away with armed inmate-guards but not given the funding to replace them with professionals, Henderson's major regret from his tenure at Angola remains that the transitional period was marred by too many unnecessary assaults due to insufficient security staff. But it would not be until 1975, the year he left Angola, that a federal court order would mandate additional improvements at the Louisiana State Penitentiary *and* the finances to implement them.

The stress of struggling with the constant crises common to any penitentiary setting, particularly in the face of budgetary constraints and Louisiana's traditional conservative resistance to progress, has tested the mettle of every superintendent and warden since Angola's earliest days, driving some to seek release in recreations like the fighting of game cocks or extracurricular amours, driving others to drink, and Henderson would admittedly have his own brush with the bottle, but only for a brief period. His record at Angola was recognized throughout the country as one of unquestioned excellence.

In 1972 the house of representatives of the state of Louisiana approved Concurrent Resolution No. 294 commending C. Murray Henderson for outstanding performance of his duties as warden of the Louisiana State Penitentiary, recognizing his innovative programs and improved facilities while praising him as "a nationally recognized expert in the field of penology" who from the day of his appointment "applied modern techniques of penology pursuant to his belief in the individual worth of a man and his innate ability to change, always with a view toward the rehabilitation of the inmate so that he may become a useful and productive member of society...."

One Sunday afternoon in October 1975, Henderson received a call from the governor of Tennessee, asking him to return to that state as commissioner of correction in charge of a department controlling several dozen juvenile and adult facilities. Henderson was ready to leave Angola, and did. During his tenure in Tennessee, he opened new facilities and made great strides toward increasing legislative and public appreciation of correctional problems, though his improvements would be overshadowed by the scandals involving the administration of Governor Ray Blanton.

Untouched personally by the troubles, Henderson stayed on at the request of the new administration until a replacement could be found, and then returned to Louisiana to take over as chief executive officer of the Feliciana Forensic Facility, the state institution for mentally ill criminal offenders which, like Angola, needed a firm hand to guide it away from outdated abuses and into the twentieth century. After eight years there, he had managed to turn the facility into one of the best in the country and had even gotten it accredited, previously considered an impossibility.

C. Murray Henderson thought he had retired from corrections for good on August 1, 1988, at the age of sixty-eight. Then the idea for this book came up, and he was back in the fray, selecting with great care those cases to be spotlighted and hoping his comments in print might have some positive impact on a system which continues to cry out for improvement.

"The broad cross-section of cases we've chosen to research and present in detail here represents various problems connected with the criminal justice system," the warden comments. "One prisoner, Jack Favor, for example, was obviously innocent, and information available to the judicial process from the very beginning of his ordeal could have cleared him before a miscarriage of justice cost him his health and seven years of his life. Other cases represent different types of psycho-pathology or sociological background factors, as well as historical prison practices blessedly replaced by more progressive methods these days. In nearly all of these cases may be observed the failure of some community agency to provide the necessary assistance or intervention; in the Ortego case in particular, early intervention by community resources might have prevented such a tragic outcome not only for the victim but for all members of the Ortego family as well. Throughout the chapters runs a repeated refrain stressing the significance of establishing a minimum-sentencing standard in Louisiana and the absolute necessity for an effective rehabilitation effort wholeheartedly supported by everyone from the inmates on up through the highest corrections officials."

Comments by former warden Henderson, pertinent to those representative criminal cases examined here, follow each individual section, shedding additional light on the situations and lending an expert's perspective. Most of the individuals he knew personally and well; one came through the system before his time, but all of their stories provide an opportunity for comment on the history of corrections, some potential solutions to its continuing problems, and those persons courageous enough to try to make improvements in it over the years.

Anne Butler

I

The Heel-String Gang and the Angel of Mercy

Besides a couple of mundane black hearts, career criminal Wallace McDonald sports a big tattoo on his left forearm lamenting "Born Too Late To Win" and one on his right forearm boasting "Too Damn Tough To Die." They tell the story of his life.

Born into a welfare family in Camden, Arkansas, in 1927, his father a "heart invalid" who rarely worked, McDonald grew up during the Depression, when the daring escapades of colorful criminals like Dillinger and Bonnie and Clyde made them much-admired heroes to deprived school kids. Though he says, ironically, that he was always stuck being J. Edgar Hoover during childhood games of Cops and Robbers, Wallace McDonald confesses, "I didn't even think it was wrong to steal until I got sent to the penitentiary. That was all we knew."

The boom years of war production brought an offer of work for his mother in a munitions factory in Louisiana, so the whole family moved in 1941 to Shreveport, where Wallace finished tenth grade before beginning his long association with the law. Several stints in the juvenile detention facility at LTI-Monroe were capped by a sentence to the federal reformatory on a charge of interstate car theft; it was at the National Training School in Washington, D.C., that he finally earned his high school equivalency diploma.

Car theft also sent McDonald, barely twenty, to the Louisiana State Penitentiary at Angola in 1947 for what would be the first of many stays there. Arriving at the worst possible time in the prison's history, McDonald would soon find himself inadvertently at the forefront of efforts to expose the brutality, overwork, and deplorable living conditions in a facility gaining national notoriety as America's worst prison.

Sprawling over 18,000 acres of rich river bottomland and thick timber on the east bank of the Mississippi River, vulnerable to floodwaters and surrounded by the rugged Tunica Hills wilderness area, Angola, as the country's largest maximum-security prison has been familiarly known through the years, was purchased in 1901 when the state at long last called a halt to the deplorable practice of leasing out its convicts to private profit-motivated lessees. The old lease system had seemed to the conservative, economy-minded voters and politicians of nineteenth-century Louisiana to be the perfect solution, at least for several decades, to the problem of what to do with state criminals. By leasing them before the turn of the century to big private operations like that run by Major S. L.

Vicinity map of Louisiana showing West Feliciana Parish.

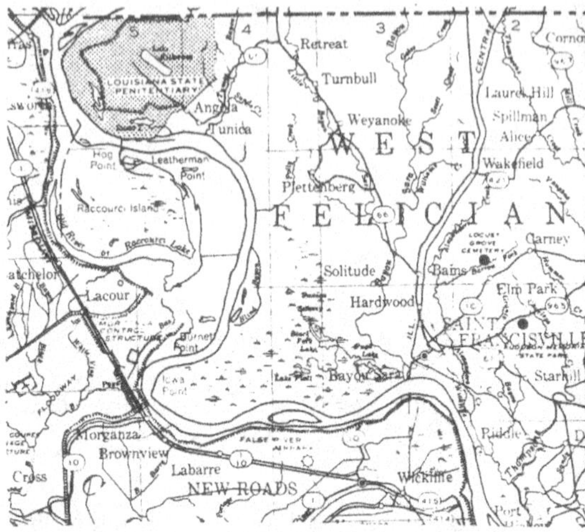

Louisiana State Penitentiary (shaded area) in West Feliciana Parish.

Major S. L. James
(Courtesy Anne Shoemake)

James at Angola Plantation (part of the current prison property), the state divested itself of the responsibility to house, feed, clothe or oversee prisoners, while at the same time actually bringing income into state coffers from their labors. Unfortunately for the prisoners, the lessees were uniformly interested only in seeing their personal profits soar, and did not care a fig that inmate death statistics leapt skyward at the same time due to brutal treatment and cruel overwork; in one of the worst years, more than two hundred convicts perished.

Even after the state terminated the convict lease agreements and resumed physical control of its inmates, abuses left over from lessee practice continued. New arrivals and first offenders were consistently thrown in with hardened career criminals and sex offenders, and "convicts" as young as seven years of age remained in the penitentiary until 1910, with the 1917 inmate census listing at least two black youngsters under the age of twelve, and thirty-one blacks and one white prisoner between twelve and sixteen, according to Mark Carleton's *Politics and Punishment: The History of the Louisiana State Penal System.*

Like the lessees, the penitentiary administration continued to classify new arrivals primarily according to their ability to perform heavy physical labor, then sent them out in gangs supervised by gun-toting mounted inmate-guards to build up the state levee system or to toil from dawn to dusk in penitentiary cotton or cane fields and sugarmill. Still, the motivation remained more to decrease the cost of upkeep, perhaps even turn a profit, than to teach the incarcerated, most from urban non-agricultural areas, any usable skills with a view toward rehabilitation or preparation for being productive members of society upon release.

Angola was, in the words of LSU history professor Carleton, "an economic and sociological anachronism." Its remote location sixty miles upriver from the nearest metropolitan area at Baton Rouge, its inadequate budget and consequent low pay scale, plus the abuse of political patronage, had ensured that what few paid staff the prison did have were, for the most part, untrained, unprofessional, and unfit. Under the supervision of camp captains, who dispensed floggings and other harsh punishments at their discretion with little interference from wardens, were no more than a few dozen underpaid guards to oversee several thousand convicts; they were supplemented by hundreds of convict-guards, armed with rifles and shotguns and under orders to shoot to kill anyone foolish or desperate enough to attempt escape.

Wallace McDonald would naturally be one of those who would try. Back in Angola for burglary and already a veteran of at least one escape attempt from reform school, he joined a group of thirteen convicts digging an escape tunnel. Caught, whipped severely and locked up in the old "Red Hats" cellblock for troublemakers, who wore straw hats with the crowns painted bright red for easier identification in the field, McDonald and seven other tunnellers would soon gain notoriety as what he calls the original Heel-String Gang.

The above picture, taken in 1949, shows the old front gate to be further east than the present front gate. Formerly known as the Tunica Gate, it has been the Main entrance for over eighty years. (Photo courtesy *The Angolite*.)

The Administration Building at Angola about 1951.
(Photo courtesy *The Angolite*.)

These buildings stand on the site of the slave quarters of the old Angola Plantation. The buildings, built in 1939, housed as many as 400 to 600 inmates on the top floor. The kitchen, dining room, showers and toilets were on the first floor.

The Red Hats, so named because incorrigible inmates housed here wore straw hats painted red. Built in April 1935 it was Angola's first cellblock and was used continuously until 1955 when the main prison was constructed. After that the building was used as a disciplinary cellblock and site for executions. It last housed inmates in 1972. (Photos courtesy *The Angolite*.)

This 1940s photo shows an icebox in the kitchen of one of the old camps. Angola made ice in 300 lb. blocks. The ice would be broken up and used to keep items cool in these boxes. Not until the fifties were refrigerators used. (Photos courtesy *The Angolite*.)

Old Camp Kitchen, circa 1940s (below). While the food in the 30s and 40s may not have been prepared to suit the taste of a gourmet, there was usually plenty of it. These gas pots were used to cook greens, peas, beans or cabbage grown on the penitentiary farm. Usually there was a gallon jug of blackstrap molasses on every table, made at the Angola sugarmill. Breakfast consisted of pancakes or biscuits and syrup. Lunch was greens, potatoes and cornbread. Supper was usually the same as lunch, with meat being served once per week.

Preparing cabbage for a meal in the 1940s. Inmates ate much of the food grown on the penitentiary farm. Here inmates clean cabbages in one of the old kitchens. (Photos courtesy *The Angolite*.)

White dormitory, probably in Camp E, during the years when the penitentiary was segregated. The above photo shows dormitory conditions before 1955. In such crowded conditions security was impossible, making rape, stabbing, and murder an everyday occurrence.

Inmate showers, probably at Camp C. Three legislative investigations in the 1940s recommended that the dormitories be demolished and new facilities built. This situation remained, however, until Camp C burned to the ground in April 1955. Below: These toilets, probably located at Camp A, were old when this picture was taken in the late 1940s. They nevertheless provided for the needs of four hundred inmates.

(Photos courtesy *The Angolite*.)

(Photo courtesy *The Angolite*.)

Camp D, the women's camp, was built in 1901 to hold thirty female inmates. These wooden dormitories (example above) were used until 1958 when the women were moved to Camp F, renamed "The Willows." In 1961 female prisoners were moved to a facility at St. Gabriel, La. Below, women make pinstripe (trusty) uniforms in the early 1950s.

(Photo courtesy *The Angolite*.)

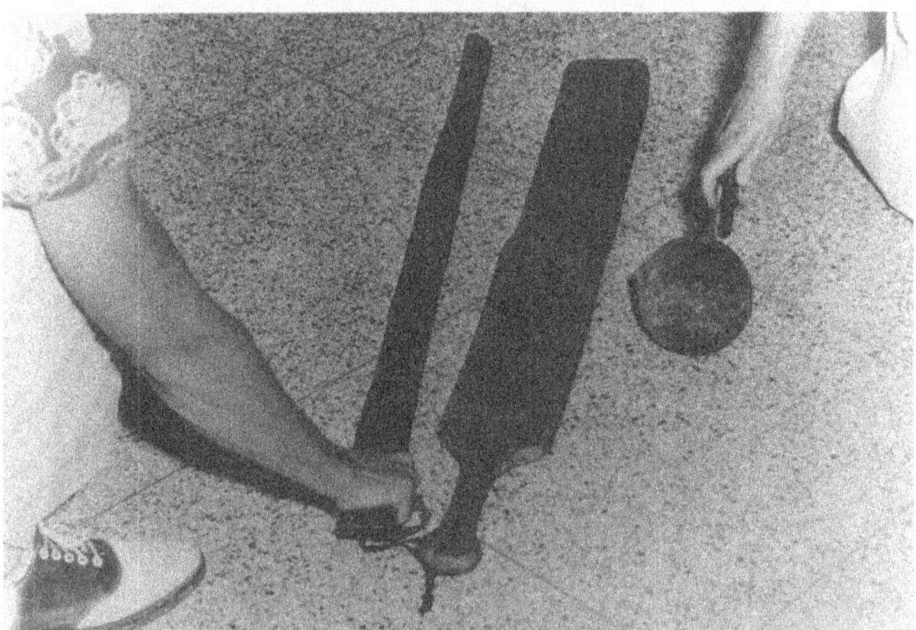

The Hole (isolation) at Camp A (opposite, above) in the late 1940s. The camp captain determined length of inmate's stay. Inmate was given a biscuit, greens, and a cup of water per day. A bucket served as a toilet. Opposite (below): paddles and belts used on inmates before reforms introduced. Right: Inside a cell of The Hole, 1952. There were no provisions for plumbing, water, or light. The only sources of ventilation were a small grill on the door and a pipe in the roof. The bed in this picture is unusual; normally, there was no bed in a cell. Below: The Hole was demolished a few minutes after the above picture was taken. (Photos courtesy *The Angolite*.)

He tells it this way. "There was two brothers, 'Big Marse' they called one, Clifford Leake I think his name was, and 'Little Marse' Leake; they were line pushers, and they were tough. You got exactly what you asked for. We was out in the field hoeing cane, hoeing grass out of the sugar cane, and one of us walked out to the quarter drain or the edge of the ditch. One of them guards cut down with an automatic rifle and blasted his hoe handle. And 'Big Marse' he come down in the field and told us, 'All of you old tunnel diggers, Warden Easterly done issued orders to kill all of y'all so he can close y'all's records.'"

Though he would several months later be pictured in the New Orleans *Times-Picayune* telling an investigative committee that in all his twenty-three years at Angola he'd never lost his temper, hit or cussed prisoners, or had a prisoner resist him, "Big Marse" Clifford Leake would be identified by some of the heel-stringers as the man who beat them. Other free guards would later comment that "Big Marse" was so handsome he reminded them of big-screen heroes like Rock Hudson, but inmates remember the two brothers as tough bosses of the "big line" (in which convicts were hustled on foot to and from their work in the distant farm fields) who had little formal education.

Stories circulated of a sanded section of two-by-four lumber "Little Marse" customarily carried to discipline inmates and impress new arrivals, and one former inmate recalls that "Little Marse" had to keep track of the number of inmates under his supervision by means of a unique system of his own devising. Apparently unable to count, "Little Marse" would put a pebble into his pocket for each convict checked out to his charge, later removing a pebble for each as he checked them back into the fenced compounds at nightfall.

Fearing for their very lives, the tunnel-diggers knew, McDonald says, "they weren't joking." They considered their options, which were sorely limited. Their contact with the outside world was next to nothing, and closely supervised at that. Only an act of such desperation as to make it eminently newsworthy might attract the attention of the press and thence the public, and only the press and public were capable of raising an outcry strong enough to influence the administrations of the prison and the state. Eight of these men decided, toward the end of February 1951, to savagely sever at the ankle the Achilles tendon running up the back of one leg, thereby permanently crippling themselves and ruling out future hard labor in prison fields where a supposed escape attempt would make it easy to "close their records" without fear of censure.

"We decided to try to get the news to the outside," McDonald remembers, "by cutting our heel strings and then trying to get the word out from the old hospital. I had an old GM razor blade with a stiff metal top, a single-edged blade. It didn't hurt much, just a little sting, but when that tendon let loose and flew up your leg, you could sure feel that. There were eight original heel-stringers, and I was one. The heel-slashings were built up by all the media hype, but it was strictly a personal thing; there wasn't nothing political about it. The heel-stringing wasn't no more political than the man in the moon.

"They hauled us over to the hospital. We didn't have no doctor then. Mrs. Mary Margaret Daugherty was the nurse; without her, we was dead. She was the only doctor we had back then; without that nurse, we'd have been crippled. She reached up in there and pulled that tendon down, then sewed it back together. We smuggled letters out to the *Shreveport Times* and the New Orleans *Picayune* to tell them what was going on, and Mrs. Daugherty stood up to the warden when he came with a bus and convict-guards to get us.

"All of us had a spare razor blade and we just pulled the other leg up and whacked it too. There were eight double heel-stringers [newspaper accounts of the times say ten]. After the warden left, we sent word to Camp E and Camp H to send us some heel-stringers, and they started cutting, too. I think all together there was nearly forty [newspaper accounts say thirty-seven]. Three original ones I remember were Ace Olsen, Johnny Folkes and a Sullivan. We were crippled for awhile, and I still feel the effects forty years later, but when the papers published the stuff we sent out, Governor Earl K. Long sent troopers and a commission to Angola."

When reporters questioned the hospitalized heel-stringers shortly after the news of the slashings broke, the men all told the same story. "We just couldn't stand it any longer," the *Times-Picayune* quoted one. "We'd rather be here [in the hospital] than take the beatings we have to take over there [in the prison camps]." Prison officials attempted to divert the focus of the incident by alleging it was connected with a plot to poison guards with cyanide stolen from the hospital (a dog, fed one suspicious sandwich, died), trotting out a newfound prison physician (an ENT specialist later hired as a consultant there) who called the heel-string injuries "not necessarily" permanent, and making allegations of homosexual jealousy, power struggles and publicity seeking among prisoners.

The committee Governor Long named to investigate allegations of brutality was composed of thirty-four members, mostly with media or law enforcement connections, and was chaired by Dolph Frantz, editor of the Shreveport newspaper which first broke the news of the heel-cuttings. Under the guidance of Frantz and vice-chairman Margaret Dixon, longtime prison reform advocate and managing editor of the Baton Rouge *Morning Advocate*, committee members refused to allow the focus of their investigations to be diverted from allegations of mistreatment and inadequacies in prison facilities and policies.

McDonald describes what the investigative commission members and the newspaper reporters swarming all over Angola found: 2700 convicts of all types were crowded together in unsanitary wood-floored dormitories in close rows of double bunks, where gambling was the main recreation, violence settled all differences, hot water was available only when the sugarmill was running, clean clothes were issued once a week and meals consisted mainly of cornbread and vegetables, the guards having confiscated what little meat was issued. The menu, reporters were told by convicts, did vary from day to day; "some days we get white beans, some days it's red beans."

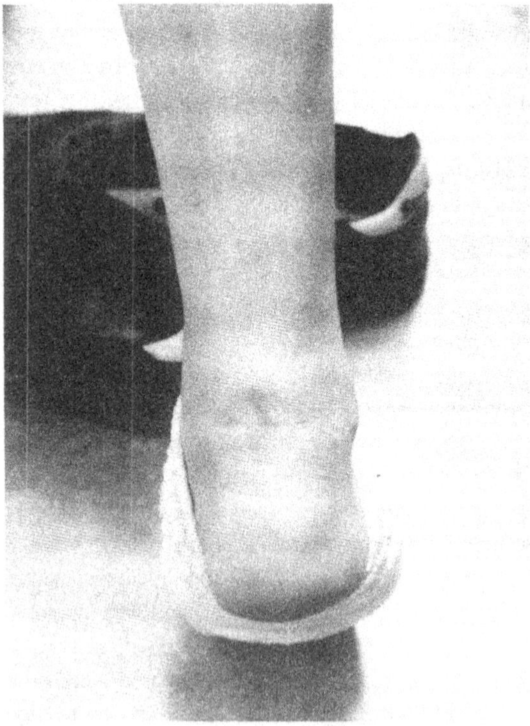

Above left
Wallace McDonald in 1949

Above right
Wallace McDonald in 1990

Opposite
McDonald's slashed heel

Above: Members of the prison enquiry committee gather at Angola to begin their investigation of prison conditions. Seated, with glasses, is committee chairman Dolph Frantz. Standing behind Frantz is vice chairman Margaret Dixon. Below: the committee tours the grounds of Angola. (Photos courtesy *The Angolite*.)

One repeat prisoner, Wilbur "Blackie" Comeaux, described Angola as a place that "ain't fit for hogs," describing how "in the 'long line' we had to run out to the fields and run back, and a lot of us couldn't keep up with the [guards'] horses. Older men got whipped because they fell back. I saw men eat out of bloody plates; the blood come from their own heads." One inmate who had talked to newspapermen was "kicked around like a football" by a guard captain afterward, according to Comeaux, and another was shot in the arm for leaving the work line to "attend a necessary function" in the fields. As for the heel-stringers, Comeaux said, "Those cons don't want to be beat to death, and with a lot of them that's what they get.... They try to kill the cons on the farms." When the first heel-cuttings occurred, Comeaux insisted, Warden Easterly was in one of the camp offices, where he saw him, not off the farm and "distracted by family illnesses," as claimed to reporters.

The investigative commission also discovered at Angola one Mary Margaret Daugherty, considered by the inmates as their "one ray of hope" whose bright light shone through the murk. In her courageous testimony Daugherty described the situation at Angola as a "sewer of degradation" where "sex offenders, stool pigeons, homosexuals, degenerates of every type, and psychopaths and neurotics are huddled in bedside companionship with the new arrivals in huge dormitories that as one inmate described to me are filthy and stink like the hold of a slave ship. On every side the eyes of the newcomer rest on scenes of abnormality." Angola, Nurse Daugherty asserted, was "still in the dark ages, isolated and remote." Without adequate rehabilitation, which she insisted should be the aim of imprisonment rather than simple punishment, "convicts gaining their freedom stagger into a strange world outside with which they cannot cope."

An Irish lass who "really wanted to be a doctor, but back then they frowned on lady doctors," Nurse Daugherty had studied for her profession in Beaumont, Texas, where she had relatives, graduating from nursing school in 1942. She had gone to Angola, after some private duty, and after she married an employee. "When I married him, he was working up there, and I wasn't too elated about going up there, but it was his job, and it was a state job, and he seemed to like it. He was captain of the hospital, so that's why they insisted on asking me to take the medical side of it over. I was the first nurse to nurse at the Louisiana State Penitentiary," she recalls, "and there were no doctors there at the time.

"I was there seven and a half years until I resigned in 1951 after the commission investigation. I was about the first one called up by the committee investigating the heel-slashings, and I asked why, because there were many people there with thirty and forty years' service. So they told me that the reason they had called me was that they had had about 300 or 400 men come through the committee room before they started investigating, and only about ten of them did not mention my name. 'See the lady,' the inmates begged them, 'see the madam,' 'see the nurse.' And I was ready to testify. Of course the press was there, and they asked me if whatever I said could be printed. And I said, 'Yes, whatever I say can be printed *and proven.'*

"So I went on from there. It wasn't very pleasant, but I didn't appreciate the fact that these fellows—they were hard criminals and so forth and so on—but I don't think that they deserved the brutality that they got. And of course no one saw that any more than I did. There were no doctors there. There were no doctors that *wanted* to be there. And so it was up to me. I did a lot of things that I probably didn't have any business doing, but it was either take the ox out of the ditch or let him drown. And I've had one or two doctors to say that they wouldn't bother with these old cons. So the heels, that started when all of this brutality came up.

"There were about eight of the inmates came into the hospital. They had been whipped in the fields that day, and somehow or another had gotten this razor blade, and each one of them had cut his Achilles tendon and passed it [the blade] on to the other. And the warden was looking at them and there was the sheriff looking at them, there were several of them there, and I just crunched, I just couldn't know what to do. Because they knew that if they cut that Achilles tendon, they couldn't walk. So there was no doctor there. I couldn't *get* a doctor. And I just said well, we had a nice set-up in the operating room where we did surgery when we had doctors, like appendectomies and hernias and things of that nature. So anyway I sewed them up; there was no one there that could help, and I couldn't just let them ... what could I do? I knew what I *could* do to help them, because I had a lot of experience in the operating room when I was a student. In fact they used to sneak me up the back stairs in the afternoon after hours when they'd do surgery at the hospital where I took nursing training, because they knew I liked to help with surgery, and I spent five years in surgery at the Baton Rouge General. So I sewed them up and then I gave them the tetanus shot, and they all got well. The Achilles tendon, when you cut it, it falls apart, so you have to reach down with the hemostat to hold one part so you can suture the rest of it. They may walk with a limp, but they are fortunate to walk at all.

"I'm sure the heel-stringing was caused by mistreatment," she continues, though she told the committee that she did not believe the self-mutilations were done simply to escape whippings or beatings, but rather were desperate acts, "the culmination of many things joined together to destroy their morale and warp their minds." Today she still feels that way. "I still feel that there's a way besides being brutal. I know some of them have committed some horrible crimes, but I think, maybe not all of them but some of them could be re-evaluated and given a chance. Like I say, I don't condone what these men have done, but then I don't have the right to brutalize them, either. There must be a better way. The way I feel about it, there is no problem that cannot be solved; there's some way, some how, to get around it, if you just sit down like normal human beings and talk about it."

The brutality to prisoners which so offended Nurse Daugherty stemmed mostly from the free guards, not the convict-guards; "the others would get them if *they* tried it." The problems were with "mostly the guards that were in the field with the prisoners. A lot of them couldn't even write their names, and some of the inmates would come maybe from New Orleans or Shreveport or some of these areas and did not know what a cane knife looked like. And they'd say, 'Well, Boss, show me how to cut the cane.' Well, then, it was 'Blankety blank blank blank,' from the Boss. And of course the boy would say, 'Well, Boss, I don't know.' Well, then, they considered that to be talking back to the Boss, so then the inmate was whipped or he was punished in some way or another."

A lack of education and professional training colored the relationships of these free guards with the inmate population under their control. "I'll give you one example," says Nurse Daugherty. "I had one boy that worked in my yard; I didn't want them [convicts] in the house. And this Christmas, he got a check for $5 from one of his family, one member of the family. So I said, 'John,' I said, 'here's a check that you got for Christmas, and if you sign it, I'll get your money for you.' So he put his X on there and he smiled, and I said, 'Well, you're happy about getting this check.' And he said, 'No, Miss,' he said, 'that's not what I'm smiling about.' And I said, 'What's so funny?' He said, 'Well, last time I got this check,' he said, 'the Bossman said, *Here, old nigger, sign this and I'll get your money*. So I put my X on there. And the Bossman, he said, *What do you mean, putting my signature on that check!'* I mean, I heard so many things like that."

Punishments were cruel and sometimes bordered on the sadistic. "There was one man that I knew, that I saw, apparently he was out of New Orleans," recalls the nurse, "he was about a twenty-two or twenty-three-year-old boy and did not know anything about cane knives, and he told the Boss. So he got some vile language thrown at him. I think he spoke up, but anyway when he came in from the fields that afternoon, the guards put him out on the post, outside of I think it was Camp A that was close to the hospital. They had his hands fastened up on the post, with his feet barely touching the floor, all night long. And they gave him a big dose of castor oil. And he was messed from the top to the bottom. And I saw that as I drove up, and I called out to the warden and I told him about it and I said, 'Please, take this man down and let him come to the hospital and let me see what the problem is.' I had the orderlies that were in the hospital cleaning up freshen him up and put him in a bed. Of course that was when he told me he didn't know what a cane knife was. And that the guard had told him that he [the guard] had been off that weekend and found his [the inmate's] wife to be a good bed partner. See, these are the things that I would hear, but they were afraid to tell anyone else. I couldn't do anything about it, except medically, which I thought was my duty. At that time I was the only one they had to turn to."

Into even the worst of the camps and dormitories, Daugherty could carry her mission of mercy without fear, even when the guards themselves were afraid to accompany her. "I even went into the Red Hats," she says of the notorious holding facility for Angola's worst offenders. "There was one boy there that was in a coma, and the guards said it wasn't safe to take him out. I said, 'Well, if he's in a coma, either come here or I'll come there.' So I went into the Red Hats. The boy had diabetes, so I gave him some insulin and he snapped right out of it. Oh yes, the guards were afraid to go in. Yes. But I didn't mind going into the Red Hats. The odor, though, would knock you down. They had just little bitty rooms with a toilet, and they had to bring in the water to flush it; they got their drinking water from the same place, too. That's all they had in there."

That was only one of many times the nurse ventured in where guards feared to tread. "A lot of the problems there came from the dope and the girl-boys [homosexual relationships]. The convicts would fight over the girl-boys and dope. In the kitchen at Camp E, that was the bad camp at that particular time, they were fighting over a girl-boy. One of them had a cleaver, and he hit this man right in the chest. But not before the other man got another knife before he fell, and he hit this man in the forehead, across the forehead, but didn't reach the bone. So of course the one that had it through the heart, he dropped right there. And there was no doctor there, no doctor, so they called me up. And the guards were all around and they said, 'We're afraid to let you in, because they might use you as a hostage.'

"They were all standing in a row. And Charlie Frazier was the head inmate; they knew about Charlie, what he did. So I had the ambulance there and I was thinking, so I said, 'Well, let me talk to the men.' So I said to the inmates, 'Well, there's one man on the floor and from the looks of it, he's lost so much blood he's not living, he's dead, and the other man is going to die. So I'm going to take both of them to the hospital, but first,' I said, 'I just want four men, two to take this one and two to take the other, and I would like the others to move eight feet backward.' So I went in and brought the two men in the ambulance, no problem. The inmates knew that I didn't approve of what they'd done, but they also knew if they got in a fix, as far as my profession was concerned, that I was going to do what I could to help, which I did. I can't see someone dying and not doing anything about it."

Nurse Daugherty tried desperately to get a doctor to come to Angola, but was successful only to the extent that some New Orleans Charity Hospital interns would spend off weekends at the prison, though by the time of the commission investigation there was a nominal Angola physician who stepped forward to testify for the warden (he did admit he had only been employed there briefly). The doctors from the surrounding area, she recalls, were not always enthusiastic about coming the long distances to Angola even to treat the free people or guards who lived on prison grounds.

"There was this prison guard," the nurse remembers, "he was up on the guard tower and he was cleaning his gun, and he made a mistake. I guess he put the gun the wrong way, but he shot this muscle, down to the bone, and they brought him in to the hospital. His blood pressure was down to nothing, and I couldn't get a doctor. There was one doctor from Jackson that finally agreed to come in. I pressure-bandaged the guard and started an IV and I checked his blood to see if he needed some, which he did, so we got about four pints of blood. By the time the doctor got there, the patient had no pressure at all, just about fifty over nothing, so I explained that to the doctor. And the doctor stood right there with his arms folded.

"So I said, 'Well, doctor, would you like me to remove the pressure bandage or what would you like me to do?' He said, 'Well, little miss, you've done everything,' he said, 'and he's gonna die anyway, and I've got to get back to my office.' So I called the Charity Hospital in New Orleans and I explained the situation, so they said to put him in the ambulance and bring the blood and they said, 'You come with him.' So they took me in the operating room and they gave him about six pints of blood, and the man I'm sure is living today. When the inmates would come in, I'd always take a sample of blood, and if they had syphillis, which back then so many of them did, well, then I'd have to do the spinal tap on them and we'd treat them. These are the things that I did."

If the doctors from the outside world did not relish coming into Angola, Nurse Daugherty, word of whose compassionate skill had spread beyond the gates, did not mind stepping out into their world. "I even had to deliver babies," she remembers. "They had the women's camp at Angola at the time. Of course, when an inmate's baby was delivered, the family come got the baby. But when they found out up in the Tunica Hills that I could deliver, they used to call me out there, too. They had a poor midwife; she called me at two o'clock in the morning and she said, 'Miss Nurse, I can't birth this baby.' So I said, 'Well, where will I find you?' And she said, 'Well, her husband will be down the road and he'll have the lantern.' So the lantern was going, just aswinging in the darkness, and I got there and the man said, 'Miss, can you ride a horse?' And I said,'Yes, I can ride a horse.' So I had to go way up into the Tunica Hills to deliver this baby. The mother already had about eight or nine, and you know what they had on the bed? Paper! Of course I had brought my own OB pack and I had everything that I needed to deliver children. It was about that time when MacArthur, I think, was going back down to the Philippines. So the mother said, 'Can you give me a name for this baby?' And I said, 'Let's call it General MacArthur.' They like those kinds of names anyway. I guess I delivered about eight or nine babies anyway in the Tunica Hills."

Besides utilizing her nursing skills to help suffering inmates, the nurse tried to help in other ways as well, sometimes relying on woman's intuition. "I know of one case when I was there, I'm not going to mention names," she says, "that he was in for rape, a fine boy, good education, college education, and he happened to be my typist. And there was someone come in for rape that day, and the big tears run down his eyes. I said, 'Well, I know that you're thinking about the past, but just ask the Lord to forgive you and just forget it.' But he said, 'Mrs. Daugherty,' that was my name then, he said, 'I did not rape this woman; I dearly loved her.'

"And he said there were twelve men on the jury, and all the others wanted to hang him or electrocute him, whatever it was, but one said no, so he got life. And after listening to his story, I went to the priest and I went to the minister, and I told them all about it. In fact, I talked to my husband first, and he said, 'Now, honey, you can't believe everything that they tell you,' and I said, 'I know this, but somehow or other in the back of my mind there's something different here.' So they did re-open the case, and when they re-opened the case, the mother went all to pieces and so did the daughter, and come to find out that the mother was in love with the boy, and the daughter was told to holler rape. And the boy was released. It's just things like that that I did to try to help."

The compassionate and caring Nurse Daugherty made an outspoken witness for the Citizens' Committee appointed by Governor Earl Long to look into allegations of brutality and mistreatment at Angola, but not before the prison warden tried to talk her out of testifying. Appointed in 1950 by the governor, Warden Rudolf Easterly had a background in farming and had also been a sheriff and state legislator representing Livingston Parish, giving him sufficient political acumen to know he would be in hot water should conditions at Angola be inspected too closely.

"I'm sorry to say," Nurse Daugherty reveals, "Warden Easterly came to my house and spent about two hours that night to tell me that there was nothing wrong, that he knew I was going to be called before the committee and all I would have to do would be to say that everything was ok and nothing was wrong. And he said, 'You'll have a job, you'll have a job for the rest of your life, and you can name your price.' And what I'm telling you is the truth. So I listened, and I talked to him and I talked to him.

"So about ten o'clock that night—I know the poor fellow is dead now—I said, 'Well, I'm looking at so many hundreds of inmates just looking at me to tell the truth, and I'm looking at a handful of politicans to tell me everything is ok. And I'm a registered nurse; I'm proud of my nursing, and I plan to keep it up. And I'm not going to lie for anyone.' So I said, 'Now, you don't *have* to put me in front of that committee.' And he said, 'Well, they're going to ask for you.' And I said, 'Well, I'm sorry.' So that's how that went."

And when this lovely blue-eyed Irish lass stood up to tell the truth as she saw it to the Citizen's Committee investigating the prison, she blistered their ears and opened their eyes to the horrors of America's worst prison. Brutality in the form of whippings and beatings, and the total lack of rehabilitation were Angola's worst problems, Nurse Daugherty testified, followed closely by political interference. The prison was "a political football and dumping grounds for the state of Louisiana," where patronage abuses assured the continuation of a staff almost totally untrained and unqualified for work with prisoners.

For her efforts in demonstrating to the committee how rampant drugs and immorality were in the prison (she produced as proof an envelope of heroin and pictures of nude women procured for $5 behind bars), she was threatened with prosecution by the longtime local sheriff, Teddy Martin. Nevertheless, the determined nurse told all she knew as truthfully as she could, and then, on April 3, 1951, to deprive Warden Easterly of the pleasure of firing her, she resigned to keep from ending her career "by being fired by an arrogant, uncouth, narrow-minded, unprincipled bigot."

In despair at the thought that the committee's findings might be ignored, Mrs. Daugherty issued a resignation statement asking, "How can I continue to fight against such power? If the committee's recommendations are to be discarded, what can I do here alone?" Citing the constant turmoil at the prison since Easterly took over as warden the preceding August, the nurse bitterly denounced what she called his haphazard policies and said, "With him now in sole charge, I have no desire to stay at Angola to witness the carnage in human lives and taxpayers' property that can be wrought by petty despots and rotten politicians."

Some two weeks later, the committee released its findings, concurring that the heel-slashings had resulted from excessive brutality and recommending a number of long-needed reforms at Angola, including the establishment of a rehabilitation program, the hiring of a qualified penologist free of political influence to act as warden, abolition of corporal punishment and dungeons, a merit system for hired personnel, segregation of first offenders and incorrigible or perverted convicts from the general prison population, removal of the women's camp elsewhere in the state, prompt action on clemency recommendations, and stepped-up efforts to eliminate drug trafficking.

It would not be until the administration of the next governor, Robert F. Kennon, who made prison reform one of his highest priorities and furnished millions of dollars to fund improvements in physical facilities and staff, that much attempt was made to implement many of these improvements. But the winds of change were blowing, kicked up by the Heel-String Gang and their outspoken Angel of Mercy.

Mary Margaret Daugherty, now Mary Margaret Daugherty Charouleau, twice widowed, has retired from a lifelong career in nursing, but remains just as outraged as ever over the abuses she witnessed firsthand at Angola in the forties and early fifties. When told that inmates at Angola, forty years later, still talk about how she helped, she says quietly, "Well, I tell you, I wouldn't want to go through that again. I don't really even particularly want to talk about it. I think you'll find everything I say was so. I have nothing to hide, let me put it that way. The only support I got was from the inmates and of course the reason why they supported me was because they knew I was going to try to do something to help them, and that was why. But that was it. I did what I could and I tried; I reached out for help and couldn't get it."

And grayhaired Wallace McDonald, who at age sixty-two walks with a barely discernible limp, is back at Angola, serving a sentence of up to fifty-five years for an armed robbery that netted $220, after which a Detainer would place him under the jurisdiction of the Florida Department of Probation and Parole. Proud of the notoriety gained when, working in the modular furniture unit of a Florida prison, he welded layers of sheet metal around a forklift to make a veritable tank which he drove right through the front gate, guards shooting off all the paint, McDonald is a veteran of numerous escape attempts, some successful. He has job skills in electronics and mechanics, has married three times and had children, but just can't seem to stay out of jail. "I've been in and out all my life," he says. "Why? Stupidity, ignorance, hard to learn. But I've always been a working man, trying to supplement low pay with petty crime. I ain't never hurt anybody in my life."

In some ways he preferred life at Angola in the old days. "Back then," he reminisces, "if you did your work, minded your own business, the people who ran the place didn't worry. They had dope back then, they had whiskey back then, they had escapes back then, and they got 'em now. Now you got better living conditions, don't work as hard and got no corporal punishment, but you ain't got no hope. You can just forget it. Before, you at least had a chance to get out."

So Wallace McDonald sits behind bars, never quite reaching the folk-hero heights of glamourized Depression-era criminals like Dillinger or Bonnie and Clyde, yet still considering himself strangely invulnerable to the guns blazing around him during wild escape tries. *Born Too Late To Win, Too Damn Tough To Die.*

The Warden Comments: Representing the birth of real reform at Angola, this heel-cutting incident was symbolic of deep and serious problems in Louisiana's correctional system, many of which stemmed from having a system which in actuality bordered on legalized slavery. Based as it was on the very same historic free-labor plantation system which in large part caused the demise of the Old South, the penitentiary at Angola as it was initially set up presented a system nearly impossible to salvage, a system from its very roots fraught with corruption, excesses, and abuse.

At the time the state acquired the Angola property to build the prison, the motivating reason was not a humane one, but rather to earn a profit. State politicians were aware that the private contractors who leased and worked the inmates before 1901 were making profits, so they felt the state could make money by it, too.

Conditions for inmates were inhumane; poorly clothed, poorly fed, forced to work long hours in horrendous circumstances, many would lose their feet from frostbite after working barefooted in frozen fields, and many more would succumb to rampant disease which ravaged the inmate population unchecked. Brutal beatings and violence would account for large numbers of additional inmate deaths each year, for many of the earliest overseers considered the convicts under their control *for* punishment, not *as* punishment.

With profit the primary goal, with the few salaried employees largely untrained and unprofessional, with armed convicted felons guarding other inmates, was it any wonder that the system was rife with abuse? Yet things had always been done that way, and a conservative public and economy-minded politicians saw no real necessity for change until the heel-cutting incident precipitated unprecedented public scrutiny of conditions at Angola.

By this period in the penitentiary's history, it was already traditional that a well-established hierarchy of resident free families in effect controlled the prison and its operations, handing down jobs from generation to generation. While there have always been some dedicated good men at Angola, there have also always been others unqualified for working with the incarcerated, and it would be from this latter group that the most shocking abuses would spring.

It was not until the heel-slashing incident that real prison reform began in Louisiana, when the administration of Governor Robert Kennon recruited Maurice Sigler as warden

Maurice Sigler
(Photo courtesy *The Angolite*.)

and Reed Cozart as superintendent at Angola. Both had excellent credentials as professional penologists as well as experience with the federal prison system, and they did a remarkable job in transforming Angola from a totally unstructured prison lacking written policy or procedures, rules or regulations.

When I came to Angola in 1968, I could still see evidence of their administration, although many of the improved policies they implemented were no longer being followed; at least the outline was there, and it provided a foundation to build on. The problem in Louisiana corrections has traditionally been that even when a recognized professional is at last brought into the system, funds to institute his suggested improvements are not forthcoming, thereby thwarting real lasting reform.

As for Wallace McDonald, he's reasonably intelligent and possesses several skills that should have enabled him to be gainfully employed, yet he appears to have been

Governor Robert F. Kennon at the 1954 groundbreaking ceremonies for the new prison.
(Photo courtesy *The Angolite*.)

institutionalized as a result of his many years of incarceration in both juvenile and adult institutions. It seems almost impossible to change the attitudes of prisoners with long histories of deviant behavior who have spent years in juvenile institutions and been exposed to crime early. He continues to exhibit some characteristics of the sociopathic personality, rationalizing his behavior by blaming others for his misfortune. He blames the system, relating in outrage that he "got five years for stealing a *pack of cigarettes,"* for instance. He also blames his wife, saying he had accumulated enough money to buy some rental cabins on Toledo Bend Lake and let his son operate a hunting and fishing business there while he sat back and drank, but his wife wanted the money for a nightclub, and this disagreement led to her reporting him for robbery.

At present, however, McDonald, like most prisoners approaching middle age or older, seems to have burned out, reaching a stage I call, for lack of a better term,*"criminal menopause."* Usually by age forty or fifty, these men stop fighting the system and become productive members of society, losing their desire to get rich quick or get something for nothing. Crime, after all, is a young man's game for the most part.

McDonald's tattoos are of interest. Why would one pursuing a life of crime want to have tattoos which make him so easily identifiable? This is symbolic, I think, of people who are self-defeating; they unconsciously seem to want to be caught and punished. Prison becomes *Mama* to them, although they protest their imprisonment, and they will do unthinking things that will return them to prison, like leaving a wallet or other identifiable personal article at the scene of the crime. When I was warden at Angola, I arranged for Charity Hospital dermatology residents to remove inmates' tattoos for free to enhance their employability; what grocery store, for example, wants to employ as a meat-cutter someone with LOVE and HATE tattooed across his knuckles? Unfortunately the state has now outlawed any cosmetic surgery since a recent highly publicized testicle transplant for a rapist or some such reason. Possibly this was a misunderstood learning experience for surgery residents; at any rate, it is the way good programs get killed.

Medical treatment has traditionally presented problems at Angola. When I arrived as warden there were two doctors and several consulting specialists on the staff. The hospital was set up for some surgery, but there were no nurses, only inmate technicians. After Mrs. Daugherty left in 1951, there were no other RNs until 1973. It was difficult to recruit them; I remember the first nurse I was able to hire was actually an LPN, but she did an outstanding job. There were several Cuban doctors, one of them the best doctor I have ever met, and he saved many lives that otherwise would have been lost. When they first arrived in this country, these foreign doctors could only obtain institutional licenses and had to practice in institutions, with not much hope at that time of receiving a full license. Compared to the old days, Angola is now medically well staffed.

Angola has come a long way since Nurse Daugherty was there. She is in a large part responsible for many changes made at that time as well as those effected since then in the system. Governor Earl K. Long appointed a committee of outstanding members who recommended some positive changes for Angola, but had it not been for Nurse Daugherty, the inmates' testimony alone would not have had much impact. She gave it credibility. Without her, I doubt that much would have been changed.

Nurse Daugherty and the heel-slashers combined really instituted reform in the prison system, which unfortunately has been kind of schizophrenic since that time. I am reminded of a quotation from St. Augustine's *Confessions* in which he stated that as a young man, he used to pray, "Give me chastity and continence, but *not just now.*" That seems to be the story of corrections in Louisiana. There have been reforms, but whenever we take two steps forward, we make one step back.

2009 Update:

Wallace McDonald died in February 1999; he was not buried at Angola. Mary Margaret Daugherty is also dead. The Red Hat cellblock was listed on the National Register of Historic Places in 2003.

II

The Queen Misses Tea

"The graciousness and charm of the Old South," said the writeup in the October 20, 1948, Baton Rouge *Morning Advocate* in the inimitable flowering of prose which customarily graced its society section, *"was in evidence yesterday afternoon at Afton Villa, beautiful old plantation home known throughout this section for its loveliness, as Mrs. Wallace Percy entertained with a large tea honoring Louisiana's first lady, Mrs. Earl K. Long.*

"The grounds of the lovely home, with their winding drive shaded by moss-hung trees, formed an inviting introduction to the exquisite beauty that marked the details for the gathering in the French gothic old plantation home. The charming hostess had used the brilliant warm colors of the fall season to accent the antique beauty of Afton Villa, and everywhere that the hundreds of guests gathered profusions of flowers were effectively arranged. Mrs. Percy, attired in a becoming black crepe formal with exquisite white orchid corsage, stood in the wide entrance hall with the honoree to welcome friends who came from St. Francisville, Baton Rouge and throughout the surrounding territory. Mrs. Long, always very gracious at the many events that have been honoring her in past months, was particularly lovely yesterday in the soft blue formal she wore, the bodice being beaded in interesting diagonal design. She, too, wore a single orchid at her shoulder.

"The tea yesterday was one of the largest gatherings of the season, and many prominent women from here and the West Side, as well as many visitors who have friends here, were among the women who assisted in the entertaining."

It sounds as if every lovely lady of any social standing for miles around was in attendance when gracious Dot Percy entertained Mrs. Long at Afton Villa. But there was *one* who was not, although she had been looking forward to the tea for weeks. Tragically, the new flowered outfit selected with such anticipation at Goudchaux's to wear for the occasion was following an entirely different path altogether.

Rubye Moore Spillman had come to the Louisiana State Prison at Angola as a young bride and had stayed there for twenty-four years. Her husband, Captain John Spillman, was in charge of Camp A for black inmates, and the family lived in a nice little white frame house at the edge of the camp with their only child, a daughter, JoAn.

Captain Spillman, born in 1900, had been at Angola all his adult life. His father, Henry Spillman, found employment there first, and son John, who as a strapping youngster farmed in the Spillman community of rural West Feliciana, joined him in working for the penitentiary at the tender age of sixteen, fudging about his youth. John Spillman would meet Rubye Moore through several of his sisters, who were in nursing with her at the state hospital for the mentally ill at Jackson. Once he caught his first glimpse of her, one fateful weekend when she visited his sisters at the Spillman home in Tunica, it would not be long before he made her his wife.

Rubye Moore, born in 1904, was the only daughter in a family of twelve children; her tiny mother was in fragile health, so most of the responsibility for raising the boys and caring for the household fell onto Rubye's strong shoulders. Rubye's daughter JoAn remembers hearing family stories of how "it didn't set too well with my grandfather when she got married in 1924. Her mother and father were living in Metairie at the time, and when she went there, Daddy went over there and I guess you'd say kidnapped her and brought her back home, and they got married."

It was a homecoming of sorts for Rubye Moore Spillman to return to the hilly Tunica-Angola area along the Mississippi River, where her grandparents, Rebecca Jane Comley and George G. Moore, had owned over 2000 acres, "in fact just about the whole of Tunica," JoAn says. This determined great-grandfather of JoAn's had fought so persistently in the Civil War that he has made her genealogical research exceptionally difficult, for as soon as he was captured and released after promising not to fight again, he would re-enter the fray using a different name, eventually fighting as George, John and Joseph Moore.

The Moores were prosperous landowners who also had stores, a cotton gin and sawmill, but the death of her husband and subsequent property auction left Rebecca's holdings reduced to a mere sixty acres, perhaps explaining why her young sons Joseph and Frank moved across the river to Pointe Coupée Parish to seek their fortunes. It would be there that Joseph would meet and marry diminutive Ella Ophelia Aldridge and father, in rapid succession, twelve children, including Rubye Moore Spillman.

Rubye was a social being who thoroughly enjoyed people. Her sister-in-law, Hazel Walters of Tunica, sister of Captain John Spillman, says Rubye was a good entertainer who loved parties and dancing. "She loved company and she liked to be *in* company," Hazel's husband Hallie Walters recounts. "She was a good housewife, and she was a good mother." And Captain C. C. Dixon, who worked at Angola for thirty-six years and whose wife was John Spillman's first cousin, says Rubye "was just as fine as she could be in my book. She always had everything shining."

Says JoAn, "Everybody says my mother was well liked and that she had a real good personality. She liked to have people around her. She had parties and played bridge and bingo. She liked to entertain, always had plenty of people. At our house, in the dining room we had one of these big long oak tables, and we had company a lot."

Everyone who knew Rubye Spillman mentions her love of flowers and the beautiful gardens she had the inmates cultivate around Camp A. Hallie Walters says, "Camp A had about two acres or better of flowers. Oh, Rubye was a gardener, all right. She loved them flowers, she did. She just loved to work with those flowers. To her, that camp was a bouquet." The gardening was also a business proposition as well as beautification project for Rubye. JoAn recalls that her mother "used to raise turkeys and flowers. She raised chrysanthemums and gladiolas, then would take them to Baton Rouge and sell them to Hunt's Florist."

JoAn also recalls that on the trip to Baton Rouge to purchase a new dress for her mother to wear to the tea at Afton Villa for Governor Earl K. Long's wife the next day, Rubye must have just sold some flowers, because she had "a wad of money." Yet for some reason she did not pay for her purchases at Goudchaux's, which included the dark dress with big flowers for the tea, accessories to go with it, and a black coat with a fur collar, as well as a blue taffeta dress and plaid skirt and top for JoAn. Instead, she charged them, meaning she was still in possession of the "wad of money" when she returned home.

Rubye Moore Spillman
(Courtesy JoAn Spillman Oubre)

Perhaps this cash contributed to what happened next. Or perhaps it involved forty-four-year-old Rubye's domineering personality. Used to having unlimited labor and to getting immediate response to orders since coming to Angola as a bride, Rubye Spillman kept the inmates hopping. JoAn recalls her mother lovingly, but adds that she "was a perfectionist and she liked to have everything just so, and she was very hard on me. I can remember any number of times I got spankings from her."

Rubye Spillman was also hard on the household staff. "She made sure the inmates did what they were supposed to, and she was adamant about what she wanted done. I guess she bossed them around pretty good," recalls Patsy Welch Dreher, childhood friend of JoAn's whose father was also an Angola captain and whose family lived on the prison grounds, too. In those days there were only two disciplinary measures doled out to inmates who got out of line, whippings with a heavy strap or solitary confinement in so-called dungeons. "They just had the spankings and the hothouse; I knew a lot more that went on than they thought I knew. Daddy was nice and easy going until you got his temper up, but I never wanted him to spank me because I heard what went on at the camp," JoAn remembers, "where they had inmate guards. Of course that doesn't go over

Capt. and Mrs. John Spillman
in their garden.
(Courtesy Hazel Walters)

Camp A
(Courtesy JoAn Spillman Oubre)

too well nowadays; people don't even like to think that they had those at the time. The hothouse was just a little boxy brick structure in back of the camps where they put the inmates; they fed them bread and water, and I don't even think they had anything to lie on, or even room to lie down at all. There was no ventilation except through the bars on the door; that was the only opening."

In spite of what was going on with some of the more unfortunate or more unruly prisoners in the camps, Patsy and JoAn recall happy days of an idyllic childhood in this unlikely spot, with inmates to do the cooking and cleaning inside the free homes and all the yardwork outside, cultivating flowers and vegetables in the rich river bottomlands, taking care of the horses and other pets, almost "raising the children," in the words of Hallie Walters. Says Adele Wilcox Percy, whose father was a prison employee in the forties before becoming parish sheriff and whose entire family lived on the grounds, "All of us had those black inmates working in the house back then, and we never thought a thing of it."

JoAn says her own children are jealous of the childhood she had at Angola, and she says, "It *was* wonderful. I was the princess and my daddy and mother were the king and

Inmates of Camp A showing off some produce of the farm. Mr. Cobb Germany (center with cane) was head gardener for Camp A.
(Courtesy JoAn Spillman Oubre)

queen, and we had servants, and we didn't want for anything. And I was Little Miss Jo, or they called me Curly or Shirley, like Shirley Temple, because I had curly hair. And it was just a storybook childhood."

Only occasionally was there trouble in paradise. Once, JoAn recalls, she and her father narrowly escaped death when an inmate poisoned their milk. "My parents were having a dinner party one night, and Mama had invited their friends the Robertsons. Mother was a very good cook; she didn't *have* to cook, but whenever she prepared something, it was really good. She had a gumbo that night, and everyone had tea except Daddy and me; we drank milk. At that time they still had the dairy at Camp A, and some convict over there must have gotten a grudge against my father, because we were both so sick we threw up constantly all night. They had glass milk bottles, and you could see pink in the bottom. You know, it was rat poison, and milk is an antidote for rat poison, so all it did was make us sick."

There had also been the tragic events of May 1936, when trusty Wilfred Lindsly shot Captain N. J. Himel after slitting his wife's throat in the bathtub, escaped in the family car and was later cornered by a posse on a sandbar in Little Bayou Sara, where, after a shootout, he fatally wounded himself in the left breast with a pistol after his shotgun jammed. Two prison guards were accidentally shot during the chase, and seventeen-year-old local resident Billy Wade was slain by a guard while going to the grocery store on an innocent errand for his mother.

Nevertheless, Patsy Dreher remembers, "Angola was a pleasant place to live back then. A vegetable cart came by every morning. What you didn't get in pay, you got in benefits. You could get your car fixed, get your clothing laundered, had free housing, didn't pay for utilities. It took me a long time to learn to turn off lights after we left there. You could get inmates as cooks, yard boys, house boys; you could have two or three of them if you wanted. We had an old cook named Leon who cried like a baby when he got paroled; he said ours was the only home he'd known in a mighty long time."

One of the inmates who worked for Captain Spillman and his family was known as Dummy. JoAn recalls her attachment to him. "He was an old black man who had been at Angola ever since he was just a young boy," she says, "and while he was there they had beat him to the point where he couldn't talk; he was deaf and dumb. We had quite a few of the inmates working for us. Dummy was sort of like a handyman for my father, and

JoAn Spillman and trusty on the porch of the playhouse at Camp C.
(Courtesy JoAn Spillman Oubre)

JoAn Spillman, trusty, and the horses Star and Prince.
(Courtesy JoAn Spillman Oubre)

he would meet me at the end of the road to the house when I'd get off the schoolbus. He was always there, and I had a little dog named Napoleon, and they were my constant companions. My father was very protective of Dummy, but he loved to pull tricks on him. Daddy was quite a prankster and he'd get these exploding cigars, and Dummy loved cigars. Daddy would say, 'Here, Dummy, you've done a good job today, here's a cigar,' and he'd put that cigar in his mouth and start smoking, and that thing'd blow up. He couldn't say anything, but poor thing, you could tell he was aggravated."

Another trusty-inmate who worked for the Spillmans for some thirteen years was a tall, slim mulatto named James Bruce. Previously sent to Angola for burglary in 1935, Bruce had worked for the family until paroled, and had apparently performed his duties so well that they requested his services again when he was re-convicted in 1945 from New Orleans with a twelve-year sentence for stealing $200 hidden in a tin can under a bed by his housemate in one of the projects.

Aged thirty-nine, Bruce served as houseboy and cook, cranking homemade ice cream for the annual backyard birthday parties JoAn hosted for all her little friends who lived on prison grounds. She especially remembers her twelfth birthday, for it was her parents' twenty-fourth anniversary celebration as well and is preserved in captivating photographs, including a shot of her mother in one of the flowered dresses she loved. At another memorable party in the area, one of the guests was a seventeen-year-old livewire who lived across the river from Natchez but was temporarily staying with relatives at Angola; JoAn recalls having more fun riding horseback with him the next day than playing spin the bottle at the party. She also says he sure could play the piano. His name was Jerry Lee Lewis.

JoAn and Patsy both think that perhaps, looking back, James Bruce may have been "a little strange." JoAn says that even at age twelve, she was aware of homosexuality and sexual perversity being part of the shadowy world of inmate camp life, "but I didn't associate that with James. We had one inmate in the house that was like that, and I knew, because he would take my iron and ironing board and use it, my mascara and noxema, but I never did know whether James was like that or anything. Come to think of it, he might have been a little prissy." He was also one of the stars of the prison "minstrels," in which he took female parts in wig and women's clothing. JoAn recalls seeing him do so on those occasions when she accompanied her father as he escorted inmates to perform in different places like Jackson and Pineville.

Another thing JoAn clearly remembers about James Bruce is that he was "always whistling or singing; you'd have thought he was the happiest person in the world. And if you said, 'Well, you're awfully chipper today,' he'd say, 'Well, might as well be,' or something like that." He was also, she says, "a very good worker, kept the house immaculate, cooked good food and everything, and I didn't see where there was any problem. He worked for us for a long time." Born in Texas, Bruce was married, a Catholic, and at 5'10" never weighed more than 130 pounds.

Hallie Walters, who would later be kidnapped by an escapee himself, recalls that the Spillmans bought tobacco and other necessities for Bruce, and says they "had to have been getting along all right or they couldn't have kept him for thirteen years. But that's one thing about a convict, you can't trust him. I don't care how good you treat him or what you do for him, he's still a convict. He can steal a box of matches and go to the penitentiary, but when they put him behind those bars, he's a dangerous man."

James Bruce walked with a limp, dragging one foot, and was said to have had a steel plate in his head from some earlier injury. And from what JoAn has since learned, her mother was sometimes less than kind and patient with him. "From what I gather from other people and family members, she was mean to him," she says now. "I don't have any firsthand knowledge of it, because all I know was how she treated me; at twelve years old, I wasn't interested in anything else. But she used to hit him with a broomstick when he didn't do something that she wanted."

James Bruce was working at the Spillman home by Camp A on that fall Tuesday, October 19, 1948, as Rubye Moore Spillman, in excited anticipation, began her preparations to attend the Afton Villa tea for Blanche Long. According to JoAn's memory, she should have still had the "wad of money" from her flower sales the previous day in Baton Rouge. JoAn had her own treasures in the house as well, a bank full of dimes and a birthday card she had received from an enormous white ex-inmate called Sap, which was a train whose wheels were filled with dimes. These, as well as several watches, would never be seen in the Spillman house again.

Whether it was the temptation of the money or some unkind treatment which precipitated the day's tragic events will never be known. At eight o'clock that morning, Rubye Spillman eagerly spoke by telephone to her close friend Mrs. J. H. Robertson, wife of a prison guard and dinner guest the night JoAn and Captain Spillman narrowly escaped poisoning, about the Afton Villa reception which they, together with another Angola friend named Mrs. Kemper, would attend that afternoon. When Mrs. Robertson called two hours later, James Bruce informed her that Mrs. Spillman had already left in a car with another lady. Rubye's niece, arriving to help fix her hair for the tea, was similarly turned away.

Bruce served noontime dinner to Captain Spillman when he came in from the camp, telling him the same story. When JoAn came in from school, she went to spend the night with a beloved cousin and favorite playmate, Johnny "PeeWee" Peterson at Camp H. First, though, she had to enter the house to collect a few overnight articles and clothes. "Well, I noticed it was kind of odd," she recalls, "that James was sitting on the front porch, on the steps. We had a front porch that went all the way across the front of the house. They had made a room out of one end of the porch with sliding windows, and that was my bedroom. A door went from the porch into my bedroom, and one went from the porch into my mother and daddy's bedroom, and there was one going from my mother and daddy's room into mine. Well, I went into the house to get my clothes. There was a great big heavy armoire set cattycornered in my room, because there wasn't room to put it straight, and the door that went into my mother's room opened up where it would conceal the side of the armoire. So I went in there and I got my clothes, and I was just fixing to come out again when James came in, you know, to the door like he wanted to see if he could help me or something. But I didn't think anything of it and went on to my cousin's."

After serving supper to Captain Spillman, James Bruce left the house around 7 p.m., ostensibly to return to be locked up for the evening in the inmate camp. He never made it. Captain Spillman, under the impression that his wife was visiting elsewhere on prison grounds, retired for the night around 8:30, as was his habit, being under the care of a doctor for a heart ailment and high blood pressure. It was not until a posse, hastily convened to search nearby canefields and woods after James Bruce was discovered missing in a routine check of the lockup camp, alerted Captain Spillman of his escape, that it was realized that Mrs. Spillman was also missing.

Newspaper accounts of the time report that Capt. Spillman was awakened sometime around 1 a.m. by three members of the search party, prison guard captains Clyde Morgan and C. C. Dixon along with Dr. James Monroe Smith, former president of Louisiana State University who himself served time at Angola after being caught up in the scandals of the Leche administration in 1939, later returning to the facility as its first serious director of vocational rehabilitation. Captain Dixon today denies being present at that point in the search, saying he had been called back to the sugarmill where trouble was brewing, literally, with inmates making beer and whiskey.

So it must have been just Captain Morgan, Dr. Smith and Captain Spillman who, their calls for Mrs. Spillman going unanswered, began the search of the house which had culminated by 2:30 a.m. in the discovery of her limp body, clad in a nightgown, hidden behind the armoire in daughter JoAn's bedroom. Her neck had been broken by a sharp blow to the chin, which caused her death. She had also been stabbed seven times with a sharp instrument like an icepick, probably after she was already dead, judging from the comparatively small amount of blood present. When she was found, she had already been dead about seventeen hours, since sometime Tuesday morning, according to Deputy Coroner P. A. Niebergall's inquest report.

The bloodied prison uniform of James Bruce was discovered just outside the Spillman home, and Angola superintendent R. H. Lawrence said there was "a strong indication that Bruce had escaped while disguised in the new clothes Mrs. Spillman had planned to wear to a reception on the day of her death." Her new flowered dress, gloves and shoes were missing, along with cash, watches and JoAn's dimes, and when Capt. C. C. Dixon rejoined the search party, having controlled the situation at the sugarmill, he "backed off from the house and found a woman's shoe track that went into the sugar cane, and I tracked it over there to right in front of the Catholic church, and I found her shoes."

It was right in the middle of sugar cane season at Angola, the largest and most demanding undertaking of the year at the prison where, in the words of the late Margaret Dixon, managing editor of the Baton Rouge *Morning Advocate*, "they tell time by the calendar instead of by the clock. From early fall until late January, most attention is paid to this work. The cane crop this year brought in 10,534,000 pounds of sugar," Dixon would write after harvest in January 1949, "and most of the profit goes to the farm revolving fund. Three carloads a day are shipped and the time and energies of most of the 2000 or so prisoners as well as that of the authorities is devoted to the cane crop."

But the all-important cane crop played second fiddle for once, as a posse of more than 300 prison guards, state police, sheriff's deputies and armed volunteers, many of them on horseback, spread out through the heavily wooded area surrounding Angola and followed the penitentiary bloodhounds on the trail of the escapee James Bruce, fleeing in flowered dress and gloves after discarding the high-heeled shoes, no doubt in the interest of speed. The *Morning Advocate* of Friday, October 22, reports that "cane cutting began Tuesday, but was halted Wednesday and prisoners were herded into stockades" where skeletal guard crews could watch them while the rest of the prison guard complement joined the search.

While searchers described the rugged terrain of the Tunica Hills as having "woods so thick that a man used to the woods can almost hide under a posse's nose and never be found," the prison bloodhounds soon picked up the trail where Capt. Dixon had left off, leading the posse to the banks of the Mississippi River. There they found Mrs. Spillman's dress and gloves, the ones she had so eagerly anticipated wearing at the gala Afton Villa reception. One newspaper account, quoting West Feliciana Sheriff Teddy Martin, described the abandoned dress as belonging to JoAn, but she refutes that. "He didn't take any of my new clothes," she insists, "because I wore the blue dress my mother bought me at the funeral home, and I wore the plaid suit there too, so I still had both of the outfits that she bought me. The dress left on the log would have had to be one of hers, because he wouldn't have been able to fit into any of my clothes at the time; I was too small. He was tall and thin and sort of chocolate colored."

The search party also found evidence of a heavy log having been pushed into the river, seeming to indicate that Bruce had entered the water using the floating log for bouyancy in an attempt to cross to the other side of the Mississippi, but this might also have been a diversionary trick to give the escapee time to double back onto the penitentiary grounds. Farther downstream by a clump of willows, footprints were soon discovered and identified as Bruce's by guards who said the trusty dragged one foot to leave an easily identifiable pattern. The chase team also found an abandoned bottle containing the remnants of the mixture of turpentine and garlic which the savvy Bruce apparently had used to confuse the tracking bloodhounds and throw them off his trail.

Capt. C. C. Dixon and bloodhounds search for James Bruce.
(Courtesy C. C. Dixon)

As the search for Bruce continued in the rugged hillcountry, spreading along both sides of the Mississippi River and as far south as East Baton Rouge Parish, with a reward of $500 offered for his capture, false leads and frustrations took their toll. After five days, one hundred prison guards and employees were pulled back to Angola, and Sheriff Martin, who had led the chase since it began, was sent home to rest "on doctor's orders." JoAn, meanwhile, had finally been told the tragic news.

"Finally my cousin PeeWee couldn't keep the secret any longer, and he said, 'JoAn, I'm not supposed to, but I got something I think you ought to know,' and I said, 'What's that?' and he said, 'They can't find your mother.' And I didn't know what to think about that. But I remember later on I was either sitting or lying in one of his double bunk beds when my Aunt Emma, that was PeeWee's mother's name, my father's sister, came in and she told me that they had found her. And I don't remember much after that except the funeral.

"They wouldn't let me see any papers and wouldn't tell me what was going on. I was just twelve and in the seventh grade at the Tunica school, and for years I didn't really know too much of the actual details. Of course I wasn't in any condition to think of it, and nobody ever tried to get any help for me. There was only one man who said I should have had some help, and that was my schoolbus driver, Mr. Pittman, who was very special to me and is married to one of my cousins. I guess back in those days people just didn't go to a psychiatrist whenever. When I went to school after that I didn't learn anything; I wasn't interested in anything. I can remember the first day going back to school after it happened and the reaction of the kids. The teachers passed me, but my mind was a blank."

Continuing, JoAn searches her memory. "I just didn't know why or for a long time *what* had happened. From what I can understand, my mother was sitting at her dresser, not dressed yet, probably combing her hair, getting ready to go to the tea. And, I don't know, maybe he just walked in on her, and she was like that, and she probably cussed him out; she cussed like a sailor. And he might have just gotten mad and went back in there and did it. I don't know. Like I say, she was a big woman and she was strong. I have seen her handle herself real well. She was bigger than he was, as far as that goes. But if it happened like it said in the paper, he probably must have slipped up behind her and broken her neck, and then stabbed her and wrapped her in a sheet and put her behind the armoire. And then he took the money and all my dimes, my watch and an old watch that Mama had that didn't run, and he put it all in his pocket, which would have weighted him down. And after he served Daddy's supper and went back toward the camp, I guess he just kept on walking. Our house was about a good distance from the camp, and by this time of the year they'd have cane, so he could have gone through the cane and nobody would have seen him."

Capt. C. C. Dixon and Powder (Courtesy C. C. Dixon)

Captain C. C. Dixon, who would lead Angola's chase team for many years, learning in the process to second-guess most escapees, surmises along similar lines. "Bruce wasn't trying to just escape; he done what he *wanted* to do. In prison, they just say 'what the hell.' It appears like what he did was directed against her personally. From all accounts, she was pretty strict on him, made him toe the mark, and I guess he didn't like it."

The hunt for Bruce continued into its second week, with penitentiary officials releasing information indicating that he was a "feminine type" who delighted in playing female parts in amateur theatricals at the prison and might still be disguised, as he had escaped, as a woman, for Superintendent Lawrence said "he was good at impersonating women in shows for prisoners." Captain Dixon recalls, "We searched the banks of the river to find where he came out, but he didn't come out. I guess it was two weeks later when the body come up. 'Course that ended the chase."

It was not until Saturday, October 30, that the drowned, decomposed body of Bruce was found at 3:30 in the afternoon by Joe Smith, a light tender from Morganza, Louisiana. Setting out river navigation lights in the Mississippi about three miles north of Morganza, Smith was puzzled by the large numbers of buzzards circling overhead and rowed to investigate. The gruesome Halloween discovery was the body of Bruce, partially visible, floating in the muddy waters of the Mississippi clad in women's undergarments, silk hosiery, a blue dress, green sweater and the woman's wig he had used when playing the part of a female in prison theatricals.

Officials surmised that Bruce had entered the river some twenty-five to thirty miles upstream near Angola, hoping to float across the river holding onto a large log and land on the opposite side, where he could make good his escape disguised as a woman. The current where the Lower Old River enters the Mississippi probably proved his undoing, they speculated, for it is strong enough to give even boats trouble, and must have torn him from his log. Captain Dixon agrees. "It would be hard to swim the river in a dress or any other way, not that river. I doubt if he could even swim. But I guess he figured that river was cooler than it was gonna be if they ever caught up with him."

The coroner's inquest ruled death was caused by accidental drowning, and Sheriff Teddy Martin boasted that he "could identify the body by a bullet wound he himself had inflicted in 1936 when Bruce had tried to escape." Feelings at Angola were understandably running high. Hazel Walters recalls there were rumors that Bruce had been killed by Sheriff Martin or her brother Capt. Spillman, so Martin made sure the inquest conducted by Pointe Coupée Parish Coroner Dr. James C. Roberts specified the unviolated condition of the body. While babysitting at another guard's home, JoAn would unwittingly see photographs of the convict's body on the sandbar where it was found. She also recalls hearing that after Bruce's remains were brought back for interment in an unmarked grave in the prison cemetery at Point Lookout, guards were posted throughout the night before his burial because "Daddy had threatened to go over there and burn his body."

Her father, she vividly remembers, "was outraged by it, and the trauma about it in itself probably did increase the chance of his having a heart attack. He had several heart attacks before he actually passed on five years later. My father had high blood pressure and I think diabetes too. My daddy was a sick man. And he had worked up at Angola for thirty-seven years when he died. He wanted to retire; he had the years, but he didn't have the age. He was only fifty-two years old when he died, and at that time you had to be fifty-five years old to retire, no matter how many years you'd worked. In the early fifties,

Capt. John Spillman and daughter JoAn
(Courtesy Hazel Walters)

they were making changes at Angola and Daddy was set in his ways, too old to change, and he was apprehensive about what all was gonna be expected of him. We had gotten up to the gate one time, literally, furniture and everything, to leave, I remember that. When the administration would change, they would be saying who was going, and if the warden went, usually a lot of the free people would go, too. But they told Daddy to go back, they wanted him to stay. They knew he was a good man.

"I guess you could say," Captain John Spillman's devoted daughter JoAn muses poignantly, "that Angola actually killed him too."

As this book is being written, JoAn Spillman Oubre and personable Alcide Joseph Oubre, Jr., her husband since 1980, live in Morganza in a shady backyard close enough to lend a hand to his wheelchair-bound mother. In their tidy trailer, JoAn has the bulky armoire behind which her mother's body was concealed, the dressing table at which she was probably seated when she was killed, and a scrapbook overflowing with invaluable photographs of an early era at Angola, showing activities, historic structures, favorite inmates, beloved family members and friends. The pictures must help during her periods of what she calls partial amnesia, and she says she is working on her own to regain lost memories.

JoAn's children are grown and on their own, and she is a doting grandmother, enjoying her large, lively family after having been an only child herself. Retired from state employment, including two separate periods working at Louisiana State Penitentiary at Angola, she finds that her current enthusiasm for genealogy and the resulting requisite research demand renewed contact with family members from whom she had kept her distance in recent years, and seems pleased by the re-establishment of family ties.

After her mother's murder and her father's death five years later, when she was just sixteen, JoAn had lived somewhat unhappily with her Spillman grandmother in Tunica, right next to Hazel and Hallie Walters, for the two years until she finished school, and then she moved to Baton Rouge. She explains the unusual spelling of her name as a compromise. "When I was in school I said my name was 'JoAnne,' then I cut the 'e' off, and then I looked at my birth certificate and it said 'Joan.' But my daddy wanted me to be named 'JoAnn,' and he called me 'JoAnn.' So I figured 'JoAn' is the closest way to get 'JoAnn' and 'Joan' together."

It was not difficult for her to return to Angola to work, she says. "At the time I went back, I was separated and had four children to raise, and they were paying good money. I guess it sounds crazy, but I had some good memories there, besides what actually happened. There has been so much negative said about the old ways at Angola, and I know myself firsthand that there was a lot of mistreatment.

"But there was good there, too. It was *home."*

The Warden Comments: The story of inmate James Bruce and the family of Captain John Spillman represents the close and convoluted relationships stemming from the practice of having free families living in close proximity with Angola inmates in outcamps within the penitentiary's borders. While these relationships and inter-dependencies were often touched with warmth and mutual respect, they also provided opportunities for revenge and abuse from both sides.

It never made much sense to have guards and their families living so close to the scattered inmate camps on Angola, and in the mid-fifties Warden Maurice Sigler supervised construction of the consolidated village where such free residents are now clustered, well removed from inmate areas. For these families, times have changed drastically since the days of James Bruce, when the free existence at Angola was probably the closest thing to a feudal system in America at the time, the guard captains being the lordly aristocrats and the inmates as the downtrodden serfs.

Although inmate house servants were discouraged after Mrs. Spillman's murder, they remained in the homes of the exective staff. While I was warden at Angola, there were no serious problems with inmate household staff, other than minor personality conflicts between prisoners. Psychological testing and careful review of records could certainly permit selection from several thousand inmates of those who could be good household workers without presenting security problems.

Surprisingly, murderers are actually the best prospects for working outside the prison or at homes, and have the lowest rate of recidivism of any group of offenders; First Lady Elaine Edwards, during her lengthy tenure in the Louisiana Governor's Mansion, insisted that mansion staff be drawn from such offenders. While I was serving as warden at the penitentiary in Nashville, Tennessee, we made a study of thirty-seven murderers whose death sentences had been commuted to life imprisonment. After release from prison, only three of the thirty-seven were ever arrested again, and then only for nonviolent property offenses like burglary or check writing. Usually murder is committed in the heat of passion and discharges something within the psyche, with the result that the individual rarely repeats the offense.

When I first came to Angola as warden, it seemed to be established policy to use homosexuals as houseboys, perhaps with the idea of protecting families, though I felt this could create more problems than it might solve. Associate Warden Hayden Dees, the classification committee member representing security when I arrived, informed me, for example, that he could identify homosexuals on sight, by the shape of their noses. When General David Wade was appointed as the first director of the Department of Corrections, he began the recruitment of professional prison psychologists and qualified classifications officers which was expanded under my administration, hopefully ensuring the adherence to more professionally recognized standards of inmate categorization.

Inmate shows like the ones in which James Bruce performed were also discouraged after I arrived at Angola. There was no useful purpose to be accomplished by men dressing up as women and trying to be seductive to other prisoners. Often it was impossible to tell that the men were not women, and they performed in a very seductive manner which made straight prisoners, trying to do their sentence without trouble, uncomfortable. To replace such theatrics, self-help groups like Dale Carnegie, Great Books clubs, Jaycees and religious clubs were encouraged to better help prepare individuals for outside living. A well-rounded recreation program stressing sports, crafts and discussion groups in the library was also established during my administration.

Sugar cane season at Angola, the time during which this crime was committed, was historically the busiest part of the year, with grinding starting right after the World Series, which all inmates received time off to watch. Once the grinding began, it had to

Players in a Camp A minstrel show of the 1940s. Inmates in dresses are males. (Courtesy Frank Blackburn)

Sugar cane harvest at Angola in the early 1940s.
(Photo courtesy *The Angolite*)

continue without interruption twenty-four hours a day, maintaining the same high temperature throughout the process to keep the sugar flowing. There was often inadequate supervision at the sugarmill because of employee shortages, and, as Captain Dixon mentioned, this was always a real problem. The inmates took full advantage of this situation to brew homemade libations by taking cane juice and adding some yeast to bring it to quick fermentation. They then drank it as beer, or sometimes they could distill it into rum. On one occasion a real nice little copper still with a gas burner was found in the loft of the sugarmill in full production.

When checking out a call from the sugarmill late one night, I found that both prisoners and employees had been imbibing. Since it was absolutely vital that the grinding continue without interruption, so the sugar did not crystalize and gum up the works, the inmates responsible for production could not be locked up, nor could the guards be disciplined at that time. Of course I read the riot act to them and stayed with them until the next twelve-hour shift arrived. Deliberate sabotage could also be a problem during grinding time; once a wrench was thrown into the mechanism and it cost $25,000 to bring an engineer from Houston to correct the damage.

The growing of sugar cane at Angola was summarily discontinued in the seventies under reform-minded Corrections Secretary Elayn Hunt. Five thousand acres of cane were plowed up, the sugarmill dismanted and sold to a Brazilian firm. The idea initially was to move toward a program which would better meet the rehabilitative needs of prisoners returning to predominantly urban areas, but soybean cultivation under agri-business director Ross Maggio soon replaced cane instead of the vocational and industrial complex I had hoped for.

In the early 1950s, inmates load a truck with sacks of raw sugar bound for a nearby refinery. During harvest seasons in the 1930s and 1940s, inmates in gangs of one hundred men set about cutting the sugarcane crop. These groups were called the "long lines" because of the number of inmates involved. They worked from "can to can't," or from the time they could see in the morning until it was too dark to see at nightfall. (Photo courtesy *The Angolite*.)

James Bruce, about whose personality and problems we have too little information, apparently had a steel plate in his head and walked with a limp, indicating at least the possibility of a head injury, which can cause marked personality change. Since Bruce had been released and then returned to prison not too long before his murder of Mrs. Spillman, perhaps such an injury occurred while he was out, lowering his threshold for frustration. His seemingly cheerful demeanor might have camouflaged a growing internal rage at his treatment by Mrs. Spillman, which at the time was only generally accepted practice.

JoAn mentions inmate punishments as being harsh at Angola at this time, but these too were only generally accepted practice, probably no worse here than at other Southern prisons. Back in the forties, the only punishment besides solitary confinement officially administered at Angola was the strap, though some guards seemed to stretch the definition of *strap* to include all sorts of weapons made of shaved-down sections of lumber, pipes and other materials.

Prisoners did not have due process concerning violation of prison rules, the regulations being whatever the officer in charge decided to make them. Prisoners did not have access to the judicial system, they were not allowed to file writs, and, had it been permitted, few prisoners had the necessary materials to do so. One of the first writs that led to the recognition of inmate rights was filed on toilet paper. It was accepted by the court. Improvements in this area of inmate life at Angola would be a long time coming.

2009 Update:

JoAn Spillman Oubre is still alive. Nurse Mary Margaret Daugherty would later reveal that James Bruce probably suffered from syphilis and its resultant brain damage, and that Mrs. Spillman had been warned against having him work in the home.

III

Cajun Country Siren Song

It has a bittersweet and haunting beauty, this desolate stretch of southwestern Louisiana in what is called Cajun country. The flat open prairieland along the mutual border of Allen and Jefferson Davis parishes is filled mostly with rice fields which seem to stretch forever, the horizon broken only by the towering hulks of huge tin rice mills, many now abandoned. Canals snake into the rice fields bringing the vital water necessary for life and growth, its flow controlled by locks.

The area's largest city, Lake Charles, was once a favorite hiding place for pirates like Jean Lafitte, who in the early nineteenth century made good use of this safe haven just inland from the Gulf of Mexico coastline, though the intricate maze of cypress-shaded bayous and murky moss-hung backwaters now yield fish and furs, oil and alligators rather than pirate treasure.

The early French settlers here, isolated by spatial and cultural barriers from mainstream American or even Southern life, struggled to preserve their heritage, continuing the customs and speaking the tongue of their ancestors far away across ocean waters, and their descendants remain in closeknit inter-related communities to this day. Older residents, most of them Roman Catholics, are as apt to carry on conversations in Cajun French as in English, while another unique element was introduced when a group of Coushatta Indians settled near Elton, bringing their own traditions and skills.

People here learned of necessity how to create their own entertainment, how to "pass a good time" in celebration of even the most mundane occurrences in daily life. Labor Day in Kinder, which still calls itself the "Crossroads to Everywhere" even though a new interstate highway has syphoned off the main flow of traffic between Houston and New Orleans, is marked with the Sauce Piquante Festival in honor of that hot heady Cajun cooking which can make even an old shoe palatable. In Basile, proudly billed as the "Swine Capital of the World," the coming of cool fall weather is celebrated with hog slaughterings in time-honored fashion, and November brings the Louisiana Swine Festival.

But for boys entering the difficult rite of passage from childhood to adulthood, the Kinder-Elton-Basile area back in the late fifties and early sixties must have lacked a certain yearned-for excitement. The siren song of the swamps which had ensnared their elders into lifelong love-affairs with the ways of the bayous held less appeal for this new generation; they wanted a faster pace of life, more excitement than homegrown Sauce Piquante and Swine festivals had to offer.

These adolescent yearnings would make them far too vulnerable to a siren song of an entirely different sort, an unsettling and discordant melody blending elements of life as they knew it with bizarre disharmonies shocking to the whole community. It was a song of raw sex and sensuality keened by a woman known in tabloids of the times as *"la belle dame sans merci,"* the beautiful woman without mercy.

The story of this secret siren song, whose haunting strains threaded tendrils of treacherous influence through closeknit communities, beckoning altar boys from the church and athletes from the playing fields, would not begin to unfold until early on the morning of Sunday, June 24, 1962, when Wilford Kirkland, an employee of the Kinder Canal, would make a grisly discovery.

Checking the water level and locks along the canal which conveyed water from the Calcasieu River to flood thousands of acres of rice fields, about four miles southeast of Kinder on property reported to belong to rice farmer T. H. Mayes, Kirkland's attention was attracted by a sound as if "a fish was jumping" near a wire fence. Instead of a fish, what he found was the mutilated body of young Gerald Davis Fontenot, naked, hands and feet bound behind him, throat slashed, head battered by a blunt instrument, and castrated as cleanly as any young hog destined to become Easter Sunday ham in this Swine Capital of the World.

A pool of blood was discovered on the canal bank, and a single-edged razor blade was found near the water's edge. From the murky waters of the canal, investigating law enforcement officials soon recovered a bloodstained pillowcase and Gerald Fontenot's clothing, untorn and neatly bundled, a sock carefully placed in each shoe. Allen Parish deputy coroner Dr. Paul Shorts ruled the case a homicide, and efforts began immediately to determine just exactly how Gerald Fontenot had spent his last hours, and with whom.

At nineteen, Fontenot was already out of school and on his own, spending the week in Beaumont, where he had a job trimming trees from powerlines and highway right-of-ways, then returning on weekends to Elton, where he had grown up. His half-brother Russell Sonnier remembers that Gerald quit high school before graduating and worked at a series of shortlived jobs before finding permanent work in Texas. Times were pretty tough for the family, and they had to rely on Sonnier's grandmother, Mrs. Lena Sonnier, to put a roof over their heads.

"We lived with my grandmother as far back as I can remember," Sonnier recalls. "When my mother and Gerald's dad separated, she got married to my dad and Gerald started living with my dad's mother, too. He called her MawMaw just like I did, and she supported me and my half-brother, my half-sister, my dad and his wife, mostly while living on welfare. My dad was an alcoholic and just drank; he didn't have a good steady job or anything." Gerald's father was a merchant marine who would eventually be lost at sea; when his mother would remarry, as she did a number of times, and move, Gerald remained in the only home he had ever known, that of his step-grandmother in Elton.

A stout smiling woman whose dark hair was customarily pulled back from her lined face in practical fashion and whose faded print dresses were covered by sturdy aprons, MawMaw Sonnier worked miracles to feed and clothe this large family group on a check Russell remembers as being $35 a month. Her rustic wood-frame house had only four rooms and no indoor bathroom, just an old outhouse in the yard. Food was sometimes so scarce that the black family across the road would share the bounty when they killed a possum or other wild game, and stylish new clothes were hard to come by.

Russell left Elton High in eleventh grade, at least partly because of embarrassment at not having adequate clothing, and says the same thing had happened to Gerald, three years older, when he returned from a juvenile detention facility after serving a brief sentence. Gerald, like most teenaged boys, "was kind of wild," Russell remembers, "and when he was around fifteen or sixteen he had to go to LTI at Monroe for about eight months or so, for nothing really big. He had gotten in trouble a few times, and I think he and some other boys had stolen a garden hose or something like that. When he came back, they tried to put him in the same grade as me, and that didn't set too well, so he quit school."

Even with his job in Beaumont, Gerald could not afford an automobile, so he was on foot when he set out looking for excitement on the night of Saturday, June 23, 1962. Before he left Elton, however, he reportedly made a seemingly casual offhand remark which would return to haunt his MawMaw. "In case anything happens to me, I want to be buried in the Elton Cemetery," she would later repeat to others as his last words to her.

For a dollar's worth of gas, some Elton youths drove Gerald to nearby Basile, about eight miles east of Elton, on that hot June Saturday night, reportedly to visit a girlfriend. After staying an hour or so, Fontenot returned to Elton by 9 p.m. and was seen purchasing a drink. And there investigators lost the trail. There were false leads—a discarded bloodstained army jacket turned out to have been the result of an automobile accident involving a cow, an early-morning sighting of Fontenot with two men in Kinder on Sunday was disproved, and more than fifty interviews in Louisiana and Texas turned up not much more than kind words for Gerald, a likeable kid with a slim build, deep dimples, big ears, an infectious grin and a lively sense of fun.

And then, suddenly, somehow, the name of Anita Guidry Ortego began floating around, whispered to investigators in Beaumont, overheard in Crowley supermarket gossip indicating that police should *"cherchez la belle dame sans merci."* If officers wanted to find out what had happened to the Fontenot youth, the conversations reportedly went in French, they should look for a one-armed man and a beautiful woman with no mercy.

Two factors seemed to break the case, tying the murder of Gerald Fontenot to these two bizarre characters. One involved breaking the code of silence among teenaged boys who had succumbed to the siren song of sex emanating from the Elton household of slight, darkhaired Anita Guidry Ortego, aged twenty-nine, and her husband Abel, a forty-

Gerald Fontenot
(Courtesy Russell Sonnier)

five-year-old veteran of World War II who had lost his left arm in a tank explosion, drew a disability pension, and worked as a rice dryer in a mill from which he could spy on his home with binoculars from upstairs windows. The other break in the case involved charges filed against the couple for aggravated rape of a twelve-year-old girl.

Russell Sonnier, Gerald Fontenot's younger half-brother, was one of those teenaged boys who finally talked. "I first went out to their house when I was fifteen or sixteen, I guess," he recalls. "It all got started with young kids drinking, listening to people talk, then calling the Ortegos up and Abel would say, 'Yeah, come on out.' Seemed like everybody in that town knew about it."

Perhaps the adults remained uninformed, but the kids soon spread the word among their own peer group. Sonnier had known Abel Ortego as a pillar of St. Joseph's Catholic Church in Elton, where he was an usher and Knights of Columbus member and his son served as an altar boy. Ortego lived in the country outside Elton, about a mile north of town, and had for years raised hogs, remaining so strong and proficient with his single arm that he was considered expert at castrating the young boars, necessary to tame the flavor of the meat. But after the death of his first wife, by whom he had four children, Ortego's life spiralled downward.

"I never thought anything of it until we got rumors of this happening," Sonnier continued. "I only went to his house once, and as far as we were concerned, he was a real nice, nice fellow. When I went, there was five of us boys. Abel's kids were gone, so we all went in the house and sat in the living room. Abel came in and said, 'Well, boys, what are you here for?' And we didn't know what to say. Finally he'd say it, and we'd say, 'Oh, *yeah!'* And Anita'd be sitting there too, and he'd make her get undressed and go in the bedroom, and he'd stand on the side of the bed and watch. This was the way he got his kicks."

Louisiana State Police Troopers Dallas Bertrand and Jack LeBlanc, called in to assist local law enforcement with the investigation, began taking statements from young boys in the community who had visited the Ortegos. "This was the sad part about it all," says Bertrand, who had been a criminal investigator for the sheriff's department for ten years before working on this case as a state policeman. "These were boys who'd been with her and him both." Calling Gerald Fontenot "a good boy, good looking and well liked by everybody," Bertrand remembers that "before this broke, you had scuttlebutt, people gossiping about it, because this had been going on and wasn't something that happened overnight, but the kids weren't gonna say nothing to grownups. They'd tell their friends, sure. But as far as law enforcement, I don't think nobody knew. I sure didn't, and hell, I was working there."

Statements from teenaged boys implicated the Ortego couple in a bizarre sex scandal, involving voyeurism, group orgies, homosexuality, and even the entire Basile Bearcats football team *en masse*, if reports can be believed. "This was not for money," Bertrand explains, "just sex. They didn't charge. Abel was a homosexual, and he'd let these boys go with his wife as long as they'd go with him."

There was even talk of other attempts at mutilation. Gerald Fontenot's mother, Mamie Reed, recalls, "Before it happened to my little boy, some boy friend of his went over there to Anita's place and they tried that on him, and when they started cutting him, somebody knocked on the door and they let him go. And after that he told his daddy what had happened."

Dallas Bertrand says, "'Course lots of the rumors weren't true, but you had a certain group of boys going, and say one week it's five of them, then first thing you know, they'd talk about it, and the next week it grew, and so on. You got lots of young kids involved, some as young as thirteen. And in their statements, them boys didn't pull no punches; that's where we got to the nittygritty of this thing. Jack LeBlanc and I were the ones who broke this case, along with the sheriff's department chief criminal deputy Jack Sirman, and it was these boys who put the icing on the cake with their statements."

Russell Sonnier did not know where Gerald was going on the night of Saturday, June 23, 1962. "We never went there together," he says of the Ortego house. "I didn't know where he was that night, but after they found out he was murdered, to tell the truth I never did say anything to anybody, but Abel Ortego was the first person I thought of."

Allen Parish Sheriff John C. Durio, in the sheriff's department for more than thirty years, says his predecessor in office and other law enforcement agents began to get the same premonitions. "This happened on Saturday night," he recalls, "and on Sunday afternoon we were at the Ortego house with permission to search. We knew, mostly from questioning people, that while this was not a public place of ill repute, they seemed to team together to solicit prostitution, though no one ever reported it. This house was sitting out there, and a lot of kids were always going through it. When this thing went down, our questioning led right to them. We knew that Gerald Fontenot had been seen in this house many times."

The questioning also led to the filing of charges of aggravated rape of a juvenile against Abel Ortego and accessory charges against Anita, who was alleged to have held the child while her husband assaulted her, allowing law enforcement officials to confine and question them. Anita, born August 14, 1932, was said to be a nice-looking young woman, 5'2" and barely over 100 pounds in weight. She was considered by most observers the weaker of the two, and soon broke under questioning, asking to make a confession. Her forty-eight-page statement was signed on July 9.

In it, Anita Guidry Ortego stated that she had known young Gerald Fontenot for some time and had been intimate with him on numerous occasions, including the night of June 23, when she had initially seen him in Elton and he had asked permission to visit her home. According to the confession, Anita returned home to seek her husband's approval, then returned to pick up Fontenot, and, with the consent of Abel Ortego, had sexual relations with him at her home while Abel looked on.

Abel Ortego and his wife, Anita Ortego
(Courtesy *The Oakdale Beacon*)

Mrs. Ortego said she then left the home long enough to transport Abel's teenaged daughter and a friend from a youth dance to a neighbor's house, returning to find Fontenot lying naked on the bed, with his hands and feet bound behind him. Asked by her husband to help him move the unconscious Fontenot to the kitchen, Anita complied and said that the couple, working together, then emasculated the boy, wrapped him in a raincoat, put him into the back seat of the family car and drove him to the Kinder Canal, where his body would be found the following morning. There, on the canal bank, Anita Ortego said her husband cut Fontenot's throat with a single-edged razor blade and the two of them pushed him into the water. When he continued to struggle, Ortego told his wife to bring from the car the lug wrench with which he beat Fontenot on the head, and then held him under water until his struggles ceased. Into canal waters the couple threw the boy's clothing and also his testicles, carefully transported from the Ortego kitchen.

Within the week, Anita Ortego's husband Abel would make his own shorter confession, in which he attempted to lay most of the blame for the murder of Gerald Fontenot on his wife, saying he was so drunk he did not know what he was doing and just followed Anita's orders, adding that "she seemed to enjoy it" in some sadistic fashion.

By five o'clock that fateful Saturday afternoon, Oretgo said, he had already nearly finished the half-pint of whiskey purchased at lunchtime and sent his wife out to buy another when she dropped off his daughter for an overnight stay at the home of a friend. Around dark, he related, Anita left their home near Elton again to take the girls to a dance in neighboring Kinder and returned. Ortego himself got in the car and drove around town, saying "it was so dull I came right back home," returning his attention to his whiskey bottle and the television set. Anita then drove into town several more times looking for action, apparently finding none.

Abel Ortego had run out of whiskey again, he relates, and sent his wife to town for more, then told her she could "make a round to Basile" if she wanted. When she returned half an hour later, she showed him the can of beer she'd bought and told him she hadn't seen anyone she knew in Basile but had seen Gerald Fontenot hitchiking on the road on her way home. She had not picked him up, but said he wanted to visit the Ortego home.

"No, let's sleep tonight," Ortego reported he told his wife, at which point the telephone rang. It was Gerald Fontenot wanting to know if a visit would be permissible. Ortego said he told the youth, "Yeah, come on ahead," then gave his wife permission to pick him up, which she did.

When Fontenot arrived, the men shook hands, sat down on the sofa and had a drink together, according to Ortego's confession. Then Anita beckoned her husband from the bedroom, where she, speaking softly, "asked me for us to tie him up now," Ortego said, "and as she was talking about tying Gerald up she grabbed herself between her legs and quivered and had a climax."

According to Ortego, he tried to divert his wife's attention. "I told Anita, 'No, go get Gerald hard and give the poor boy a piece,' and in my own mind I thought this would satisfy her and she wouldn't want to cut his nuts out." While Anita and Gerald Fontenot were in the bedroom, Ortego said he tried to get up but was so drunk he fell to the floor. "I got back up on the sofa and stayed there until Nita came out of the bedroom," he continued, "and she came to me and asked if I wanted to cut his nuts now. I told her, 'No, go on and play with him' until it was time to go get the kids and be damn sure she was in Kinder in time to pick up the kids because I was too drunk to see about them."

When Anita Ortego left around 10:30 or 11 p.m. to pick up the teenagers at the Kinder dance, Ortego said she told him that when she returned, "We're going to cut his nuts out." He stated that he managed to get off the sofa and into the bedroom to fetch the whiskey bottle, taking a big drink while noticing that Gerald Fontenot was asleep, naked, on the bed. "I don't know what made me do it," Ortego confessed, "but I stumbled over to the chest of drawers and opened a drawer and got some ropes out that we had in the drawer to tie packages with, and walked on my knees to the bed and in this position, on my knees, I tied Gerald Fontenot's hands together first and then tied his feet together."

Ortego than dragged himself back to the sofa in the living room, where he lay until his wife Anita returned and woke him up. "Nita looked toward the bedroom," Abel

Ortego continued, "and when she saw Gerald tied up she put her hands between her legs and did the same thing as she did when she talked about cutting Gerald's nuts out."

The couple then returned to the bedroom together, where Anita woke Fontenot. The youth, naked and bound hand and foot, naturally wanted to know what was going on. "Wake up, boy, and come here, and you'll find out," Anita reportedly told him, pulling his feet and legs to the floor and sitting him up on the edge of the bed. With one of the Ortegos supporting him at each side, Fontenot was propelled into the kitchen and stretched out on the floor between the sofa and the heater.

There, taking her husband's belt, Anita Ortego struck the youth several times. "I was good and drunk all this time," her husband's confession relates, and Anita reportedly criticized him for it. "Nita told me that he wasn't tied good and told me that when I was drunk I couldn't never do nothing right, so she went somewhere and came back with an electric cord," with which she trussed Gerald's bound feet and hands together behind his back.

The Ortego confession continues to relate that Anita "got up and went somewhere, and when she came back, she rolled Gerald over on his back as far as she could and reached down and grabbed his sack and pulled and played with it. She called me over there and I slipped down on my knees on the other side of Gerald, and Nita grabbed one of Gerald Fontenot's nuts and squeezed it out tight. She handed the razor blade to me and told me to cut his nut out. Why I did it, I don't know, but I took the razor blade and cut the nut out by slitting the sack."

The act was repeated on the other side, then Anita Ortego, who her husband said was "climaxing again" during the procedure, took both testicles and put them in the kitchen sink, where she washed them and commented on how pink they were. Gerald Fontenot, meanwhile, had apparently been aroused by the excruciating pain and was "hollering," according to Ortego. "While I was washing my hands, Gerald called me and said, 'Abel, what are you going to do, let me bleed to death?' I told him no and told Nita to get ready, we were going to take Gerald to the Kinder Clinic."

With a pillowcase stuffed between his legs to slow the flow of blood, Gerald Fontenot was moved to the back seat of the family car, along with his neatly folded clothes and his testicles in a paper sack. "I started to drive," Ortego confessed, "but Nita told me I was too damn drunk to drive, so I got in the right side of the front seat. Nita got under the wheel and drove. She asked me what road to take and I told her to take the back road. We passed the Indian Church, through the Indian settlement, and came out to the Richard brothers' road. I made the remark that we would come out by Clyde Chachere's place. I remember passing Fruge's home and Odom's barn and I don't remember any more until Nita had stopped the car and opened the door and told me to get out."

The car had arrived not at the Kinder Clinic, but at an isolated spot on a gravel road travelling along the banks of the Kinder Canal. Gerald Fontenot was removed from the back seat and, according to the confession of Ortego, never said a word until he was deposited on the roadbed and begged, "Oh, no, Abel, not drown."

Anita Ortego allegedly brought a razor blade from the car, held Fontenot's head back with one hand and passed the razor blade to Abel, saying, according to him, "Cut his neck and let's kill the bastard." Ortego said he "didn't know why, but I did what she told me to do." After a wait of a few minutes, the two then threw Fontenot into the canal. His body surfaced by a fence, at which point Anita reportedly turned to her husband and said, "When you're drunk, you can't do a damn thing right."

She then brought a lug wrench and jack handle combination from the car and instructed Abel to use it to kill Gerald Fontenot. "I got down in the water and hit Gerald in the head," Ortego's statement continued. "Nita was standing on the bank telling me what to do. After I hit Gerald in the head, I threw the wrench as far down the canal into the water as I could. Gerald slumped in the water and I held him under for awhile."

Gerald Fontenot's struggles for life had ceased. His clothing, the pillowcase used to stem his bleeding, and his severed testicles in the paper sack where Anita had placed them after washing them so carefully in the kitchen sink, all were thrown into the canal along with him. Anita Ortego turned the car around. Abel lit a cigarette. It was a little after two o'clock on Sunday morning when the couple reached their home. Abel had another drink and went to bed, leaving Anita to clean the bloodstained house. The next morning, he burned the raincoat in which Gerald Fontenot had been wrapped during the trip from the Ortego home to the Kinder Canal.

After the July confessions, an Allen Parish grand jury in early August returned four true bills against Abel and Anita Ortego, charging both with the murder of Gerald Davis Fontenot, and additionally charging Ortego with aggravated rape of a juvenile and his wife as an accessory to that crime. Trials were set for early November, to be prosecuted by Bernard Marcantel, district attorney for both Allen and Jeff Davis parishes, with help from Alfred Ray Ryder, assistant DA. Ortego's trial was to be held first, and Oakdale attorney John P. Navarre was appointed by the court to defend him. Brothers Ed and Holmes Mouser, both Oakdale lawyers, were appointed to defend Anita Guidry Ortego.

Navarre recalls that at the time, there were few attorneys practicing in the small parish of Allen, and since the Ortego charges carried at least the potential of capital punishment, only a lawyer with five or more years of practice could be appointed defense counsel. The Mouser brothers, initially intended to represent both Ortegos, asked the judge to be excused from representing Abel on the basis that there might be a conflict in their defense, so Navarre was asked to represent him. At the time, he says, "the DA was adamant that he was going to go for the death penalty, so I kept filing technical things, doing the best I could for him."

After delays caused by some changes in the makeup of the sanity commission appointed by the court to determine the Ortegos' abilities to stand trial and assist in their own defense, Dr. Paul Shorts as acting Allen Parish coroner and Dr. John Trice, East Louisiana State Hospital psychiatrist, eventually constituted the lunacy commission which on December 19, 1962, would declare Anita Ortego so schizophrenic as to be incapable of defending herself, understanding the charges against her or cooperating with counsel. Her prognosis, the commission ruled, even after confinement at ELSH since September, was "practically nil," she was not ever expected to recover and was being "permanently committed" to the forensic division (security treatment section) of the mental hospital at Jackson after the hearing in Thirty-first Judicial District Court before District Judge Minos D. Miller, Jr.

To some of the investigators involved in the case, the insanity ruling made sense for Anita Ortego, who was not yet thirty at the time of the murder, a good fifteen years younger than Abel. Sheriff Durio says now that it was obvious to law enforcement officers involved in the case that Anita Ortego was "a little simpleminded. Abel was the dominant male, naturally, and much older, too. He was a very dominant thing in her life; if he had told her to kill ten men, she would have done it. She did anything he said, including becoming a whore for all these young kids. If she'd gotten in with a good man, she'd never have gotten in trouble. She would have done anything that a person told her to do."

Former state trooper Dallas Bertrand is another who supported the insanity ruling for Anita wholeheartedly. "She was weak, see? She was a weak person," he says. "Abel tried to blame her, but we know different. She was the type of person who would do exactly whatever he wanted her to do, she was that weak. Not a bad-looking girl, woman. Abel, he was sharp. I'm sure he was like a dual personality, but he was a smart man, nobody's fool. Sick, yeah, but not his brain; he just led a dual life, a big usher in church, a World War II veteran, respected by everybody. You'd have to know Anita like I did; she was just a weak person, and I think she done just exactly what her husband told her to do. He tried to put the blame on her, but that didn't work; you could talk to her forty minutes and know she was a weak person."

Even Russell Sonnier, half-brother of Gerald Fontenot, described Anita as "kind of slow. She would do just whatever he said. People like that continue to build up to something more, eventually; it's just on their mind. Mostly we always went out there in groups of boys, you know? And Gerald was unlucky enough to have been by himself."

Defense attorney Navarre also recalls Anita as a person with "some weird ideas and a very promiscuous attitude toward sex" as well as being "of rather low mentality," but he always felt she just might have actually been the instigator of the crime nevertheless, or at least as culpable as her husband. "I had known Abel before," he recalls, "and to the best of the information I got, he led a very normal life with his first wife. Abel's family blamed Anita for a lot of his problems. During his first marriage, there was no weird sex or anything of this sort, he was well regarded by the people in the community, and apparently the first wife was a stabilizing influence on him."

Anita, on the other hand, if local talk could be believed, had earned a rather unsavoury reputation from early adolescence, and Navarre says "young men in the Elton-Kinder area knew that they could have sex with her at any time, and a number of them did, especially in the seventeen to twenty-two-year-old age group. There's nothing illegal about having sex with another man's wife, especially if he consents. I guess if some of them were juveniles there might have been charges of contributing to their delinquency, but most of them were nineteen or over and they told their friends, not their mothers."

Others in the community were not even this charitable in their attitude toward Anita. One former neighbor recalls her as having been taken in as an unwanted infant by the town jailer Tom Griffin. By the time she reached early adolescence, she was known as a promiscuous girl of low moral character who sat on the porch in front of the house where she was raised, beckoning to boys and men walking along the street. There was talk of an early pregnancy, an abortion, interracial and intergenerational relations, as well as a prominent family that was always said to extend a helping hand to get her out of trouble.

That helping hand did not desert her in even these scandalous circumstances. The "permanent" commitment to the forensic facility of East Louisiana State Hospital at Jackson lasted less than four years, during which time Anita Guidry Ortego, according to the recollections of state employees who worked with her then, exhibited little sign of mental illness, was a good worker, and involved at least one male member of the administrative staff in alleged sexual misconduct.

In February 1966 Dr. Allan M. Johnstone, clinical director and chief of staff at East Louisiana State Hospital, reported to Judge Miller that Anita was considered capable of assisting counsel in her defense, capable of understanding pending charges against her and competent to stand trial, despite some intellectual deficiency. Dr. Johnstone then requested that Anita Ortego be returned to the jurisdiction of the committing court at the earliest opportunity. By April 1968, Anita had been completely discharged from the forensic facility, returned to Allen Parish to face lesser charges and was sentenced only to time already served, walking away a free woman.

Ed Mouser, now a retired judge and the only surviving member of Anita Guidry Ortego's defense team, refuses to discuss the case, citing ethical considerations. And Anita Ortego's exact present whereabouts are unknown, though unverified sightings and rumors have placed her in such varied circumstances as working in a house of ill repute in Eunice, in New Orleans, still confined in the state mental hospital at Jackson, or living anonymously as a lawyer's wife in Oakdale. She seems in actuality to be in the Baton Rouge area, where her last known contact with the law was an arrest on a minor charge dealing with improper telephone communications in Baton Rouge in the summer of 1987.

Abel Ortego would not get off so easily. He underwent psychiatric testing from mid-September through mid-October at the East Louisiana State Hospital in Jackson, where doctors determined him to be capable of understanding court procedure and of defending himself. Nevertheless, defense attorney Navarre initially pleaded his own client innocent by reason of insanity before Judge M. D. Miller, Jr., in the Oberlin courthouse in early January, objecting to his client being arraigned without his wife and successfully quashing the first murder indictment because of an improperly empanelled grand jury for which one of the requisite witnesses was functionally illiterate.

He also petitioned the court for a change of venue for Abel's trial because of "prejudice existing in the public mind against him, growing out of articles and items of news published in the newspaper, magazines and rumors and stories circulated about in the community and the demonstrations and abuse against members of his family that the citizens of Allen Parish have become so inflamed and prejudiced against your defendant that it will be impossible to secure an unbiased jury and impossible to secure a fair and impartial trial." By this time, several sensational crime magazines had unearthed the story and released prurient national features with eyecatching titles like "The Case of the Jealous Dr. Jekyll-Mr. Hyde" and "Woman Without Mercy."

By March, however, the DA agreed, according to Navarre, to let Ortego change his plea in the murder from insanity to guilty without capital punishment, for which he was formally arraigned "after prior fixing" on March 11, 1963. Abel Ortego's qualified plea was accepted in the presence of District Attorney Bernard N. Marcantel and Alfred Ray Ryder, assistant DA, representing the state, and John P. Navarre, attorney for the defendant. District Judge Miller rendered judgment in favor of the state of Louisiana and against the defendant Abel Ortego, whom he sentenced to serve the remainder of his natural life in the state penitentiary at Angola, Louisiana.

Before the judgment was rendered, however, the state, in the person of Bernard N. Marcantel, entered into the court record its reasons for accepting such a reduced plea, a move the DA said he felt necessary "in view of the widespread interest in this crime and the shocking nature of the act." Commending the fine investigative work of Sheriff Bill Cowart, Trooper Dallas Bertrand and other involved law enforcement officials, and insisting that the state did not "in the least minimize the heinous nature of this crime," Marcantel stated that he felt the acceptance of the plea without trial was "in the interest of justice and beneficial to the people of this parish," adding that "the shocking nature of the evidence that would necessarily be brought out in a trial would scandalize our beloved parish and district and many innocent people would be hurt."

Reminding the court that Anita Ortego had been "permanently committed to East Louisiana State Hospital at Jackson," thus depriving the state of use of her confession and evidence based upon her statements, Marcantel also pointed out that the state's case was predicated substantially upon Ortego's confession, and consequently some consideration should be given him for his cooperation with investigators. Ortego was also, Marcantel pointed out, intoxicated at the time of the crime, a homosexual with "certain mental attitudes inimical to the interests of organized society," a sociopathic personality and a pathological liar, besides having lost an arm in the service of his country which "no doubt also tended to warp his thinking."

While sanity rulings of the time would not permit excusing defendants because of such mental aberrations, Marcantel said, they and the fact that the victim was involved in an illicit relationship with the defendant's wife should be considered "at least mitigating circumstances in determining the premeditation necessary to constitute the crime of murder." A trial would not only be costly but hurtful too, and might well reach the very same verdict in the end.

Abel M. Ortego, whose children were subsequently raised by his sister, was sent on March 13, 1963, to the Louisiana State Penitentiary at Angola, where he remained in protective custody in Camp H, partially because of his known homosexuality and partially to shield him from the violence even hardened criminals usually visit upon perpetrators of crimes against children. He would not leave for nearly two decades, until his death from a heart attack on September 15, 1981, at the age of sixty-four. The charges of aggravated rape of a juvenile girl were left pending and were never pressed, the feeling being that the murder charges would suffice to remove the defendant from society.

Thus it was never officially revealed to the public that the child Ortego molested, in his last act of perversion as a free man, was his own.

The Warden Comments: The strange case of Abel and Anita Ortego demonstrates that justice in the state of Louisiana has not always been equal-handed, as the symbolically balanced scales purport to show, and that a defendant with even a small amount of influence and the right connections can often beat the system. There has always been a reluctance to prosecute women, but the inequity of sentences and time served by the two major perpetrators in this case represents more than that traditional hesitation.

Cases like this are what cause offenders and even the general public to have little respect for the criminal justice system. It is obvious to even the most casual observer that the two defendants received inequitable treatment under the law, in a legal system which promises fair and equal consideration to even the most indigent and inarticulate of defendants. Anita's mental disability, questionable at best, should not have precluded her being at least tried by a jury and considered for the same punishment meted Abel, once the treatment facility returned her to the jurisdiction of the court as capable of standing trial for her offense, for her culpability in the crime certainly seemed to match his.

This case points up the need for more uniformity in sentencing, the same sentence being handed down for the same crime in the absence of mitigating circumstances. At

Angola, I recall having two second-time drug offenders, for example, one doing fifty years and the other a single year for the same possession charge. While in Tennessee I served as chairman of a committee composed of judges, district attorneys and members of the legislature, charged with developing a uniform system of sentencing for that state. Eventually enacted, the presumptive sentencing system we developed prescribed certain fixed sentences for particular offenses, which nevertheless differentiated among first-offender crimes, second-offender crimes and multiple-offender crimes, becoming more severe with each progression. The judge could deviate from the set sentences only after recording pertinent reasons. This assured equality in justice to a greater extent, though perhaps there is no fool-proof method.

In Louisiana, however, we were not even successful in bringing before the legislature the model sentencing act designed by the National Council on Crime and Delinquency. Justice Joe Sanders of Louisiana had served on the committee that developed this model legislation back in the late 1960s. Shortly after Edwin Edwards was elected governor the first time, Secretary of Corrections Elayn Hunt and I had a meeting with him. I had brought along a copy of this progressive legislation, which I redesigned to meet the specific needs of Louisiana in a number of ways, one being in the establishment of a fulltime professional board of parole, outlining educational and career qualifications for board members and so forth. Gov. Edwards was enthusiastic about the legislation and the possibility of successfully steering it through the legislature at that time, but Mrs. Hunt demurred, saying she would rather think about it, perhaps make some changes, and possibly present it to the next session of the legislature. Making timely decisions was never Mrs. Hunt's strong point. Unfortunately, the time was ripe then; by the next session, there were other problems, and the momentum had been lost. That was the last I ever heard of a model sentencing act for Louisiana.

The classification process upon entering prison determines a prisoner's needs both treatment-wise and security-wise. Upon his admission to Angola, Abel Ortego was confined to Camp H for inmates needing special protection. Prisoners convicted of such heinous crimes as Ortego's usually have a difficult time in prison. Child molesters and other sex deviants, as well as people who have killed in a horrendous or especially heartless fashion, are at the lower end of the social strata of the prison class structure, on the upper end of which are armed robbers and murderers whose crimes involve little or no premeditation or brutality.

To the best of my knowledge, Ortego led a rather lonely life in prison, mixing little with other prisoners. On my regular inspection visits to the camp dining room where he worked, his eyes always seemed to follow me as I moved around the area, and I was never sure whether it was me watching him because of the nature of his crime or him watching me because of the authoritarian position I occupied. Although Ortego was never caught in any homosexual activities, it was common knowledge among camp authorities that he always had a young "gal-boy" on the string, for whom he would buy small luxuries not easily obtainable in confinement. Ortego's financial position was much better than most prisoners, thanks to the compensation he drew for a service-connected disability.

As far as can be determined there was never any communication between him and Anita after he was confined to the penitentiary. The forensic facility, at that time part of the East Louisiana State Hospital, was located in Jackson, some thirty-eight miles from Angola. From all reports, Anita's adjustment at the forensic facility during her strangely brief stay was more than adequate, though her old behavior patterns must have continued to dominate her personality, for she and a male employee in a supervisory position reportedly carried on an illicit and decidedly illegal liaison which eventually resulted in the employee's departure.

One of the real mysteries of this case is the fact that this woman, who was a party to one of the most brutal murders ever committed in the state of Louisiana, was released at such an early date. When committed she was said to be schizophrenic, and her chances of recovery were considered almost nil. Many patients who have committed much less serious crimes and have recovered find it almost impossible to gain release, and at that particular point in time, the early sixties, patient rights were not a paramount concern. Even now, it would be difficult to gain release for a patient in similar circumstances, even after a lengthy period of treatment.

It would appear that Anita has had somebody powerful interceding in her behalf all along the way. Talk around her hometown has always alluded to an illegitimate connection with a prominent and powerful family there. To this day, almost thirty years after the crime, it remains nearly impossible to obtain much concrete information on her. The public records of her confession, sanity hearings and commitment, subsequent release and court hearings, probation arrangements and other judicial rulings are reported unavailable by the Allen Parish clerk of court, whereas Abel Ortego's records are readily furnished for research. There are still those, obviously, who continue to feel that certain portions of Anita's story need to be covered up, and they apparently still have the power to do so.

IV

Have You Ever Learned to Love a Cowboy?

It is probably Willie Nelson's plaintive ballad which best sums up the dichotomy of the all-American cowboy, especially the verses that go like this:

Mamas, don't let your babies grow up to be cowboys,
Don't let them pick guitars and drive them old trucks,
Make them be doctors and lawyers and such.
Mamas, don't let your babies grow up to be cowboys,
They're never at home, and they're always alone
Even with someone they love.

Cowboys like smokey old poolrooms and clear mountain mornings,
Little lost puppies and children and girls of the night,
Them that don't known him won't like him
And them that do, sometimes won't know how to take him,
He's not wrong, he's just different, and his pride won't let him
Do things to make you think he's right.

The cowboy, this bigger-than-life buckeroo, came riding out of the Wild West into the American consciousness at a time when homegrown heroes were hard to come by, and for generations afterward every freckle-faced boy and a lot of little girls too included chaps and spurs and Stetsons on their Christmas wish lists, even those with nothing softer to straddle than broomsticks or sawhorses moseying along concrete canyons.

There was something about cowboys which commanded respect, these hard-honed men from a harsh demanding world, oblivious to pain or fear, able to withstand fierce winter blizzards or dry sun-parched desert summers, sometimes beaten by the weather but rarely by anything else. Like the tough Texas longhorns which learned to live and even thrive on the sparsest and most forbidding of range conditions, cowboys were survivors.

Jack Favor
(Courtesy Ponder Favor)

From earliest childhood they were molded and marked by the wild West Texas landscape, the wide-open spaces where the winds howl and whine and turn creaky windmills drawing life-giving water from underground pools, where the stinging, blinding, wind-driven sandstorms etch character lines on the exposed faces of rocks and cowpokes too, where winter's desolate harshness hangs icicles from barbed-wire fences and handlebar moustaches alike before giving way in warmer weather to the most wondrous blankets of blossoming wildflowers to color anyplace in the continental United States.

If the land was one of contrasts, so too were the men molded by life there, incredibly strong and brave, yet strangely vulnerable and soft-hearted at the same time. Of just such contrasts was a cowboy named Jack Graves Favor made. Had he been marked only by strength, only by bluster or bravado, his story might not hold such interest.

Jack Favor was born in 1911 in Eula, Callahan County, Texas, growing up with three brothers and a sister on the family's Z Ranch and early exhibiting such roping and riding skills that even as a youngster he was already breaking wild horses for a Turkey Creek outfit and by the age of twelve was being paid a man's salary by the famous Harris Ranch. Filling out his 6'2" frame, he would soon enough be lured into the rough-and-tumble world of championship rodeo, where for decades his would be the name to be reckoned with in steer wrestling and bronc busting.

Throughout the forties and fifties Jack Favor would be world-champion steer wrestler four times and runner-up champion on fifteen ocasions, travelling the circuit with other contestants between the big-time rodeos in Denver, Houston, Fort Worth, Chicago, San Antonio, Detroit, and even New York, where the month-long show in Madison Square Garden was the pinnacle of cowboy competition, widely known as the World Series of Rodeo.

In one Houston arena Favor would set an unbeatable world record by bulldogging a steer in an incredible 2.2 seconds, and in Madison Square Garden one night he won $18,000 for becoming the first to ride a hunk of four-legged fury called Hell's Angel, the greatest bucking horse that ever lived. With typical cowboy nonchalance, Jack spent a few thousand dollars of his winnings in celebration with his friends, then boarded the train home with the rest of the cash stuffed into a battered old suitcase tied shut with piggin' string, used by ropers to bind together three legs of roped calves in arena competition.

It was also in New York, in 1947, that a couple of Blue Bell Corporation executives walked up to Jack Favor in a hotel ballroom and commented on what a good-looking pair of jeans he was wearing, offering to purchase them for $100. Right there and then Jack peeled off the pants, handsewn for him like all his fancy cowboy duds by tailor Rodeo Ben. A pattern was cut from the pants and Wrangler bluejeans were born. Blue Bell Wranglers and other companies used to throw parties for the cowboys to keep them entertained in New York, and Jack Favor was often hired as bouncer for these shindigs, keeping the peace and not averse, when necessary, to using skills honed as heavyweight boxing champ during several hitches in the Navy.

Like all good cowboys, Jack had a tremendous tolerance for pain. When school was out, Jack's wife Ponder and their three children often travelled with him to rodeos; other times he would take turns taking one child at a time. Jack's son Tommy remembers being alone with his father when Jack broke his arm at a rodeo somewhere in Texas. Because of the swelling, Jack couldn't drive, so "he put his arm in a bootjack and yanked it back into place, put a metal cast on it and then an ace bandage, and propped it up on a pillow. I was eight years old," Tommy remembers, "and we had this 1958 Oldsmobile 98 pulling a shotgun trailer with two horses. And Daddy said, 'Son, it's 135 miles. You got one red light. Stop when you get to that red light. Drive us home.' This was at night, and I was sitting on a suitcase so I could reach the footpedals and see over the dash of that big Oldsmobile. I got us all the way to Arlington before I hit the power brakes and jackknifed the trailer. We went around and around. And Daddy said, 'Son, I think I can handle it from here.' He drove on in, backed the trailer up, told me to unload the horses, and that was it. I never heard him moan or cry."

It had been at another rodeo when Jack had his first real date with Ponder, though they had seen each other a few years earlier. "It was in '38 or '39," Ponder recalls fondly, "first time I ever saw him. I was walking down the street. He had on a white cowboy hat with a black braid around the brim, and I had never seen a hat like that. I never did look at *him;* I was looking at that hat. I mean I turned around to look at the hat, and he turned around to look at me, and his first wife was with him and she jerked him by the arm. I looked down then and laughed, because that was the first time I'd really seen a man there; before, I'd just seen the hat. It was about two years after that that I met him; I remembered it because he still had on that same darn hat, and meanwhile he and his wife had divorced."

Their first date came about by accident, when Ponder and a girlfriend asked another cowboy for a ride to a rodeo in Granbury without knowing that he and Jack were travelling together to cut expenses. "So directly this cowboy walked up and asked me to dance," says Ponder with a twinkle in her eye, "and when we got on the floor, he says 'I just thought I'd tell you that if I take you to the rodeo, I'm bringing you back.' Well, actually I was going up there to see another cowboy I had met. So when we went to the rodeo, there was an afternoon show and a night performance. Jack was a contestant. So after the first show, we went to this little old joint that had one of those nickelodeons and we danced all afternoon until it was time to go to the rodeo. And when we pulled up, I saw this cowboy that I had been going up there to see, and he came over to the car. Right quick Jack says, 'O.B., I want you to meet my wife.' Well, O.B. just turned around and left, so I was stuck with Jack."

Jack had told cowboy buddies the first time he had laid eyes on her that Ponder was the best-looking woman he had ever seen and he was going to marry her. "'Course he just happened to have a wife at that time," Ponder says. "Pearl was seven or eight years older and it was a battle royal. Every time they had a fight she'd pull off her shoe and hit him in the head with the spiked heel on it, and she'd wind up in the hospital." Daughter Jane says, "Daddy never laid a hand on Mother." "Well, I never took off my shoe, either," interjects Ponder; "that makes a difference."

By 1941 Jack and Ponder had married, beginning a relationship of love and trust and faith which endured until Jack's death in late 1988. Even today Ponder speaks with great affection and admiration of her husband's physical strength and toughness, his love for children and kindness to people in general, his great courage and dark sturdy good looks, fetching photographs to show "what a handsome dude I married." Echoing these sentiments are the couple's three children, Jane, Janice and Tommy, who speak of feeling secure just being in their father's presence, of being taught to fight back and survive, of Jack's credo 'Winners never quit and quitters never win.'

And they laughingly recall his sense of humor too, how he would call a whole long list of "widow ladies" early each morning to check on them, inquiring enthusiastically about their sex lives, much to their simulated horror. "Have you ever learned to love a cowboy?" was his favorite question for everybody, Jane remembers.

Tommy says, "Daddy found humor in everything, except maybe when I branded the dog. We were playing cowboys and Indians one time, and my grandmother told me and this boy named Larry Maynard to burn the trash. We come and got Daddy's branding iron and stuck it in the fire and got it red hot. And I got Daddy's lariat rope out. He had a boxer dog that he just loved named Rusty, and I tied that dog up with this lariat rope and piggin' string, and I got that branding iron real hot, and I went out there in my Randolph Scott chaps and my six guns and all and I put my foot on that dog and I branded him. That branding iron went SSSSS and that dog went to bellowing. Well, I said, 'that's for real, get the garden hose!' So I started trying to scrub the brand off with some Tide soap and some water, and that dog's going nuts, 'course he's hogtied and can't go nowhere or bite or nothing.

"So I told Larry, 'That's not gonna wash off.' And he said, 'No, you burned him plumb down to the meat, that's there forever.' And I said, 'My Dad'll kill us. What are we gonna do now?' And he said he didn't know, so I said, 'Let's camouflage him!' So we got the leaf rake redhot and striped him like a zebra, rolled him over and striped him on the other side. So now he looks like a zebra with an F branded on his hip. We turn him loose and he starts doing these flips out there and bellowing, and I run put up my guns and everything. Daddy comes home and he looks out the window and he says, 'Ponder, what in the Sam Hill is wrong with that dog?' And all of a sudden I hear 'Tommy Ray, come here, boy!'" Not until Jack ended the dog's suffering would anyone else involved in the situation receive well-deserved attention, for animals were all-important to this cowboy.

Jack Favor and daughter Jane, 1944.
(Courtesy Ponder Favor)

Even before Jack had left the Favor ranch for the rodeo circuit and a family of his own, he had already been inculcated with the hard fast rules of living and surviving in West Texas, rules he would apply to whatever situation he might find himself facing wherever his travels took him. Favor's daughter Jane would later delineate these rules. First came the all-important livestock; you fed and cared for the cattle and horses first, because if you did not take care of them, they would not take care of you. Their needs had to come first, even before yours, and if you reached a point where you could not feed them or take care of them, you gave them to somebody who could or you put them out of their misery (dogs included).

Next rule was that you cherished and took care of your womenfolk. Ponder says she never saw Jack start a fight in his life, but if anybody ever hit him first, he'd sure finish it right there, especially if it involved one of his beloved girls. "We had this neighbor one time who was so mean and ugly to me when Jack was off rodeoing it was pitiful. And when Jack would come back in, I'd tell him and Jack would say, 'Well, honey, just pray for him.' He didn't believe I was having all this trouble," Ponder remembers.

"But one day Jack was just home from the hospital where he'd had a double hernia operation, and you know men don't stand up very straight after that. And he was walking around without his boots on and the neighbor didn't know he was there, so he came over to the fence and started giving me what-for. Jack heard him and came out, and Jack was holding onto a tree, talking to him. Well, this neighbor made the mistake of calling Jack a son of a bitch. Jack held onto that tree and hit him once and knocked him plumb back under another tree, then he stepped over the wire fence. The neighbor said, 'You're on my property,' and Jack said, 'Yes, I am' and hit him again. Then we got into the car and went down to the police station and Jack told them what he'd done and paid a fine. The policemen told Jack they'd had all kinds of trouble with the man and said if he paid the fine, no charges could be filed. And that's what they told the neighbor when he went down there after he got his face sewn up. You just felt secure when Jack was around. He protected his womenfolk. Period."

And the third rule of life in West Texas, the one which would come back to haunt Jack Favor in his later years, was that you did not leave a man stranded on the side of the road; life was hard and the weather harsh in this part of the country, and if you were lucky enough to be driving, you picked up the less fortunate on foot. "I've seen him pick up a hitchhiker and give him his last $5, and I'd say, 'Now Jack, what are *we* gonna do?' and he'd say 'We'll make it,' and we always did," Ponder recalls. Jack would remember his own days of hitchhiking between rodeos when he was just starting out on the professional circuit, and he always recalled his gratitude whenever someone would stop to offer him a ride. He returned the favor all his life. But one time he got more than he bargained for.

This was after diabetes and the beginnings of heart trouble in middle age convinced Jack to more or less retire from active rodeoing. Though he had just as often judged and produced rodeos for Tommy Steiner and other big rodeo companies while serving as a founding director of the Rodeo Cowboys Association, Jack's years as a contestant had taken a toll. Even a hard muscular body like his could take just so many years of diving from a hard-running quarterhorse onto the long horns of tough wily range steers to wrestle them to the ground, or balancing atop a bone-jarring bucking bronc while raking its shoulders with spurs.

In 1961 at the age of fifty, at his last competition in Texarkana, Jack had thrown two steers in a respectable 6.9 seconds, then thrown his old straw hat into the grandstand and announced, "That's the last one I'll go to, boys." Jack Favor, world-champion cowboy, settled down to life as a husband, father and highly successful four-state travelling salesman, hawking everything from eyeglass fittings to water repellent franchises on the road and managing a succession of automobile dealerships at home.

A Houston, Texas, salesman named M. A. Wyter (or Wyche, according to some accounts) had contacted Jack about becoming Louisiana distributor for a product Jack handled called Sure-Fits, bands that fit around eyeglasses to prevent slippage. Jack sold the Sure-Fits wholesale, twelve to a card for $3 a card, and Wyter wanted one hundred cards delivered to him in Shreveport on April 17, 1964. On his way from Tulsa, where

Jack had been setting up a franchise for a water repellent represented by Therma Chemical Corporation, he stopped for lunch in Muskogee, Oklahoma, on April 16 and picked up two hitchhikers headed in the same direction.

When the trio arrived in Shreveport at 11:30 that evening, Favor pulled into the Alamo Plaza Hotel Courts, where he registered under his full correct name and gave the correct license plate number of his Pontiac, EW 4438. He was given the last vacancy, room 306, at a rate of $9.50. As there were two double beds in the room and the two hitchhikers had nowhere else to go, he invited them to share the room overnight. Jack left early the next morning to meet his salesman out on Hwy. 80-West in the White Swan Cafe across from the state fairgrounds, but not before he had driven the two hitchhikers across the Red River bridge to Bossier City so they'd have a better chance of getting another ride without being picked up for vagrancy, something Louisiana law enforcement officials were notoriously tough on.

One of the hitchhikers had mentioned having fought bulls as an inmate rodeo clown in 1960 or 61 at the Oklahoma State Penitentiary at McAllister, a rodeo which Jack had in past years helped Jim Shoulders produce, but Jack had made his last appearance there in '59; he remembered it distinctly because his shoulder had been cut and dislocated then. He had never seen either of the hitchhikers before, and Jack Favor figured this would be the last time he would see or hear from these two fellows again.

He was wrong. Some eighteen months later, on September 1, 1965, Jack Favor was selling cars at an automobile agency in Fort Worth when a Texas Ranger, accompanied by a deputy sheriff from Bossier Parish in Louisiana, Chief Deputy Vol Dooley, approached him and showed a warrant for his arrest. "What for?" Jack asked. The answer was murder. Double murder.

The two hitchhikers Jack had picked up on that April 1964 Shreveport trip had not been such nice fellows after all, it seemed, though it took Jack awhile to figure out the connection. The two turned out to be Floyd Edward "Chigger" Cumbey and Donald Lee Yates, both ex-convicts with lengthy criminal records, and the minute Jack had deposited them in Bossier City, they had begun preparations for a robbery-murder which they committed in nearby Haughton, Louisiana, that same afternoon. A third party was somehow involved in the commission of this heinous crime. And Floyd Edward Cumbey said the name of that third party was Jack Favor.

Victims of the crime were Mr. and Mrs. W. R. Richey, who for five years had owned and operated a fishbait stand in a building adjoining their home in Haughton, selling minnows, goldfish, crawfish and bait. Mr. Richey, fifty-six, had previously operated a bait business at the foot of the old traffic bridge in Shreveport. He was known, according to Bossier Parish Sheriff Willie Waggonner, to keep large sums of cash in the safe in his home, as well as the cash register in his bait stand.

On the afternoon of April 17, 1964, someone entered the Richey bait stand in search of that money and murdered the couple gangland-execution-style, lying them across the bed in their home, placing the same pillow in turn over the head of each, and firing at point-blank range with a .45 automatic. A neighbor, Edward Barnes, discovered the bodies about 6 p.m. Bossier Parish Coroner Dr. C. H. McCuller performed a partial autopsy on Mrs. Richey to secure the slug which mutilated her skull at its entrance and mingled feathers and hair with brain matter; the bullet which killed Mr. Richey was recovered from the mattress beneath his body. No fingerprints or other incriminating evidence could be found at the scene. Dr. McCuller called the crime one of the most brutal he had investigated in his eleven years as coroner, and Bossier Parish law enforcement officials immediately began a search for the perpetrators.

It would not be until nearly Christmas 1964 that a break in the case would lure Chief Deputy Vol Dooley to Carthage, Missouri, where Floyd Edward Cumbey sat awaiting trial on yet another burglary, a career con-man at age thirty-one, figuring ways to stack the deck in his favor. His record, he knew, would not look good to a jury: bad conduct discharge from the Air Force in 1956, armed robbery and burglary conviction that same year resulting in seven-year's probation, a marriage that lasted all of twenty days before he took off on a crime spree with Donald Lee Yates and Billy Dean Brown culminating in an Idaho arrest for interstate auto theft and a sentence of five years in South Dakota's state prison for burglary, back to the Oklahoma State Prison at McAllister for parole violation from 1960 to 1963. Multiple-offender status would now earn Cumbey lengthy sentences, he knew. He decided to try the time-honored criminal tactic of turning state's evidence, cooperating with authorities in return for favored treatment. He had little to lose, and he found some receptive ears back in Louisiana, where elections were looming and an unsolved double murder reflected poorly on the investigative abilities of both DA and sheriff.

After Cumbey's Missouri trial ended with a hung jury and a mistrial, he voluntarily returned to Louisiana with Deputy Vol Dooley and began, in prison parlance, to sing like a canary. For the authorities he spun a tale of robbery and murder in Haughton, naming Yates as the triggerman inside the Richey home and Jack Favor as the instigator of the actual shootings while he himself merely drove the get-away car and stood lookout, "jiggering" or "holding the point" while watching out for the arrival of customers or the return of a couple of black employees seen earlier at the bait stand. The robbery, Cumbey said, netted only a disappointing couple of hundred dollars' worth of old-time and foreign money, not the $30,000 promised when the crime was planned at the shady Cheyenne Club in Tulsa on April 15, when the trio supposedly had been given pistols, maps and instructions.

Inside the Bossier Parish jail, Cumbey was spinning other tales for the benefit of impressionable fellow prisoners, claiming to have been the only convict ever to successfully escape from the infamous prison at Alcatraz (which just happened to have been already abandoned by that time), boasting that he was on the FBI's prestigious list of Ten Most-Wanted Criminals, advising novices on robbery techniques, and alluding to a plan to get even with Jack Favor for his involvement in an abortive gunbattle with police that supposedly resulted in the death of Cumbey's brother (alternate versions had Cumbey's brother killed in a car wreck or an ambush, or Jack's brother or a nephew who was a Texas Ranger being responsible instead of Jack himself, while at one point Cumbey denied even having a brother, much less one killed by police).

Floyd Edward Cumbey earned the reputation among Bossier jail inmates as a "head-runner," always shooting off his mouth, and a "snitch," yet he continued to receive favored treatment from authorities, having the run of the jail and free access to luxuries, according to later testimony by not only other inmates but parish authorities as well. Ponder Favor was told by one of the jailers, a fellow named King, that Cumbey had open-door privileges in the jail and a private cell to which girls were brought, and was escorted to a restaurant for steak dinners. "That jailer told me if he was me he'd do something about this, but what could I do? I didn't know what to do. I'd never even paid a fine in my life. I didn't know how to go about doing stuff like that," she says. On a trip to Texas for Jack Favor's extradition hearing, if later accounts from parish officials can be believed, Cumbey and Dooley shared not only a motel room but bottles of liquor and women as well. On the same trip, Cumbey was heard to threaten the lives of witnesses appearing for Favor.

Jack meanwhile had put together what he felt sure was incontrovertible evidence that he had nothing whatsoever to do with Cumbey, Yates or the crime they were said to have committed in Haughton. His only fault, he insisted, had been picking up the hitchhiking men, something he called "a bad habit I got" and one in which he had been indulging his entire life. He arrived at the November 12, 1965, extradition hearing in the Texas secretary of state's Austin office armed with receipts for gas purchased in Fort Worth and Oklahoma the day of the murder, receipts he kept for tax purposes in cigar boxes at home. He also had with him former rodeo star Willard Combs and his wife, who testified they had visited with Jack and a man named Jerry Rippentau (a Phillips 66 Oil Company agent to whom Jack gave a ride from Dallas to Tulsa) at their ranch near Reynoldsville, Oklahoma, on April 17; a ticket for a $3.33 lunch at a Reynoldsville barbeque restaurant which had to be charged to mutual friend Willard Combs when the proprietor could not make change for Jack's $20 bill; the cafe owner Laura Drennan (in some records rendered as Dernell) herself; and other witnesses who could verify Jack's presence in Oklahoma at the same time when Cumbey said he was in Louisiana committing a crime.

Yet the judge, after hearing Cumbey's testimony, ordered Jack Favor extradited to Louisiana. As lengthy appeals dragged on, Jack lost patience with the slow-moving judicial process in October 1966 and called Bossier Parish District Attorney Louis H.

Padgett, Jr., volunteering to return to Louisiana in an attempt to clear his name. "If I come down there and take a lie-detector test and pass it, will you drop these charges on me and let me alone?" Jack asked Padgett. Padgett said he would. Extradition still pending, Jack set out for Louisiana immediately, accompanied by a friend and as much cold cash as he could put his hands on in case he needed to pay for legal services in the neighboring state.

He thought he would be back home in Arlington, Texas, that evening. Instead, he was ushered into the Bossier jail, locked in a dank, foul-smelling cell, and refused permission to take a lie-detector test. The DA sent a message that the only way he would come down to the jail would be for Jack to agree to confess to the murders. No statement was taken from Jack, who would not see Padgett until his court appearances began months later; in the meantime Jack would have lost more than fifty pounds.

Trial was eventually set for April 1967, some three years after the commission of the original crime in Haughton. With fund-raising help from rodeo producer and longtime friend Tommy Steiner, sufficient money was raised to hire respected attorney Joe T. Cawthorn of Mansfield to defend Jack. Cawthorn told the family that for $10,000 he thought he could win the case and would go all the way to the Supreme Court if necessary.

The trial would be heard in Twenty-sixth Judicial Court of Bossier Parish, Judge O. E. Price presiding. Star witness for the state, of course, would be one Floyd Edward Cumbey, whose testimony would miraculously now be exact as to locations, dates and times, where in Austin he had been able to recall few of the specifics. Cumbey's threats against witnesses at Jack's initial extradition hearing had scared at least a few of them into sitting out the trial. Jerry Rippentau, who had ridden with Jack from Dallas to Tulsa on April 17, had died of a heart attack. And Cawthorn had advised Jack not to put Oklahoma cafe owner Laura Drennan on the stand because she was black and would therefore not, he said, be a credible witness in a state like Louisiana.

Nevertheless, an outpouring of support came from Jack's friends and associates, a number of whom insisted on travelling at their own expense to appear voluntarily as witnesses for the defense. The atmosphere around the trial was less than hospitable for Jack's supporters. Ponder and the children, travelling on a tight budget which allowed them a single meal a day, felt hostility everywhere they went. "The local people, they acted like we were pond scum, basically," Janice Favor Kitterman remembers. "Everybody knew who we were, and they weren't even nice to us at the motel."

"It was like we were suspect, like we were criminals," Tommy remembers, recounting how their home phone was tapped and he felt it necessary to check his mother's car for bombs and loose wires before she drove it, after hearing that a contract was out on family members. "Here I was sixteen years old, when I needed my Daddy the most," he says, "and the state of Louisiana was trying to take him away from me. I built up a terrible resentment. When we'd go into the restaurants there in Bossier, if they found out who we were, they wouldn't wait on us, or they'd sit there and stare at us and talk about us." Daughter Janice remembers most the cold close-set eyes of Floyd Cumbey. "He's scarier than Charles Manson," she says, "and at that trial, they literally let him roam that courthouse, and he'd come by where we were sitting out in the hall by the water fountain, to get a drink of water, and he'd just let the water run and glare at me. You talk about some cold eyes; I've seen snakes that have warmer eyes than him."

And Jane, who just had her fourth child five weeks before the trial began and who was having nightmares that someone would drive by with a machine gun and mow down her kids as they played in the yard, was horrified at the trial to see her great big father weighing less than she did. "I had never in my whole life," she recalls, "been able to walk up and put my arms all the way around my Daddy, he had such a big barrel chest and stomach out to here, and now I could walk up and put one arm around him, he was so skinny. And when I saw that, I can't express to you the rage I felt." Adds Janice, "It was just sheer cussedness that kept him going. They had him on so much medication he moved like a walking dead man. He looked like he had no blood." But, Jane adds, "he never ever quit, he never ever gave up, and he never ever bowed his head. He knew who he was, and it didn't matter if anybody else knew it or anybody else accepted it or anybody else believed it."

Attorney Cawthorn made the most of the differences in his client and the state's star witness. Calling Cumbey "a habitual criminal since his childhood days" who had been escorted by Vol Dooley from Missouri to the Bossier Parish jail on August 10, 1965, under a cloud of four hold orders from three other states where charges were apparently pending, Cawthorn grilled the chief deputy as to exactly what promises had been made on his office's or Padgett's authority in exchange for Cumbey's testimony against Favor. When Dooley denied holding out hope of reduced sentencing or other special dispensations, Cawthorn asked, "Then it is your testimony as an old and experienced officer that a man who has been in crime all his life freely, voluntarily, without hope of reward to your knowledge, admitted a crime that would cause him to be electrocuted under his admission without your promising him anything?" "He didn't ask us," Dooley answered.

Cawthorn made much of the fact that Cumbey, "a man who has been convicted, charged, tried, pursued, a habitual criminal...was given the right and the permission to make a voluntary statement," while Jack Favor, who surrendered voluntarily, who was shown to be clear of criminal record by an FBI background check, and who asked of his own free will to take a lie-detector test, was not given the opportunity by the district attorney or sheriff's department to answer questions or make a statement in his defense prior to trial. Dooley, describing for Cawthorn the hundred or so interviews conducted in investigating the Haughton murder case, admitted that not only had no statement been taken from Jack Favor, but also revealed that Mrs. Richey's former husband Frank Powell, "tried in this very court for manslaughter for beating a man to death" and represented at that trial by Louis Padgett, Jr., had not been questioned concerning the deaths of his former wife and her present spouse.

Legal maneuvering by the district attorney prevented the introduction as evidence of the sales slip showing that Jack Favor delivered one hundred cards of Sure-Fits to M. A. Wyter on April 17, 1964, at the White Swan Cafe on US 80 in Shreveport; since the slip was a duplicate, without Wyter himself, who could not be located, the DA called the document "self-serving and not admissable." The gas receipts showing Jack had been far from Haughton at the time of the murders were also ruled inadmissable in the absence of the gas station attendants who had signed them.

Even character witnesses for the defense were hampered by Padgett's constant badgering insistence that witnesses on the stand report no personal associations, only whether they might have heard other people discuss Jack's reputation in the community for truthfulness. That did not stop these determined friends of Jack Favor, like G. Alfred Brown, pastor of the 2800-member First Methodist Church Jack attended in Arlington, or Troy Wright who testified that Jack managed one of his car lots, buying and hiring and handling thousands of dollars, or devoted neighbors Mr. and Mrs. J. J. Lewis.

Tommy Steiner and Mrs. Tommy Steiner, owner-operators of the World Champion Steiner Rodeo Company, related their close associations with Jack Favor over many years, with Tommy testifying that his father had hired Jack to teach him the ropes as a young man and that together they would handle thousands of dollars in prize money. "One time at Corsicana, Texas," Steiner related, "the prize money exceded $10,000. Jack had it all in cash in his pocket and he helped me to do the paying off, and there wasn't even any question in their minds that he might keep some of it in his pocket. He never did come up short one time."

Other old rodeo associates insisted on testifying as well. Gene Pruitt, secretary-treasurer of the Rodeo Cowboy's Association, travelled all the way from Denver at his own expense to testify that "Jack Favor is a man to keep the peace, not cause trouble," and colorful world-champion steer-wrestler James "Big Jim" Bynum, aptly described as being "big as a side of beef," enthusiastically dramatized his heartfelt statement that "Jack Favor would pull his shirt off of his back and give it to you." Tommy Favor recalls with relish that particular testimony: "James Bynum tore his shirt off, said 'Jack Favor would give you the shirt off his back,' and grabbed his shirt and just ripped it. And Judge Price said he was gonna fine him for contempt of court for undressing. He's a big man, James Bynum is."

Jack's daughters Jane and Janice both testified that he had been a good Christian father and a non-drinker, while Jack's devoted mother-in-law, aged seventy-nine, said if she had had a son of her own "he couldn't have been any better than Jack." Ponder Favor, his wife since 1941, described her marriage as wonderful and Jack as a good father, a good husband, a good provider. "Has he been a good husband to you?" she was asked by Cawthorn. "I wouldn't change a hair on his head," she answered.

Padgett did his best to restrict the testimony of Jack's character witnesses, attacking as unqualified Harold Huddleston who admitted that, though he had known Jack for years and gone to church with him, he had never really sat down and discussed his character with others. Padgett asked, "Wouldn't it be correct to say you've come here in the interest of Jack Favor, to be fair about it?" Huddleston answered, "I've come here in the interest of what I think is justice." District Attorney Padgett responded, "I see, and that would be in the interest of Mr. Favor?" Answered Harold Huddleston determinedly, "In my opinion it is synonymous."

If the DA attempted to minimize the impact of testimony by Jack Favor's family and friends, the defense attorneys Joe T. Cawthorn and his assistant J. B. Wells expended no less effort in discrediting the state's star witness, Floyd Edward Cumbey. A fellow jail inmate, Jerry Gates, was brought in to testify that "a snitch is like Mr. Cumbey is trying to do to Mr. Favor." Another inmate, William Raymond Teasley, said he had offered to testify for Jack because "I don't like for somebody to be bum-rapped," not because Jack gave him $15 for cigarettes the day he left for Angola. "That's nothing," Teasley insisted, "Jack gives a lot of people who leave jail money."

And it was brought to the attention of the court that Cumbey had been allowed, in a highly irregular move, to enter a plea of guilty to murder without capital punishment during the noon recess prior to his testimony, on the day after the trial began and while jurors were still being selected. Said Wells to the jurors, "I've tried a lot of cases, but I've never seen as much going on as I have in this one. Here's a man [Cumbey] that's been out there in that jail practically a year, he comes in here while you gentlemen are out eating lunch, I was out eating lunch, Mr. Cawthorn was out eating lunch, pleads guilty. Gentlemen, in my opinion, I know why he pled guilty. He wasn't about to take that stand until he had done had it nailed down that he wasn't about to take the chance of getting that hot seat."

At this point, Donald Lee Yates had not been arraigned for the crime and was in federal custody at Fort Leavenworth, Kansas, serving a twenty-year sentence for bank robbery. A slight redhaired, tattooed multiple offender who was born in 1937 and had been in trouble with the law since he was a teenager, Yates was brought for this trial to Bossier, where he supposedly staged sit-down and hunger strikes until he was removed two days later from the local jail to the nearest federal house of correction at Texarkana. This removal took place before he could appear in the case, but not until after Cawthorn said Yates had told defense lawyers Jack Favor was not involved in the crime, testimony objected to by Louis Padgett, whose objection was subsequently sustained by Judge Price. Ponder Favor says, "They brought Yates down, but they found out that he was gonna tell the truth, so they took him to Texarkana and locked him down. They told everybody that he was so bad their jails wouldn't hold him, so they had to put him under heavier security. But they weren't about to let him testify."

Continued Wells to the jury in Jack's trial, "Why was Cumbey saying so and so? That louse hasn't been sentenced yet; that's why he will say any durn thing they want him to. Give me ten minutes with him and I'll have him saying anything I want him to...And these men are well qualified. Now I'm not saying they are telling him to lie. I'm saying they are saying we want this information and that information, and he's been a con all his life, he knows the ropes, he knows what they want and he will give it to them to satisfy them."

Even Cumbey admitted, to a certain extent, what was going on. Under cross-examination by J. B. Wells, Cumbey was asked, "You maybe saved your own neck by testifying and entering a plea of guilty yesterday with permission of the district attorney, didn't you?" Cumbey answered, "As far as the electric chair goes, I guess I did save it that way. What I meant about saving my life, there are some certain friends of mine...people like that ever gets to me or could get some hard people to me, I'm dead, because I'm what you'd call a snitch." He also admitted knowing that pleading guilty without capital punishment meant life imprisonment, which in Louisiana at that time translated roughly into only ten years and six months of actual time behind bars.

Both defense attorneys derided Padgett's insistence that Cumbey had genuinely repented of his life of crime and begun to tell the truth. Said Wells, the district attorney had "brought Cumbey in here with everything but a Bible in one hand and a flag in the other. Now they can scrub that bum down with a $4 brush but that's what he is. Look at him. Would you meet him on a dark night?" And why, Wells wanted to know, had the DA's office, faced with three men charged with a deadly crime, prosecuted the one upstanding citizen instead of "two convicts with records a mile long?" Why also, Wells asked, would a world-champion rodeo star, well known and widely recognizable across the country, register in a motel under his own name, giving his correct home address and license tag number, and walk around in easily noticeable cowboy clothing, if he had evil intent? "Well, now, how idiotic can you be when you are coming to commit an armed robbery?"

Cawthorn in his summing up contrasted, on one side of the ledger, Jack Favor as a Christian family man who was an honest businessman and had served his country honorably in the armed services, getting several Navy ships shot out from under him during World War II, and, on the other side of the ledger, "this little convicted thief, this little convicted burglar, this little rat that's a menace to society, and if the district attorney had the conscience that I believe he should have, he should have tried him, electrocuted him and got him out of society; instead of that he takes the position that this little feller who has robbed and robbed and robbed and robbed deserves another chance."

"Gentlemen of the jury," Cawthorn continued, "you've got to have the heart of Hitler, you've got to have the conscience of Stalin, you've got to be without a soul that you look to your God to save, to resolve the testimony we brought here against this defendant in favor of the testimony of this little lying thieving lowdown rascal." Jack Favor was a church-going man, Cawthorn reminded the jury; on the other hand, "Mr. Cumbey, or Cumbey, I wouldn't call that rat *Mister* anyplace, if you turned him loose in a church with the collection plate, do you know what the minister would eat on next week? Hot air, if they didn't have a treasury. Yes siree." Jack Favor, it had been graphically testified to, would give you the shirt off his back, Cawthorn reminded the jurors; Floyd Cumbey, "this cantankerous little thief...that carries these pistols along like you'd carry a corsage to a wedding...Do you know what Cumbey would do with your shirt? He'd steal it and probably stick you in the back, and that's the difference, gentlemen of the jury."

The first trial of Jack Graves Favor for the murder of Mr. and Mrs. W. R. Richey of Haughton in April 1964 began on Monday, April 24, 1967. On Friday at noon the Bossier Parish jury received the case, and by 9:30 a.m., Saturday, April 29, the jury returned a verdict of guilty without capital punishment, a verdict carrying an automatic life sentence. Witnesses recount that the jury first reported that it was unable to reach a verdict, at which point the district attorney told the judge that if he could speak to jurors in the hall a moment, he was sure he could straighten things out; he apparently did, with, strangely, no objection from defense attorneys.

Jack Favor's attorneys filed motions for retrial which were unsuccessful, and Jack was sentenced to two life terms to be served at Angola. The day before he was transferred, he suffered a serious heart attack in the Bossier Parish jail. That did not stop authorities from loading him into a police car and shipping him out on the long, difficult trip to the state penitentiary, where upon arrival he was immediately sent to the hospital.

When his health improved sufficiently, Jack was assigned to work in the prison hospital and the library. He also spent some time breaking horses for prison guards to ride and herd cattle with, but his favorite occupation was working with the Angola Prison Rodeo, which he transformed from a ragtag operation begun in 1965 to a thoroughly professional production attracting big-name performers and thousands of visitors, enriching inmate welfare funds through ticket and hobby-craft sales. Arena seating capacity was increased to over 5,000, and Jack's rodeo productions, every Sunday throughout the month of October, filled the bleachers to the brim. Jack was said to give the rodeo professionalism and a new vision, adding excitement with such prison rodeo favorites as the "Bust Out" when six bucking bulls and inmate riders entered the arena simultaneously, and "Guts and Glory" which saw scrambling inmates pursuing on foot an enraged Brahma bull in foolhardy attempts to detach from his horns a chit worth $100. He also revelled in the prison rodeo version of his old specialty, steer-wrestling, pitting two inmates, on foot, against a charging steer weighing 1500 to 1800 pounds.

Jack Favor (arrow) at an Angola Prison Rodeo.
(Courtesy *The Angolite*)

All of his spare time was spent at the rodeo arena, where he kept his old dog Spud. "Jack was just real lonely," recalls one inmate friend of Jack's, "and he would talk to Spud, and Spud would wag his tail and bark back at him." When Spud had a pup, Jack named it Ponder. Jack also won the grudging respect of other inmates, becoming active in the religious community and trying to aid other prisoners. Says award-winning prison journalist Ron Wikberg, "Picking up hitchhikers, that was Jack's nature, to help people. And here at the prison there were just so many people who needed help. Jack tried to help everybody. The inmates would try to get him to use his influence, because after all he was somebody, he was a well-known personality. Now some inmates didn't understand him. Jack always did everything for good, and this is a place where not everybody is good. Jack tried to change Angola and he tried to change all the inmates in it. He just couldn't do that, but that didn't stop him from trying."

Ron Wikberg in 1990.

According to the inmate grapevine, surprisingly reliable, Jack Favor was innocent of the charges against him and had been framed by a professional snitch. Said Wikberg, "Nobody likes a snitch or an informer, but nobody complains about an informer when he's doing something right or good. But in this case Cumbey was an informer who was looking out only for himself and didn't care who he hurt in the process. Jack was a very fine person. He talked like a Texan, he walked like a Texan, he looked like a Texan, he acted like a Texan, even in his mid-fifties. Jack never talked like a crook, and I found it difficult to think that he would ever do anything wrong. He never violated the rules in Angola, and he worked very hard to encourage other people to obey the rules."

It would be Ron Wikberg who would be most instrumental in encouraging Jack to re-examine his legal situation and do something about it. Not well informed on the law when he first entered Angola with a life term plus twenty-five years, Wikberg says, "I needed to get interested in it, because I wanted to help myself, and in the process I became interested in other people's cases. One day we were just sitting out there at the rodeo grounds. It was raining and we were inside the office, Spud was in there with us, and Jack was cooking us up some eggs we'd purloined from the culinary department and some baloney meat, and he was telling me about his case and about this fellow Cumbey, who was supposed to be somewhere in the prison system in Louisiana. And we found out that he wasn't in the prison system, that he'd never been received into the prison system at all.

And I said there's something wrong here, we might be able to file a writ and do something. At that point Jack didn't even know his appeal had never been filed."

Louisiana law usually allows a thirty-day grace period for the filing of appeals in convictions. This period had long since expired when Jack discovered that not only had Cawthorn not, for some unexplained reason, filed an appeal, but also that the attorney had died in the meantime. Wikberg explained that post-conviction papers could not be filed until the appeal had been finalized, so he and Jack set about going through an appeal process in the state courts, then filed their first writ. Denied by the state court system and the Louisiana Supreme Court, the two filed in U.S. district court, where Wikberg says "Federal Judge Ben Dawkins, bless his heart, he came through like a trooper. He really got interested in the case, like we had gotten interested in it."

Wikberg, who has since helped inmates file over one hundred writs and become a prison expert on legal issues, looks back on what started Jack on the long hard trail to freedom. "What really turned Jack onto the idea that something was wrong was Yates. Yates was brought here to Angola and kept at the Reception Center until he filed a petition and got his sentence reduced to seventeen years for manslaughter so he would be eligible to be paroled to his federal detainer. Yates told Jack they had made a mistake in his case, and he said Cumbey was not even here. He was the one who told Jack that Cumbey was in Oklahoma. Then somebody sent a clipping. Jack never did know who. There was no letter, no note, just a clipping from the Oklahoma newspaper saying Cumbey had killed two women there. And that's what really got us going. We had already put together a writ about Jack being denied his right to appeal and ineffective assistance of counsel, but that's when we added *collusion.*"

Jack Favor filed his writ of *habeas corpus* with the United States District Court, Western District of Louisiana, Shreveport Division, in July of 1971, all twenty-eight legal-sized pages of it laboriously typed on a typewriter put together from spare parts. The writ raised three questions: Was relator's conviction had by one sole witness' perjurious testimony? Did collusion exist between star witness Cumbey and the Bossier Parish authorities? Was relator denied his constitutional right to appeal, and to have the aid of counsel on appeal?

The part of the writ which had the most impact was that section alleging collusion between Floyd Edward Cumbey and Bossier Parish officials Judge O. E. Price and District Attorney Louis H. Padgett, Jr. Cumbey, the writ implied, had been coached as a witness against Jack Favor, and the jurors in Jack's trial had been misled as to Cumbey's character and past criminal history as well as his future sentence; jurors were told Cumbey had been sentenced to two life terms, when in fact he had not even been sentenced at all until after the trial was over and at that point, on December 11, 1967, withdrew his guilty plea to murder without capital punishment and changed his plea to manslaughter, receiving two consecutive twenty-one-year sentences for manslaughter to be served in the Louisiana State Penitentiary.

Not only was Cumbey never delivered to the state prison at Angola to serve these sentences, he was actually physically released from custody on December 12, 1967, ostensibly to continue work as an undercover agent in Oklahoma. He was driven by Bossier Parish Deputy Sheriff Vol Dooley to the state line at Texarkana and given $25 and, according to some accounts, a gun for protection. Within forty-eight hours, he had brutally murdered two women, Opel Ritchey and twenty-eight-year-old Sheila Farley, the latter an old acquaintance with whom Cumbey had left certain valuables she was apparently unable to produce when he arrived to collect them; the murder would be pinned on Cumbey after he was arrested later for armed robbery.

Jack's writ, initially denied when Judge Enos C. McClendon, Jr., of the Twenty-sixth Judicial Court of Bossier Parish refused to overrule Judge Price, began to make some headway, especially when J. B. Wells joined his efforts as attorney of record. Copies sent to newspapers led to investigative features about Cumbey and the deal he had allegedly received. A Bossier Parish grand jury went so far as to indict Judge Price and DA Padgett for perjured testimony concerning the release of prisoner Floyd Edward Cumbey. The indictments against these top officials would eventually be quashed and then dismissed due to time limitations, but Judge Ben Dawkins on May 26, 1972, ordered the state of Louisiana to either re-try Jack Favor or release him from custody.

When the Louisiana Supreme Court ruled Dawkins had overstepped his bounds, Wells appealed to United States district court, where Judge Alvin Rubin upheld Dawkins' ruling, giving the state thirty days to bring Jack to trial. The court, Rubin wrote, was convinced that Cumbey had been given assurance of a suspended sentence by responsible state officials before he testified. "It is almost unthinkable," he continued, "that state officials sworn to uphold and defend both federal and state constitutions, like guarantees of due process, should have joined in such conduct."

Ron Wikberg reflects on the collusion charges after the passage of several decades, still outraged. "I look at the whole chain of events involving these players. You had Vol Dooley, the chief deputy who later became sheriff. Then you had the judge, O. E. Price, who later moved up to the court of appeals. Then you had the district attorney, Louis Padgett, later promoted to judge. Those two eventually were indicted, but the statute of limitations had expired by one day. Somebody knew what they were doing; this was an orchestrated thing. There had to be a conspiracy, because why did they wait to make the complaint until exactly one day after the year was up? Everyone was elevated; everyone gained something out of it. Cumbey gained his freedom. Everyone gained something out of it except Jack Favor. It all started with a swift-talking ex-convict, who convinced them they had something to gain by doing this. Of course it's not unheard of in Louisiana politics for politicians to make unholy matrimonies with people for various reasons."

In April of 1974, a full decade after the murders of Mr. and Mrs. W. R. Richey at their bait stand in Haughton, Jack Graves Favor would again be tried in Twenty-Sixth

Jack Favor in 1981.
(Courtesy Ron Wikberg)

Judicial District Court in Bossier Parish before Judge C. J. Bolin, this time prosecuted by the state attorney general's office, as local officials declined to prosecute the case. The outcome this time would be different, too, and so would the entire atmosphere surrounding the fifteen-day trial. When Donald Lee Yates was called to the stand by the defense counsel and was asked to take the oath, he addressed the judge, "I'd like to say now that I don't believe that anytime during this case has anyone ever told the truth..." After finally taking the oath, Yates testified that he and Cumbey had hitched a ride with Jack from Muskogee, Oklahoma, to Shreveport, where they accepted his offer to share his room for the night, asked him to give them a ride across the Bossier bridge the following morning, and never saw him again until the two met at Angola. "At no time," Yates testified, "was Jack Favor involved in the murders. Myself, Cumbey and a third person were the only ones."

Yates also revealed that he had told a gathering of Bossier officials that "Mr. Jack Favor had received a raw deal in this court," but had not gone into detail because "I seen the people weren't interested in it...They are not interested in whether Jack Favor was innocent or not. They have a guilty verdict. That's all they want to hear." Ponder and Tommy Favor would later recount some of what Donald Yates said at the trial and in private to Jack: "He said that there was a third party involved in the crime in Bossier, someone high up in politics, whose name he couldn't divulge or he would be dead before he ever hit the street. He said he would never tell, he couldn't tell, no one could *make* him tell." Yates also told Jack that he and Cumbey were under orders to hitch a ride to the Shreveport area, kill whoever picked them up and steal the car, but that Jack was "so damn nice we couldn't kill you."

On April 19, 1974, the jury in the second trial of Jack Favor began its deliberations shortly before 9:40 p.m. After less than an hour, the verdict was announced. Jack Graves Favor had been acquitted of the murder of Mrs. W. R. Richey; the state would later decline to prosecute him for her husband's murder, citing the principle of law precluding duplicate litigation on matters involving the same facts between the same parties. Until the state declined to prosecute, the judge told Jack he could be released on $5000 bond, if he could come up with that much cash. Medical and legal expenses had depleted his savings, however, and he could not. A complete stranger, good-hearted Mr. Alfred Cloud, arose from the courtroom audience and posted a property bond so that Jack could go home to Texas with his family.

"I got him home to Arlington on a Saturday night," Ponder Favor recalls, "and we got up the next morning to go to church, and he was nearly completely dressed when he hit the floor just like a ton of bricks. I had not the faintest idea what was wrong with that man; he'd been away all those years. So I thought it must be a heart attack and I got to trying to find his nitroglycerine. He had it in that little tiny pants pocket on the side and I like to never got it out, but I put one under his tongue and he came to directly. He was hitting on a stroke, with his artery clogged and the blood not getting to his brain, but after laying there it slowly eked through and he came to. And he insisted on going on to church. He was just so weak still that I had to nearly carry him up the stairs. Well, we got in there, and of course that big church had supported him so much and everybody was just clamoring for him, so the preacher asked Jack if he would come up on the podium and speak. Jack was so weak he couldn't get up those few stairs, so the preacher helped him up there. First time I ever saw Jack Favor cry in my life, but it was physical weakness, that's all it was. Well, everybody in that church cried. We got Jack to the doctor on Monday and by Tuesday he was in the hospital."

Heart surgery and pacemakers followed, then a quadruple bypass, with Jack outlasting even the most permanent of pacemakers. "He had four pacemakers from the time he got home until he died," Ponder says, "and every time they'd put one in they'd say this would last him the rest of his life, thinking it wouldn't be long. But they didn't know Jack Favor." When pancreatic cancer was discovered, again doctors gave Jack just a few months to live. "But they didn't reckon with his competitive spirit," Ponder says. "He was the most competitive man I've ever known." Adds son Tommy, "Plus he took his horse medicine, thick black tar-like stuff that was so strong it'd melt the capsules he put it in with his pocketknife before he could get them in his mouth. Said it cured fistulas in horses, so it was good enough for him."

Before Jack Favor "went home to Glory" on December 27, 1988, in the words of a Cowboys For Christ obituary-tribute, he would have piled up staggering medical bills. When a book, *In Jack's Favor*, written with Methodist minister William B. Moody, failed to produce much profit, Jack would sue the state of Louisiana for false imprisonment and settle for $55,000, of which $28,000 went for court costs and $22,000 for medical bills. His wife and children are now working with a former television producer on a documentary version of Jack's fascinating story.

But Jack Favor's real legacy would be the memories he left behind, loving recollections of a bigger-than-life and colorful all-American cowboy, who went through an experience which would have broken most men and emerged nearly unscathed, dignity and integrity intact and without a trace of bitterness. His work for prison reform touched many lives and earned him the respect of some outstanding men on both sides of the bars; some fellow inmates followed his example and turned from a life of crime once released, while others found faith through inmate religious groups and attained a feeling of peace even while still serving time.

Jack's old rodeo pals still talk about him with affection and amusement. "Jack was a real good fellow, full of fun, and he sure rode a horse well," says Dan Coates, Triangle Bell Rodeo Ranch announcer; "I didn't see how he could have done anything like that murder, knowing Jack." Flaxie Fletcher, rodeo arena secretary for the World's Champion Rodeo Corporation—Gene Autry and Associates show and the executive secretary of the rodeo division of the National Cowboy Hall of Fame, says Jack had a wonderful personality, was great big and good looking too, and when he was the Madison Square Garden bulldogging champion, that made him the best in the US; no one who ever knew Jack could ever think he'd do something like commit murder, she insists.

Mitzi Lucas Riley, who started trick-riding in rodeos in the thirties when she was five, recalls being kind of family, everybody travelling on the rodeo circuit, and says Jack was very outgoing and had a lot of friends; he was so considerate and thoughtful of other people, she remembers, and when a groom died without any money, Jack collected funds to bury him and got everybody to go to the funeral too. Garlene Parris, who also rodeoed with Jack as a young trick-rider, recounts touching tributes paid Jack at his funeral, when the big Methodist church was packed and there wasn't a dry eye in the house.

"Jack was a person who wanted to help everybody and didn't want to hurt nobody. He was a person with not much money, but I guarantee you if some unfortunate person would go to him and say 'Jack, I need ten bucks,' he might say 'I ain't got ten bucks' but then he'd turn around to me and say 'Let me have ten bucks,' get ten bucks off of me and let the guy have it. I just knew in my own heart that Jack Favor wasn't the kind of man that would stick a pistol on people and kill them. Now he might punch you in the mouth, but that was different," says Big Jim Bynum, fellow world-champion steer-wrestler and friendly competitor. "We were just like one big happy family on the rodeo circuit back then, more of a family than the modern-day cowboys are. The people that rodeoed, they had to love the sport, 'cause the money's not that good and you could have a sizeable investment in it, a $10,000 dogging horse, a hazing horse, a car, horse trailer, all your tack. We went from rodeo to rodeo and we got to know each other and got to know our capabilities, our shortcomings, and we really had a good time. 'Course the money's a lot better nowadays than it was then, but it was kinda like if one cowboy had money, he didn't mind sharing it with some of the other less fortunate cowboys. Like I said, Jack was one of the best at that. He'd borrow money from me just to loan it to you."

When Jack Favor returned home after his wrenching nine-year ordeal with the Louisiana judicial system, Jane says the first thing he did was typical. "He was in downtown Fort Worth after he came back home, heading out of town, and he saw this really well-dressed young man in a suit with a briefcase, with his jacket...it was in the middle of summer..trudging down getting out on I-30. And Daddy stopped and asked him where he was going and what the problem was. Well, he was an attorney, he was headed for Dallas, he was supposed to be in a court case over there, his car had broken down and he didn't know what in the world he was going to do. And Daddy told him to get in, he'd take him. He took him to Dallas, hung around, waited on him, brought him back, and sent somebody to go get his car." This was attorney Steve Swander, and Ponder says, "Swander told me he'd never had anybody be that good to him in his whole life. Now that was Jack Favor. That was the story of his life."

The Warden Comments: The moving case of Jack Graves Favor serves to emphasize the dangers inherent in a criminal justice system out of control and willing to convict on even the most questionable evidence, a system which could make almost anyone its victim and run rampant over most defendants. Over-eager investigators will sometimes exhibit an unfortunate tendency to make a predetermination of guilt and then gather only those facts which support their theory, when they should instead, of course, approach any criminal investigation without preconceived ideas and gather facts objectively.

Jack's very eminence as a world-champion cowboy may have contributed to his troubles. It is always more interesting and sometimes more profitable for district attorneys to prosecute someone who is well known, especially if that offender is capable of generating publicity for the public officials involved. On top of that, an out-of-state defendant does not vote locally, nor does he have friends or supporters who do, so prosecutors run less risk of offending their own power base.

To me this case demonstrates a criminal justice system that falls well below the lofty standards set in this country for those charged with upholding and interpreting the law. They seem instead to be subverting justice, and it appears that a manipulating multiple offender is actually calling the shots. Pertinent facts and information favorable to the defendant seem to have been withheld, and even his own attorney was reluctant to submit an alibi based on the testimony of a person who happened to be black and would therefore, the attorney assumed, have little or no credibility with this North Louisiana court. Who can remember where he was one year ago and what he was doing? This is a very scary case, especially since it could happen to anyone.

Another pertinent element to be noted in this case is the danger of accepting plea bargains in exchange for testimony. I could go into the penitentiary right now and get twenty-five inmates to swear they had personally witnessed the warden kissing a mule in front of the administration building if I so much as hinted such testimony might be beneficial to their own cases. There should be hard evidence to convict, especially in capital cases. I have serious questions about the admissability of testimony by a man with such a long history of conflict with the law, especially when he is also on trial for the same offense.

Had the testimony of Floyd Cumbey not been given credence, two women in Oklahoma, in all likelihood, would be alive today, not to mention the changed outcome in Jack Favor's first trial. Apparently the only thing that really saved Jack Favor from dying in prison was the fact that an inmate writ-writer became interested in his case and pursued it until he won a new trial.

It did not take long after Jack Favor's arrival at the Louisiana State Penitentiary for the word to circulate that he had been unjustly imprisoned for a crime he did not commit.

This was the studied opinion of staff members like Dick Oliveaux, head of the cattle operation who knew Jack from rodeo days, and inmate trusties like Tandy Miller, who had the complete trust of both prisoners and prison officials. Inquiring into the circumstances surrounding Jack's conviction, Miller informed me that inmates who had been in jail with Jack in Bossier Parish attested to his innocence and felt that he had been "framed" by Floyd Cumbey to save his own hide.

Most members of the penitentiary staff were aware of the questions surrounding Jack's conviction. There was not much we could do about solving his legal problems, so our primary goal was to see that incarceration had as little detrimental effect on Jack as possible. Because of his bad health we tried to make serving his time as easy as possible. He was almost immediately classified as minimum security and allowed the run of the 18,000-acre farm.

The Angola Prison Rodeo had been organized in 1965 for the benefit and participation of employees and prisoners. No attempt was made initially to make a profit or attract the general public. However, Jack's willingness to work with the rodeo lent an air of professionalism and the promise of greater success. With funding provided by Governor John McKeithen, we purchased $5000 worth of bleacher framework offering seating for some 5000 visitors, and Jack supervised their erection and repair. Big-name entertainers, many originally from Louisiana, were invited to appear at the performances, which helped to draw crowds once the rodeo was opened to the general public. Profits from the rodeo went into the inmate welfare fund and steadily increased each year. In good years we netted something like $30,000 for the inmate welfare fund, money used to purchase necessary items for the prisoners for which no funds were officially appropriated.

Because of the respect and confidence Jack earned from all of us in the prison administration, we gave him furloughs to visit with his family and also let him travel the state promoting the rodeo, accompanied by an employee. He must have appeared on every TV station in Louisiana. He never once talked about his own problems, but rather promoted the rodeo in a straight-forward professional manner. In 1989, the twenty-fifth annual Angola Prison Rodeo was dedicated to Jack's memory, a tribute and a "tip of the hat" from penitentiary staff and inmates alike.

Besides having a lasting impact on the Angola Rodeo, Jack Favor was also active in Alcoholics Anonymous and the Methodist Men's Club at Angola, generating new interest in these beneficial programs as well as greatly increased participation. He took a personal interest in a number of the inmates and was forever trying to get some young person on the right track. We found him to be a man of integrity and high personal moral standards, and he served as a positive role model for many of the prisoners.

I attended the second trial of Jack Favor, at which it was evident that he, his family and his friends were treated with great courtesy, sympathy and respect, in direct contrast with the hostile atmosphere surrounding his first trial. Despite the many conflicting stories told by participants with varying levels of credibility in voluminous testimony at hearings and trials, our research leads us to conclude that Jack Favor was no murderer.

This view is not universally accepted in Bossier Parish to this day, however. Some involved officials there still earnestly believe that Jack Favor was the lookout man while Floyd Edward Cumbey and Donald Lee Yates robbed and murdered the W. R. Richeys at their Haughton bait stand. Current Bossier Parish District Attorney Henry N. Brown, Jr., still feels Jack was found innocent in the second trial primarily because the first trial, accomplished before he came to power, had been so badly "botched," calling that first case "an example of everything that can be said bad about the criminal justice system...an example of corruption in the system." Retired Sheriff Vol Dooley is another who still feels that Jack was a party to the crime as well, though he now admits Cumbey probably lied to and misled officials during the investigations and prosecutions, causing mistakes to be made which eventually resulted in freedom for Jack Favor.

Jack Favor never returned to Angola after his second trial, thanks to a kind stranger who paid his bond. Fellow prisoners back at the Louisiana State Penitentiary were elated, for Jack had earned their genuine respect and his release gave them renewed hope in the judicial process. A lot of the prison staff felt the same way.

2009 Update:

Jack Favor would be proud to see the rodeo he helped start now attracting more than 10,000 every Sunday in October; in fact, combined with an arts and crafts festival, it proved so popular that an April weekend rodeo has been added and a new arena with covered seating area keeps the spectators comfortable. Ron Wikberg was released from Angola in 1994 and died not long after of cancer.

V

The Yuppie Convict

Lock two strangers, both Southerners, in a room together and in fifteen minutes they'll know everything there is to know about each other. Confine two strangers who are Californians together, on the other hand, and in fifteen *days* they still will not know so much as each other's names.

This typically exaggerated West Coast sense of individual privacy goes a long way toward explaining how an intelligent, well-travelled and with-it woman DJ (a fictitious name in response to her request not to embarrass her family further) could spend nearly a decade loving and living with a man about whose background she knew next to nothing—at least until the federal agents came knocking on their door.

His real name was Douglas Bror Dennis, though most people from his earlier years knew him as Swede. But DJ knew him by another name altogether, James Walter Stevens. Stevens was an upwardly mobile, gainfully employed credit-card-carrying taxpayer in California's Silicon Valley, well thought of by employers, indulging his passion for physical fitness, doing community volunteer work and living quietly in a neatly kept doublewide trailer with DJ. Douglas Dennis, on the other hand, was a double murderer on the lam from two life sentences in the Louisiana state prison system, a system which very much wanted him back.

Now back in Louisiana, trying to reconcile two very different lives, Dennis tells his story from behind bars, the story of tragic youthful mistakes made and paid for over the course of twenty-two years of incarceration, and of the frustration of coming so close to freedom he could taste and feel it, only to be made a sort of sacrificial lamb by a vindictive DA possibly looking for some eyecatching law-and-order press to overshadow his own difficulties with the law.

Son of a newspaperman, Douglas Dennis was born in Chicago in October 1935 and by the age of six months had begun what would be a childhood of continual uprootings. Tulsa, Baltimore, Biloxi, New York City and Lansing are just a few of the cities where he recalls living as the family crisscrossed the country for employment purposes. New York he refers to as "the long spell," eight years in one spot, with his father working as a police reporter and the family remaining in Queens Village until Dennis was just one semester away from graduation at Andrew Jackson High School.

Douglas Dennis

"I was very, very disturbed about going to Michigan from New York City with just a semester left," he remembers. "I was just getting to the good part. The last semester of high school you are a big wheel. You get to wear a little beanie, a big status symbol. And I got cheated out of all that. I don't think I ever recovered from it. I really resented that. It was always move, move, move, move, then we stayed there for a long time at a very critical stage in my early development, and then right when I'm gonna reap all these benefits, zoom, we're gone again.

"I really didn't like that, much more so than the other moves, which I didn't like either. You know how a kid is...you get a few friends, a little group, it doesn't take long to get adjusted to a place, you stay there six months and you feel like you've been there forever, and then you're gone. That rootlessness was not very good for me, as it turned out, and I kept it up later; it was like a habit. I *never* put any roots down."

By the time he finished high school in Lansing, only seventeen because his good grades had allowed him to skip a grade, Dennis says he was so rebellious that he left home, worked briefly in an Oldsmobile plant, then joined the Marines. "Just as we were ready to be shipped over to Korea as replacements, this was in '53, Eisenhower flew over the battlefield there and shut the war down. He took one look at it and said it was ridiculous. So they made me company clerk in a training company in southern California, doing rosters, stocking, paperwork for the company. I don't remember why I went AWOL; I don't think I even *had* a reason. I was screwed up."

In his yellow 1935 Cadillac convertible, Dennis drove to northern California and worked as a logger in redwood country for awhile, then returned to San Francisco, stole another car and drove back down to Hollywood. Arrested, he was sent by the California Youth Authority to a vocational institution for non-violent salvageable youngsters until he was paroled to his father, then in Florida as general manager of a West Palm Beach television station. There Dennis found work in the film room and did a little announcing in his deep, resonant voice; he also enrolled in a real estate law course in junior college, even then interested in the law.

Though he had spent a furlough after boot camp with them in Lansing, it would be his first extended stay since high school with what he calls a stereotypical family of strong, non-demonstrative father and weak but loving mother, both Lutherans; it would also be his *last* extended stay with his family, though he did not know thén that thirty-five years would pass without any further contact after his parents left the Sunshine State. "My father never projected caring," Dennis reveals, "though what was going on in his head, I don't know; I can't read minds. Occasionally he would do things that seemed to indicate caring, but they were isolated. He did the old saw, took me to a ball game to see the Yankees play when we were in New York City, and I remember I wanted a bicycle real bad for Christmas one time, and he got it. So I'm not trying to paint him all black, but he was not an easy person to be a son to." In the forties, this same father, Walter Lawrence Dennis, then working as a Chicago newspaperman, had been the original model for the Clark Kent character in the Siegel-Shuster "Adventures of Superman" cartoon series. A hard act to follow.

"Anyway, I'm working at this TV station in Florida and settling in, the parole was no problem," Dennis recalls, "and all of a sudden my father moves again. Apparently it was too much trouble for him to switch an already out-of-state parole to another state, for which you have to have a job waiting. He had a job waiting for *himself,* but not one for me, and he wouldn't want to walk into a bránd new job and say, 'Oh, by the way, I've got this kid of mine on parole, have you got a place for him?' That doesn't fly. By then I was nineteen; I was able to fend for myself, that wasn't a problem. But there he was, gone again.

"At that point, my brother was eleven, my sister was ten; I was the oldest and there was an eight-year gap, which made it hard. Lord knows what they knew about me; you don't tell ten and eleven-year-old kids their brother's on parole, and if you did they wouldn't know what the hell parole was. I don't think they told them anything, and if they *did*, it was probably that I was just gone. The father, *he* knew where I was, but he never made any effort to get in touch. Matter of fact, leafing through my classification files at Angola after I came off Death Row, I found this 1957 letter from my father when I had put him on my approved correspondents' list; he wrote back a little letter, no letterhead that I remember, saying 'I know where he is, and all he wants is money and help getting out'...yeah, I wouldn't say that was *all* I wanted, but yeah, I wouldn't mind a few bucks and help getting out, who wouldn't; I'm human just like everybody else...'therefore I don't want to hear from him; I know where he is, and if I ever want to contact him I will do so.'" Apparently he never wanted to do so again.

The removal of family support had a detrimental effect on young Dennis, who remembers, "while I had the anchor, the stability of the home, I was doing OK. But when that was gone, I wasn't able to handle it. I was making it, I was surviving, but I wasn't able to handle it responsibly, for what reason I don't know." He began driving a cab in West Palm, then switched to driving a refrigerated eighteen-wheeler full of fresh flowers from the Gold Coast area to New York, returning with loads of jukeboxes and pinball machines destined for shipment to Havana.

The very private, solitary existence Dennis lived, with few intimates, was consistent with his upbringing and the repeated wrenching sadness of leaving behind childhood acquaintances with every move. "I was used to seeing people come and go, and just counting on myself," he says now. "Driving cabs in West Palm and Fort Lauderdale, it was a profession where you were on your own. Oh sure, you had a dispatcher, a boss, but when you were out on the streets, you were in control. I always have liked driving for that reason, though I didn't realize that at the time."

Finding himself out of a job at some point, Dennis took off with a couple of buddies named Blackie, an ex-con, and Cherokee, who had a car, bound for New York. "Was it Thomas Wolfe who said you couldn't go home again?" he wonders. "I discovered that was exactly true. We got up there in this old wreck, remember this is way before freeways, this is all two-lane blacktops, and we went back to my old neighborhood and drove around, and even went to the house of this guy I used to hang with in high school. We were reminiscing and he said to me, 'I didn't think I'd ever see you again, I thought you'd rob a bank or something.' I was that kind of unstable kid; I wasn't the all-American cheerleader in school."

Cherokee took off after the car died; Dennis and Blackie began hitchhiking, crisscrossing the country three times. "That was a nightmare," Dennis recalls. "I remember sleeping behind billboards, freezing my buns off, working or selling blood, but we stuck together and didn't do anything illegal, just hitchhiking. I wouldn't trade that experience for anything. It was like boot camp; you couldn't stand it when you were doing it, but looking back on it, you say it really was kinda great. I was exposed to all kinds of people and saw the country."

Back in Florida after six months on the road, Dennis hooked up with Cherokee again. They had heard wild tales of Morgan City, tiny oil boom-town on the Louisiana coast where the money flowed freely and bars stayed open all night, jobs were easy to come by and the fun never stopped. With a third buddy, they headed for the good life, only to find it as elusive as ever in this little town with the large transient population.

"I worked on a shrimp boat," Dennis says. "I made one trip out, and that was the most disgusting, nauseating, backbreaking thing I have ever done in my life, dumping those nets on deck, knee-deep in every kind of flipping, flopping, greasy, slimy thing. I have never been on a shrimp boat since. I worked on an oil-rig supply boat, and then on a rig, learning more about drill pipe than I ever wanted to know in my whole life. We were just hanging. When I was in Lansing, I'd been introduced to one of those old-time pool halls like you see in *The Hustler,* and I got to be good enough to make money at it and, more importantly, knew *how* to make money at it, which is a whole other thing. There weren't any pool hustlers in Morgan City, so I was able to make a living at it for weeks at a time, and to do that without getting your head beat in is an accomplishment."

Driving cab in Berwick, across the river, filled the nights with action, taking fares to all the area clubs. "Remember I had jumped parole in Florida, but looking back on it I really don't think they gave a damn, this kid on out-of-state parole from something called the Youth Authority. Anyway, one night this guy was drinking and didn't have the money to pay for the cab and I got upset, so he gave me this .25-caliber pistol in lieu of the fare, one of those little automatic Saturday night specials, and one bullet, just *one.* So I kept it; even back then cab drivers used to get attacked and robbed."

Not long after, Dennis got word that one of the Morgan City policemen wanted to have a few words with him. Panicking, he remembers thinking, "'Jesus Christ, my *parole!* ' I made no connection with the pistol. I was so green that I didn't even realize that if they wanted me for parole violation, they'd just come *get* me, they wouldn't *ask* me to drop by the police station when I had the time." The two buddies who'd accompanied him from Florida were in essentially the same shape, drifting from job to job, game for any kind of excitement, so the three hit the road again. "Rock and roll, away we go," Dennis says. "I found out later that all the police wanted to ask me was where I got the gun, what I was gonna do with it, and would I tell them everything that was going on all over town that I knew about. From my standpoint, that was all totally harmless.

"But before we left, we were trying to get some money, and looking back this is where I really started going batty. A couple of guys that I didn't like much owed me some money, not that much, $40 or $50 bucks, no big deal, so we went to their place. They gave me a ration of crap about the money, so I whipped out the pistol." When no money was forthcoming, a search ensued and $20 or $30 was removed from a wallet hidden under the mattress.

To prevent phone calls to the police, Dennis and his travelling companions took the other men along in the car until they got out of town, dropping them off in an isolated area. Waving an empty pistol, his single bullet in his pocket, Dennis had them remove their pants and left them in a roadside ditch. "But first, I just couldn't resist it, I pulled the bullet out of my pocket and I said, 'I really would've killed you guys, but I couldn't figure out how to do it with just one bullet.' Crazy kids, crazy kids. We took off for New Orleans, where I lost everything I had to a skinny little 190-year-old man in a pool hall, and those other guys in Morgan City went to the police."

Dennis and his two friends headed north toward Dallas in the spring of 1957, robbing vending machines in drive-in theater concession stands of petty change to pay for food and gas. They developed a routine, whereby two would "do" the drive-in while the third stayed with the car, watching out for police. In Bossier City, it was Cherokee who stayed with the car, but this time he'd apparently had enough and drove off into the darkness, never to be seen again. That was the beginning of the end of the adventure for twenty-one-year-old Douglas Dennis.

Trudging along the highway and across the Red River, the two boys, on foot and weighted down by pockets full of small change, had almost made it through Shreveport to the relative safety of the open road when the inevitable police car pulled alongside and they were taken into the station for investigation. "They can't do that nowadays, but back then, they had seventy-two hours to make a case or kick you back out," says Dennis. The boys were split up, with 6'3" Dennis put into the drunk tank.

"There were a couple of guys in there who were in the same position I was, had no money, and what they'd do, when the cops would throw a drunk in, they'd roll him. The drunks would come in and they'd fall over and go to sleep, and someone would go through their pockets. So I got to doing that. And this one guy, fat sloppy big guy, I took his stuff, $3 and a pack of cigarettes, and he finally came around like they all do, and he got all indignant.

"There might have been ten or fifteen guys in there, some in the cells, others out walking around, some laying down, some passed out, and I think somebody pointed me out to him. Anyway, he gets in my face, 'I want my money, you took my money.' He shouldn't have done that. He tried to tell the jailer, and the jailer wouldn't pay him no mind. I got pissed because he was ratting on me to get me in trouble. So I said 'here, I got something for you,' and commenced to whale on him. He tried to fight; I got a little carried away. He went down and I went to kicking him, then walked out on the tier. Then I hear the guy breathing and it just doesn't sound right, so I go back and look at him, and he doesn't look too good. So I go and get the jailer, and they get him to the hospital. Internal injuries, spleen.

"I've heard people talk about blind rages and losing control, but that's never been me. I go just the opposite. I have a temper, and I can jump up and down and scream and cuss with the best of them, but when it really gets down to unavoidable physical violence, I shut up, I say nothing, I get totally emotionless...it's all activity, moving, doing, looking. I got carried away; I didn't mean it to happen in that sense. I did too much. I should have stopped, I *could* have stopped, but I didn't stop. That's why I say it's on me."

The victim, William S. McDonald, a CPA for the IRS, would die. Morgan City authorities were returning Dennis to South Louisiana to face charges of armed robbery and kidnapping, stemming from the botched attempts to recover money owed him before his departure from that town, when Shreveport police requested his immediate return to their jurisdiction on murder charges.

Becoming a prime focus of one of the periodic feuds between the media and the police, Dennis found his case emblazened across the front page of local newspapers. "That's what sank my ship," he says, "the media always asking how the police could protect the public in their homes when they couldn't even patrol their own jails. And every time something happened, they'd resurrect me. They wanted to give me the death penalty and charged me with murder. I feel even today I should have been charged with manslaughter, because that's what it was, that's what I did. Murder is premeditated, with planning and a deliberate intent to kill. But I was the perfect patsy for everybody, from out of town, out of state, no money, nobody interested. I was just nothing, a punching bag for whoever wanted to come along and work out on me. The newspapers were clubbing the police over the head with me, and the police didn't like that, so they were gonna charge me with murder and shoot the juice to me. And there was nobody to get any help from."

Held in a tiny dark isolation cell, Dennis could converse through a toilet vent only with the unseen inmate of the cell across the hall, a black man charged with aggravated rape. "He kept saying he was innocent, and he was concerned about going to heaven, which he thought was on the moon," Dennis recalls. "I think a lot of blacks in those days got the same deal I got, *over*-charged. I was totally convinced that I was getting screwed. Not that I should have *walked,* but I figured it was manslaughter; I had no intention to kill this guy. After a few months, which seemed like forever in this little cell, they took the black guy away to Angola to the electric chair, so he did go to the moon and then I had *nobody* to talk to. It might have been an improvement."

Advised by his court-appointed attorney, whom he recalls seeing for the first time as he went to court, to plead guilty for a life sentence as opposed to the death penalty, Dennis did, a move he regrets to this day. The witnesses against him, half a dozen drifters, were predictably disappearing once they served their sentences, taking with them the state's case, Dennis says, but "I was just a kid, I didn't know that then. I know it now, but I'm not gonna go out and kill somebody. I shouldn't have pled guilty, but I did, and so I'm stuck with it."

On to the Louisiana State Penitentiary at Angola in the oppressive summertime of 1957. After six weeks of perfunctory processing Dennis was assigned to a disciplinary cellblock, which he protested, yearning for the comparative freedom of "the yard." "I'd been locked up and locked up," he says. "But you don't arrive at Angola in a vacuum; you don't suddenly materialize out of thin air. You come as part of a package, the rest of the package being what the law enforcement people where you came from think about you, what kind of guy you are, stuff that's not in the record or part of the commitment papers...was he a troublemaker, is he really a rapist even though the charge was busted down to assault, what is the real story on this guy...the word. Apparently this jailer in Shreveport, who I think later became sheriff, had told them I was a real bad boy. So they treated me like a real bad boy and put me in a disciplinary cellblock with all the other real bad boys who'd come off the yard for disciplinary problems. It was a working cellblock, so we were in the farmlines a lot."

It was on a Thursday afternoon that Dennis was delivered to his cellblock, the other "fresh fish" continuing on to the yard as trusties and big stripes. Returning from supper single file, coming out of the Control Center to get to the all-white cellblock, Dennis witnessed a fellow inmate attacked and beaten with a pipe by an assailant who leapt from the shadows and then just as quickly disappeared. It would be his welcome to Angola, and far from the last act of brutality he would be close to.

"Don't misunderstand," he says. "I wasn't part of the in-crowd. But I was acceptable, if not 'in.' I fit right in, chopped cotton, got no serious disciplinary write-ups and in six to eight months was right out on the yard." Coming from the block gave Dennis some status in his new dorm, but he found he needed money. "Money isn't that important in prison," he says, "unless you don't have *any*. You need a few dollars a week, especially if you smoke. You need some cosmetics, a bar of soap or toothpaste. They didn't supply much. The gap between issuing a tube of toothpaste was about four tubes long."

To make spending change, Dennis rolled cigarettes, getting twenty-five cigarettes to a pack, keeping five and selling twenty, then ran an ongoing inmate poker game with chips made in the tag plant out of sheet metal. "The guards didn't want us to throw it in their faces, but it wasn't a big deal and just about everybody was doing it. The ratio of prisoners to security officers was like fifty to one. We had one security officer in a little phone booth to cover the four sixty-man units of this dormitory, spread out like an H. It was impossible for one man to supervise, so a lot of them didn't even try. They could only do so much."

Dennis says he got his locker "jacked," burglarized of the booty bought with proceeds from his cigarette business and poker game, and "got very indignant about it. I made a mistake; I figured out who did it and started giving him dirty looks to let him know I knew he did it, and that mistake cost me my eye." Coming back from supper one night, an informant warned him that inmate Wesley Sonnier and his buddy Earl "BlackJack" Dupree had stolen the contents of his locker and were waiting for him in the dorm. "He said 'you better get something,' and I said 'where the hell am I gonna get something, I'm out on the walk.' He sent me to his buddy who was working leather, and he gave me a leather knife, which was just a little hooked thing. And I went back in the dormitory.

"I get right next to the first big post and Wesley jumps out of his bed. I spot BlackJack way in the back sitting down, divorcing himself from everything. Wesley pulls out a huge caneknife, and I take out my little leather knife and grab a pillow and wrap it around my arm. Wesley comes around the bed and we're standing face to face about two or three feet apart, and all of a sudden I hear something behind me. It was Donald Borland. He just came out of left field. I don't know what his story was. Best I could figure it, he was trying to make points with Wesley; he wasn't part of Wesley's little crew, just inserted himself into this.

"I started to turn, and that's when he hit me over the head with a lock in a sock. Because I had turned, the lock came around and instead of smashing my nose, it hit the glass in my eyeglasses, driving it straight into my eye. He expected me to fall over like in the movies, but I just kept turning around and took a couple of steps; he backed up and fell back on a bed, and as I got ready to hit him with my little leather knife, that's when Wesley chopped me with the cane knife." After several more savage slashes from the cane knife, Dennis had had enough and tried to make it to the locked door of the dormitory, bleeding profusely but still conscious. Re-attaching the tendons restored some use to his arm, though his eye was not salvageable.

"At the time," he recalls, "I wouldn't tell them who put my eye out; I never did, though I don't mind telling the names now, thirty years later, who cares? But before I was treated, Associate Warden Hayden Dees came and asked me who had done it. I said I wasn't going to tell, and he said I was going to stay right there in that hall until I did tell, and *then* I might get some medical attention. They shookdown the entire dormitory, since it was obvious weapons were involved and also to find any cuts or bruises on other inmates indicating participation. Well, there wasn't anything wrong with Wesley, but they did find this little hickey on Donald Borland where my little knife had barely pierced his skin, so he did five days in the hole. They never locked Wesley up or anything. They probably found his knife, 'cause it's pretty hard to hide a cane knife, but I'm sure Wesley didn't have it when they found it. They put me in CCR and left me there until Borland discharged."

After weeks in the prison hospital, Dennis was sent to CCR, restricted control cells, where he first met some of the prison's worst inmates, including Robert Lee "Tangle-Eye" George, the second person he would kill. By November of 1964, Dennis had become involved with the inmate store operations, working in the warehouse where supplies were stockpiled to fill orders from the camp stores. He recalls, "Tangle-Eye George ran the trusty-yard store operation; Big Daddy Simmons ran the big-yard store, and there was a free warehouse supervisor we called Old Man Price.

"To make a long story short, I never did like Tang, and he never liked me, going back to CCR days when I first came in. A lot of people didn't like Tang and were afraid of him, even his own 'homies.' With good reason; he'd snake you if nothing else. He'd already stabbed the barber, so we're not talking about Mr. Easter Bunny here. This guy was dangerous, there's no question about it. At the time he was the heroin connection for the whole prison, which meant he needed money. He was loaded all the time, and would come wandering in with his eyes pinpoints. Somebody in New Orleans that Tang knew had to be sending it; Old Man Price and Tang were tight, but Old Man Price on his own wouldn't have had the connections to get anything like that. Somebody was getting it physically to Tang, some security officer or captain or something; I don't know.

"I was in the office, doing the paperwork, taking inventory and all. The paperwork was the key. I was already covering up shipments to Big Daddy, and Tang wanted me to do it for him 'cause he was shooting all his profits up, but it was too much. It's one thing to skim a little; it's another to clean the thing out and expect nobody to notice. So I refused, and he didn't like that. Essentially what the deal was, I'd put them down for five cartons of Salems and send them fifty; the zero would get lost, see, and the other forty-five cartons they could sell and convert to cash money, which wasn't that difficult for the store operator.

"So that really brought the friction to a head, that I wouldn't do for him what he suspected I was doing for Big Daddy. Tang comes in one day just about quitting time, loaded out of his skull, and starts screaming at me. Old Man Price run off, got lost, made himself scarce. Tang was telling me he was gonna steal my other eye. I said 'that's it.' I went down to the yard and got a knife from Big Dad and the next morning, as soon as I saw Tang, I hit him. And I'd do it again. If he didn't get me then, he'd have gotten me another time. The guy was dangerous, in and out of prison, and would always be.

"When I hit him, he turned around and started running, and I kept stabbing him. He had really gotten under my skin with his talk about stealing my eye. When he saw there was no escape, he tried to fight, then broke away and jumped off the loading dock and got under an old truck. I couldn't get him out so I backed up the truck away from him and then stabbed him a couple more times, until I saw in his eyes that it was over, and then I stopped, went back in the office and waited for the people to come."

Longtime Angola inmates and security staffers alike suggest that Dennis' killing of George, undeniably shocking, was nevertheless an almost inevitable act of self-defense when seen in the context of life behind bars. Had Dennis not killed the other inmate when he did, they explain, he himself would surely have been killed by Tangle-Eye, and would have had to keep looking over his shoulder until that happened. However, Dennis was sentenced to death for the slaying and in the spring of 1965 went to Death Row.

"They gave me the death penalty," he says, "and I gave it back to them. It goes back to the trial. They brought me to court in the whole outfit, waist chains, shackles, handcuffs, and they kept me through the whole trial like that, plus they had a whole truckload of guards surrounding the courthouse. And I'd been reading where a California federal appellate court had ruled that in the absence of specific cause as to why a particular defendant presents a security threat, you just can't do that. So I told my lawyer, Leon Picou, to object. He said that was normal procedure, not just for me but for everybody. The judge, John Rarick, denied the objection on the same grounds, that it was standard procedure. I had it incorporated in my automatic appeal; Picou I think was good enough to take it to the Fifth Circuit, which pitched the case back, saying re-try or release, and then they offered me the standard life sentence."

It was in 1968 that Dennis was removed from Death Row and went to the big yard; he finally began to realize that it was time to think about a legitimate means of getting out of prison. "I've got two life sentences, I'm not a spring chicken anymore, I've been locked up eleven years, and I realize that just coming off Death Row I'm more than a few years away from release. But I'm *thinking* about getting out, whereas before I had never really thought about it that much, or had kept from thinking about it. I began evaluating myself overall...who am I, when am I gonna get out, why should I, what am I gonna do when I get out, things like that. I think aging more than anything else, and going through those traumatic experiences, kinda started the mellowing process."

Dennis began playing football with prison teams, got involved in inmate recreation programs and worked his way up from recreation clerk to being in effect the director of recreation, organizing programs, setting up schedules, getting teams together, ordering equipment and movies. "I *was* the recreation department," he says. "I was really into that. I was proud of it, and it really gave me a sense of satisfaction for the first time. The stores were challenging, especially when I was 'cooking the books,' but this was the first job that gave me any kind of reward aside from monetary, and I liked that. People respected me, they asked my opinion, and I'm talking about free people too. That was a nice thing to experience."

By the early seventies Dennis, through good behavior, had made it up to the trusty side of the prison, where he took a lead in integrating what had been a totally segregated inmate population. With rumors of the massive upheaval approaching, tension was building; the forced integration of school districts and public facilities would be painfully troublesome all across the South, but the forced integration of a large population of violent criminals had the distinct potential of being deadly.

To calm the waters and get things moving peacefully but quickly, Warden C. Murray Henderson sent for a small number of recognized and respected inmate leaders—trusties and big stripes, black and white. Explaining that, under the watchful eyes of the federal courts, integration was inevitable, Henderson told the four leaders that the first moves would be made on the trusty yard and big yard. They were given the choice not *whether* to integrate, but *how* to integrate; security staffers could do it by force, or the inmate leaders could handle it themselves, assuming responsibility for explaining the necessity to other prisoners and working out the particulars.

"It was a big deal, a big change, I mean this was twenty-four hours a day we'd have to live with it," says Dennis, looking back. "So we figured what he said made sense. Then we got into the details, deciding how to keep from separating the inmate 'families,' the little groups that stuck together. The families were really beneficial within the traditional prison social structure, because nine out of ten helped each other within the group to do their time without getting into trouble; the tenth group maybe caused trouble, but busting them up would mean a lot more friction."

Some families consisted of a small group of dominant friends in control, often with additional member-inmates who took the role of dependent "little kids," homosexual partners. "You start splitting that up," Dennis explains, "and you have even more trouble than splitting up groups that are just friends. If my kid goes to another dormitory where I'm not there to look out for him, and somebody moves on him, then my friends and I are gonna go straighten it out, and maybe the mover has got some friends, and that means problems. Security has always recognized that. Don't misunderstand; if they caught you in a homosexual act, you were gone, and it could result in a street charge. But as far as *knowing*, as opposed to witnessing, they knew, but they wouldn't take any action unless problems resulted. Within limits, it was accepted by security.

"We didn't want to split that up. And we wanted to keep like with like. Our major concern was that. We didn't want to empty out half the white old-folks dorm and put in a bunch of black urbs (inmates from the streets of New Orleans); we wanted to put black oldtimers in. We wanted to keep like with like, that was what we were really focusing on. So we put the black urbs with the white urbs, and the young first-offender kids together. There had been no social, work, or living conjunction of black and white inmates before; even the stores were black one day, white the next. The mess hall had a black line going in one door, a white line going in another door, and they sat on different sides of the room.

"When Warden Henderson gave us the choice, we left that room and got moving, each of us going alone into eight dormitories to give our speech, answer questions, talk. The buzz word was 'like with like.' The initial reaction from a small group was 'we'll die first;' I said 'well, you probably *will*, but we're gonna go ahead on and do this, and you guys do what you want.' They were just letting off steam. Most people grumbled, but there was no real opposition. Very few people said it was a good idea, but the momentum of those who wanted to get it done our way, together with the apathy of a larger portion, carried the day.

"We made lists and lists and lists, the Go or Stay lists; half had to go and half to stay in each dorm, with endless changes. Goddamn, the changes—'no I wanta go,' 'no I wanta stay,' 'no I don't wanta stay,' 'hey wait a minute, if he's going then I gotta go'—and for everybody that was going, I had to find somebody to stay, and for everybody that wouldn't go, I had to find somebody who would, and I know the rest of the guys were running into the same thing." Despite endless changes, lists were turned in to meet the deadline and the move was successfully accomplished all on one day, organized mass confusion with inmates pushing roller-wagons, moving beds and possessions, with a minimum of trouble. Allowing the inmates to handle the change themselves turned out to have been a stroke of genius.

After his recreation job placed Dennis on the path to becoming a recognized inmate leader, his very visible position bringing him into contact with large numbers of inmates and free guards alike, he began to focus even more on eventual release, learning watch repair and becoming involved with the fledgling law library. At this time, again because of the federal court order, there was new focus on the disciplinary process at Angola, or lack of one, which brought the Department of Corrections' first attorney, Richard Crane, to the prison to create and implement a viable, acceptable policy.

"Crane, for whom Corrections Secretary Elayn Hunt created the position, had no background in corrections but was sharp enough to know he needed to talk to the prisoners to find out what needed to be done, and we hit it off right away. He was idealistic, a child of the sixties, and very, very sharp," says Dennis. "The disciplinary process involved how to maintain discipline in a penitentiary, with all these guys convicted of everything under the sun, some of them losing their grip and others just plain evil. Most just wanted to get along, but there was a need for structure and discipline. How do you do it?

"The unacceptable approach was the old days, to federal judge E. Gordon West, though they didn't beat hell out of you any more; what they'd do, and it's essentially the same now, was that the officer would write up infractions on a pink slip, and then you'd go to disciplinary court, which consisted of the chief security officer and maybe a captain, before whom you stood while he read the report; you could say something if you wanted, and then he'd say 'isolation' or whatever. If you got isolation, you never knew for how long; it was totally arbitrary, and when they felt like it they'd let you out, though they usually tended to conform to similar terms for certain offenses unless they didn't like you.

"Crane wanted something approximating court due process but on a smaller scale and more flexible, so he could feel that each prisoner subject to disciplinary action was being given a fair hearing, which was all he was entitled to. He didn't want to do any more than that, but that's a long way from what it used to be. I was one of the people he talked to. I'm not bragging, I'm stating a fact in saying that intellectually I'd be in the top one percent of prisoners at Angola, so I was someone with whom he could speak and get something back he understood. They were also going to get into the totally innovative idea of counsel substitutes, for which the response was better from black than white inmates, many whites taking the attitude of, 'Man, you go up there and try to help these guys or speak for them and assist them, security's gonna get you.' And that's a very real thing, not paranoia; it's a knowledge of the system and how it works.

"But knowing Richard, and after Elayn Hunt came through and talked to us, I said 'well, I'll give it a try, these people mean business, at least in this area.' I won't say I was the first counsel substitute, but I was in the first group of four or five. A counsel substitute is to disciplinary court what a defense attorney is to criminal court. The mechanics of it were really quite simple, through Richard Crane's work, with help from Warden Henderson who provided the support to smooth the process. All of a sudden we had two courts. The little piddly write-ups for unmade beds and stuff would go to a disciplinary officer, a captain, who'd hear it by himself, and all you could lose would be privileges, not good-time. For major or high court, there actually was a board, with two out of three of the wardens for administration, security and treatment having to be there, rotating the chairmanship, and counsel substitutes representing the inmates."

Being a counsel substitute was time consuming but rewarding. High court met three times weekly, with the counsel substitute having to conduct pre-trial interviews with offending inmates beforehand, penetrating mental barriers, weighing sides, considering mitigating circumstances, recommending pleas and planning defense strategies just like licensed courtroom lawyers. "I'd have to extract all this; if they hadn't been written up in a year, for example, we'd plead guilty and ask for a suspended sentence, and when I'd get it, I'd feel like the greatest thing since Clarence Darrow, and it was just walking-around sense. And some of the others, mostly black, were doing the same thing. Initially, I was the only white guy, so on the call-out, I had all the white inmates. That, I stayed with until I went to Baton Rouge. I started going down to the law library and by osmosis picked up some paralegal techniques and knowledge."

Escalating violence around this time accompanied the removal of inmate guards before funding materialized for paid replacements, leaving professional correctional officers only in the perimeter guard towers and no security staff in the dormitories. But it was not fear that motivated Dennis' next move. A trusty for some years now, he had won the respect of administrative staff on up through the warden, the DOC attorney and Corrections Secretary Hunt, all of whom supported his request to transfer to a corrections work-release program in Baton Rouge, where he would be living at the minimum-security state trusty dorm called the Police Barracks and working at DOC headquarters. "I just wanted to go," he says. "I'd been at Angola for like seventeen years at the time, mostly in maximum or medium security, and I was tired of it." Normal "life" sentence at that time generally translated into ten or twelve years served, or less; even with two life sentences, Douglas Dennis felt he had paid his dues, and a lot of influential people agreed.

"I guess what they saw in me that made them support my request was sincerity, maybe maturity. When you're around someone for an extended period of time, like a co-worker in an office, you get a pretty solid basis to draw a valid perception of that person, and surely they must have seen at the least that this was a mature person who was not impulsive or temperamental, who was in control, intelligent, sincere. Why not? There'd obviously been a major modification since I'd arrived at Angola. Before, I'd had no sense of direction, no sense of consequences; it was a bit more than immaturity. Even in the Tangle-Eye incident, there had been a paranoia about losing my other eye; I was really almost a fullblown sociopath, not a psychopath but a sociopath, I really didn't care. You know what turned me around? Again I say the sixties were not a throw-away. I sat on Death Row and had subscriptions to *Village Voice, New Republic,* and that whole period was really an enriching process. I saw demonstrations on TV and watched public television channels a lot, so my mind was fertilized by that period, as were a lot of others. The seeds were planted then, that I could be more than just a Marlon Brando act-alike from *The Wild One.*"

Sent to Baton Rouge to work at DOC with Richard Crane and process disciplinary appeals from that end, Dennis would listen to tapes of deliberations and hearings, review appeals, draft decisions and hand the finished product to the attorney for his final approval. He also was assigned to chauffeur Elayn Hunt to speaking engagements out of town. "She was a political person, you see, and she worked all day," he remembers. "She worked like a mule. So when she had these engagements, she'd come down to pick me up, I'd sign out and get into the driver's seat and take her to wherever. She'd be in the back making her notes and putting her speech together, going through paperwork in her briefcase."

After a few months at the Police Barracks out by the municipal airport, he transferred his residence to the CCRC, Community Corrections and Rehabilitation Center, where a good-sized group of inmates and trusties lived while working at the Department of Corrections, taking care of cars, handling mail, doing minor maintenance, many while on probation or parole. CCRC was a type of work-release program with no bars or fences but at least nominal around-the-clock supervision, located just downriver from DOC headquarters in the Pentagon buildings near the state capitol.

"Part of CCRC was Kenny Vince, a quadriplegic and really great guy," says Dennis; "this guy has *cojones,* really an admirable guy. He was working for the state in vocational rehabilitation, not corrections, helping wayward youths who had CCRC as alternative sentencing. I wanted to go to LSU, not during working hours but after I'd put in my work day, and VocRehab paid for it because of Kenny Vince. At night, I'd sign out of CCRC, drive to LSU, go to evening classes, do research in the library, whatever I had to do. I took a full load for four semesters. My major was Criminal Justice; what else do I know? I've been a prisoner all my life. And if I'm not of some value as a corrections employee of some calibre, what else am I gonna do? Watch repair had gone by the boards with all these digitals, so I had learned a trade that was useless, like making clay pots for a living. I had a 3.96 gradepoint average."

Powerful Baton Rouge District Attorney Ossie Brown would enter the picture at this point. A flamboyantly successful defense attorney who jumped to the other side of the fence with his election as DA in 1972, Brown has been called by Louisiana political observer John Maginnis "what you get when you cross a high-sounding Baptist preacher with a fast-talking criminal attorney," and before long would himself be the subject of federal inquiries into alleged preferential treatment for the drug-suspect son of a local millionaire businessman to whom Brown was trying to sell a failing business.

The Bible-thumping Brown, Dennis says, "somehow found out I was in school at LSU, and I really don't know why he got such a hard-on, I really don't...free publicity and the ability to stomp on a defenseless target were two factors; another one, maybe he didn't like Elayn Hunt so much, she was honest and very forward, and someone like that never gets along with Ossie. I had had no connection with him before, though I had heard of him. I knew some spicy little tidbits that later came out in all the glory that he deserved, bagman that he was.

"Anyway, he made a big to-do, got me kicked out of school; I didn't do anything wrong, it was just the fact that I was attending LSU, paid for by tax money, that outraged him. The school didn't kick me out; I was withdrawn by C. Paul Phelps, who'd taken over as secretary of corrections after Elayn's death. I don't blame him. See, the East Baton Rouge district attorney is the most powerful DA in the state of Louisiana, and Ossie was not hesitant to use every ounce of power and clout that he had. I know for a fact that he went to Governor Edwin Edwards at least half a dozen times, bitching and moaning specifically about me, if you can imagine that, and I hadn't done a goddamn thing to provoke that type of antipathy."

A burglary ring operating out of CCRC and subsequent stakeouts by a state police investigator named Joe Whitmore who would later figure in Dennis' eventual downfall, an escape by another CCRC resident in Hayden Dees' DOC car which resulted in several law enforcement officers being killed, all had the effect of attracting the attention of DA Brown to the work-release facility, bent upon closing it down. Its inevitable closure returned the remaining corrections crew to the Police Barracks under more restricted living conditions. Dennis was put in charge of a DOC station wagon in which to transport the other inmates to work, which allowed him to work on weekends too. "They checked on me, those people out there. They'd call me on the phone to make sure I was at corrections headquarters. But there was never an incident, no trouble."

Returning to the Barracks for lunch one day with the other inmates, in early July 1979, Dennis was involved in a minor auto accident in downtown Baton Rouge which would prove fateful. He was not in any way at fault; the other driver was being ticketed, when who should arrive on the scene but District Attorney Ossie Brown. "Big old sad-sack Ossie, 6'7", 500 pounds, all flab, and he gets right in my face, 'You Dennis? What did you cause?' The cop tells him I'm not at fault, and Ossie tells the cop he's gonna have his job if he lets this *prisoner* get back behind the wheel of that car and drive off endangering the lives of the citizens of this parish. He was jumping up and down, 'you oughta be back in Angola, I'm gonna *see* that you get back in Angola where you belong,' really frantic. He'd just happened to hear my name on his police scanner on his way to lunch. After that, I didn't drive the car, just rode in it. And Ossie made sure that it all got in the paper for two or three days, and every article, while admitting I was not at fault, kept quoting Ossie, and he was really getting on Fast Eddie and C. Paul, really beating them to their knees with it. And Fast Eddie didn't need that; neither did C. Paul." The unfortunate Dennis, who had become an unwitting symbol of what the DA considered as uncalled-for leniency underlying Louisiana's corrections problems, would have to be removed from Brown's territory altogether and sent to Dixon Correctional Institute in an adjoining parish.

Before the accident, Dennis' focus had been on getting a pardon, and Elayn Hunt offered to help. "Which she did," he recalls with gratitude. "On her deathbed, she asked her brother, prominent Lake Charles attorney E. C. Hunt, 'get Dennis a pardon, get him out.' He promised her he would make it happen. He orchestrated a pardon hearing, with Kenny Vince and several others to testify that I should receive a commutation, time cut to time served. This was another big brouhaha, because Pardon Board met in Baton Rouge, and Ossie paid a Shreveport ADA all expenses to come down and howl about what a desperado I was in Caddo Parish and what a heinous crime I had committed, when he hadn't even started going to law school when the crime went down, some young kid twenty-four or twenty-five years old.

"Still, I got a highly publicized recommendation of time cut to time served. E.C. was a close personal friend and longtime supporter of Edwards; there wasn't a *deal*, but the understanding was that when Edwards went out of office, I'd go out with the mansion crew; it's historic that when a governor leaves, he frees the whole crew of inmates working at the governor's mansion. After the accident, E.C. said it didn't look like Edwards would be able to help me, because he was looking to come back as governor and didn't want Ossie beating him over the head with me. My contention had been that I was rehabilitated and could function properly and productively in society; Ossie's was that I would be no more able to function productively in society than Charles Manson. Everything was going down the tubes. Pardons are a political thing, and politically I was dog meat. So with all this in mind, I just said 'OK.' I just left." It was July 25, 1979.

Through a career criminal friend, he was provided with a get-away car and driver, unknown to him, to take him from corrections headquarters wherever he wanted to go. "I'd been up all the night before. That was a major move, not a light decision or done on impulse. I felt I *had* to go; I'd been in prison long enough, twenty-two years, though the last five had been relatively nice working around human beings, being exposed to normal thought patterns and a normal environment. That was not a throw-away, that was a big deal for me; without those five years, I wouldn't have lasted six months outside. I'm a product of twenty-two years in a prison environment, and I can't erase that, no matter how hard I try; without the gradual acclimatization to reality in those five years in work-release, the whole decompression there, I wouldn't have made it outside.

"In a way, I was betraying the trust and confidence of Richard Crane and also Joe Whitmore, who was running the Police Barracks. It wasn't, 'Oh, boy, let's run off!' It was a very serious move, and I really felt ambivalent about it. The bottom line was, I was forty-three, I'd been locked up long enough, and if I went back to DCI there was no telling how many more years, not months but years, I'd have to do before I'd get out, if ever. I wouldn't have run off if Fast Eddie had said I'd go when he went, but with that commitment withdrawn, I had no hope, no hope at all. So it was either go to prison for the rest of my life or an unknown amount of years, or go out and do right, not rip and run, not steal and rob and rape and pillage...go out and do *right*, do what I said I was gonna do in the first place, integrate into society, get a job and work, meet a lady, get together, just be *normal*, live like a human being. So that's what I did. I spent much of the night writing three very long letters, one to C. Paul, one to Richard Crane, one to Whitmore, doing my best to explain what I was doing, what I intended to do which was work, and why I did it, and to apologize and hope that they understood."

Dennis spent a week in a New Orleans motel, hardly emerging except to go to a mall to see the movie *Alien*, being supplied with food by a friend, purchasing a used car for $200. He then drove to Houston, where he worked day labor in a warehouse for a month, living in a weekly motel and hoarding his savings from his watch repair work.

Guatemala was his next destination. He made a nighttime crossing of the US border into Mexico at McAllen, Texas, stopping in the free zone long enough to apply for a tourist visa in the name of J. W. Stevens, the alias which matched his falsified birth certificate, driver's license obtained from the DMV in New Orleans and Social Security card, all acquired on furloughs from the work-release program because "after the LSU thing, I figured I needed a lifeboat." The major stumbling block was the absolutely critical Social Security card, requiring "spinning a little tale for the sympathetic little gal who was the clerk," coming up with a believable explanation of why a middle-aged man had never had a number. Dennis spun a long involved tale of doing watch repair in a family-owned jewelry store without ever being officially on the payroll, thus never needing a Social Security account number until his father's recent death necessitated the sale of the store and a first attempt at outside employment.

When Dennis left, State Police Investigator Joe Whitmore was vacationing at a camp on Padre Island, Texas. Cutting short his holiday, he returned and immediately took up the trail. Whitmore and Dennis had known each other from Dennis' years at Angola, meeting initially through the screening process before Dennis was moved to Police Barracks, and had a mutual respect for each other. While not by any means excusing Dennis' Shreveport crime, Whitmore says he feels Dennis was simply a big young kid who didn't know his own strength and had no intent to kill.

Of the continued support Dennis enjoyed at DOC headquarters in Baton Rouge, Whitmore stresses that he never felt an accomplice at work had physically assisted in the escape. "I don't think they helped him," he says now, "but I think they knew what his plans were, they had to, they *had* to. Mr. Phelps had no alternative but to take Dennis and put him in a barred institution, after transferring the DOC messengers back to Police Barracks didn't satisfy Mr. Brown, who had used Dennis as a model of why CCRC shouldn't be down there, even though to my knowledge Dennis hadn't done anything wrong. On a Friday Mr. Phelps and Richard Crane the attorney called Dennis in and told him that they intended sending him to DCI. That Wednesday, he escaped, and from that day in July of 1979 until December 1988, the state police expended many, many manhours in an attempt to apprehend him, but came across no solid leads."

Dennis was in Mexico, El Salvador, and Guatemala, working in various clerical or accounting capacities for small companies, picking up enough Spanish to get by on. He met DJ down there, beginning a relationship which he says gave new meaning to his life and his quest for normalcy. Born in Germany, DJ and her family relocated to the United States and lived on the East Coast after her mother, a war widow, married an American GI.

It would be a macadamia nut project which drew DJ, grown to adulthood, to Costa Rica and then Guatemala, where her second marriage dissolved and she found employment in Guatemala City with an American businesswoman who provided outlets for furniture made in cottage industries. "She'd been in business there for years, had a real good imagination and put together a really quality product. One day she came into the store and said she was bringing in another American, a cost accountant to do the finances and the books," DJ remembers, "and that's how I met Steve for the first time." The year was 1979, and Douglas Dennis was calling himself James Walter Stevens; DJ shortened it all to Steve.

"We became friends, and had been friends for almost a year before we started seeing each other," DJ relates. The friendship deepened the July evening she threw herself a thirty-sixth birthday party complete with mariachi band at the twelve-room house she shared with American roommates in Antigua, Guatemala. "At one point he told me he loved me, two or three weeks down the line, and I remember saying to him, 'don't do that, because I am going to leave, I'm going back to the States.' This had been my fourth year there, and due to the political situation and everything, I was ready to leave. He asked me where I was going, and I said Redwood City, because that's where I had been before and I had friends there. And he said 'I will see you there.'"

What was it that attracted DJ to this particular individual? "One quality was his gentleness," she says, "and his strength, stability, kindness. The friends that he has made like him, maybe for some of those same reasons He was a good worker and always pulled his share, in many instances more than his share. When he told you he was going to do something, you could bet your life on it. We worked well together and we were friends."

As far as any normal inquiries into his past history, she was told that his parents were dead and there were no brothers or sisters. "What he told me," she remembers, "was 'our life starts now, and anything that was before that doesn't matter.' And I accepted that, without any question, because I didn't want to hear about old loves or old marriages, and I'm sure he didn't either. So what he said was 'we start from here.' I am a very private person, I don't open up to many people, so we just respected each other. I do know that occasionally when I would ask questions I would not get answers, the subject would be changed very quickly, but it never led me to any suspicions. And I *never* saw any violence or breaking of the law, never even a ticket."

Visiting her mother in the East for awhile after leaving Guatemala, on New Year's Day 1981 DJ heard her sister answer a knock at the door, then announce that a surprise package had arrived for her. "And there he was, with a big bow around him, and he just came in and said 'You don't think I'm gonna let you spend New Year's alone?' He stayed two days, because that's all he had off from work." Dennis had already spent several weeks getting established in California, and DJ soon joined him there. "I stayed with my friends for awhile," she says, "because I didn't want to live with anybody, but prices had gone up tremendously in the Bay Area, so what it came down to was that I needed to live with someone, a roommate or something. And I decided, 'OK, Steve is a known quantity, I'll move in with him.' We kept everything separate, separate checking accounts, separate bills; the only thing we really combined was expenses."

After four years in a rented house, the couple purchased a mobile home in Sunnyvale. Dennis had arrived in California with no job, no living quarters, no car and a little over $2000 in cash, but was established within a matter of weeks, moving quickly. "My problem," he says, "was getting a job with no American work history. My goal had not changed: to work and integrate into society. The solution was to work as a temp." Signing up with several temporary employment agencies, Kelly, Adia, Manpower, Dennis worked at various clerical and financial jobs until Alza liked his performance so much they hired him permanently. From there he went to Louis Allen Associates, a management consulting firm, until laid off in the recession. A temporary job at Hitachi lasted a year, then he found a comfortable niche at Nidek, where he worked eight years, "always taking small steps upward, never backward, very much like a person just out of school breaking into the job market, except that I was forty-four when I began."

Upward mobility had its rewards. Working in middle management at salaries ranging up to $32,000, Dennis says, "I accumulated, gradually, the possessions others do—VCRs, TV, dishes, crystal, good suits and clothing, a nice albeit used car, own home, good furniture, etc. But most important of all was my relationship with DJ, who got me through some mentally rough times and, as I realize so very clearly now, made the whole escapade worthwhile, giving direction and meaning to my life, direction in the sense that 'things' are a means at best, not an end. If I was a yuppie, it was in the sense that I was upwardly mobile rather than materialistically oriented."

Dennis, like all longterm inmates, had a lot of catching up to do. "The biggest problem facing each and every prisoner re-entering society," he muses, "is that the years spent inside are *dead*. For example, I was inside twenty-two years; therefore, I was twenty-two years behind my peers. And the absolute best I could do was *stay* twenty-two years behind. The least important part of it is accumulating 'things.' The major part of it is the twenty-two years my peers spent building families, having children and even grandchildren, cultivating friends, building careers, travelling, enjoying, sharing, in short, *living*. I only *survived*. Don't misunderstand; I'm not looking for sympathy, merely stating a fact. Being behind is bad; knowing you can never catch up really works on you. What makes it even harder to handle is that it blindsides you; no one ever told me about this. "

Nevertheless, he and DJ made a good life for themselves. Even with a bad knee, Dennis jogged four days a week, ran in races, trained for a marathon and regularly worked out with weights, volunteering to spend Sundays as a uniformed ranger at one park where he often ran. At-home movies were other favorite weekend entertainments. DJ accepted the fact that Dennis enjoyed being around other people less than she, so she usually visited friends alone, persuading him to accompany her to parties only rarely. "We had very few people at the house," she says, "because he just didn't seem quite sociable with people. Now I understand the reason. Then, I just respected him for being that kind of person. He went to work every morning and came home every night, living a perfectly normal life. We even fought just like everybody else. He was proud that he belonged to Mensa; he had a Mensa sticker on his car, and we would go to their book swaps. We split the chores, and he was very good at cleaning up and taking care of the cars."

As manager for administration at Nidek, the Palo Alto firm that made ophthalmic lasers, Dennis impressed his bosses so much they wanted to send him to visit the parent company in Japan, all expenses paid. He and DJ had also made plans for a fantasy vacation abroad. Tempting trips, both. But both required a passport. He had applied for and received a five-year passport in Salvador in 1980, then upon expiration mailed it back in for a ten-year renewal. And then he had lost it.

The passport was the beginning of the end. "I did something really stupid; I guess we all do at some point," Dennis says, looking back on the turning point which came after nearly a decade of eternal vigilance, carefully considering every move and weighing every consequence. He returned to Guatemala on a business trip to pick up a heavy laser tube and power pack for Nidek. After a lenthy flight back to Los Angeles, an exhausted Dennis made the connecting flight to San Jose; the laser, in its coffin-sized container, did not.

"So I made fifty calls trying to track it down, it's nighttime and I've been flying all day and I've had a few drinks and I'm ready to crash, and then about a half hour later, about ten o'clock, the phone rings, just when I'm falling asleep." The laser had arrived. Because the airport in San Jose closed at midnight as part of a noise abatement program, Dennis decided he'd better pick it up right away.

"I got up, I was tired and functioning about sixty percent," he remembers, "staggered out to the car rubbing my eyes, trying to really get focused in. I had a habit of carrying a little pouch-purse that I put everything in, keys, cigarettes, wallet, passport, money, credit cards, American Express, Master-Card, Visa, Discovery, all my pennies. I had an '85 Nissan 200-SX turbo, black, and I loved that car, so I always used a car cover. And I laid my bag down on the back fin to fold up the car cover, got in the car and drove off...you know, like a woman does at the gas station, drives away with her purse on top of the car. So halfway down to the airport, six minutes from the house, I reach over on the seat next to me and panic city, where the hell is my bag? So I realize it's on the back of the car and I can't see in the rear view, it's nighttime, so I drive *very carefully*, and I pull over at the airport exit and I get out to look and it's gone."

Driving back, then walking the whole route on foot, he found no bag, but did find twenty or thirty pennies, the lost-baggage claim and his pen along the entrance ramp to the freeway right in front of his house. Dennis surmised that someone must have seen the bag fall and stopped to pick it up; he advertised for it, but it was never returned. Replacing the credit cards and driver's license, he says, was nothing; he was already on file.

But the *passport*...that was another matter. It required presenting either an expired passport or a birth certificate. Dennis had disposed of his expired passport; his phony birth certificate had been lost in the bag. "I had two choices," he says. "I could either forget the passport and just stay in the country, or I could make another birth certificate and then hopefully, the passport being a replacement, it would just slide through. Why should there be fifty people examining this thing like Sherlock Holmes; people lose their passports all the time. And I said 'well, why take the chance,' and here's another big decision.

"The first stupidity was losing that bag, but I could have recovered from that. The biggest stupidity was deciding to try to push it through...me, of all people, whose forte now that nine years have passed is computers. I've computerized two companies. Of all people, I don't realize that this isn't 1979 when the Apple was still in the garage; this is 1988, now we have all these huge computer systems and networks that are independent but they *talk* to one another. I was a dead fish, I really was, when I went through processing that thing. I sent it up there and they ran it through the computer and it set off every red light in the place. If I had just realized that the advances in personal computers, which was my forte, had to be paralleled by the advances in governmental computers...and I *knew* that, but it just eluded me.

"I had two big pressures to get a passport. Number one, DJ and I had tickets in our hands for a trip to Germany, Paris, London in March of '89. Can't do that without a passport. Second thing, my boss wanted to send me to Japan to the parent company for two weeks, everything on the company. Can't do *that* without a passport. So I had two specific pressures to get a passport, which explains that stupid decision. The rest is pretty prosaic."

Contacted by a special agent for the State Department who invited him to drop into his office in the federal building in downtown San Francisco, Dennis knew it had all blown up. "I'm really in shock, and I've spent so much time being normal that I don't know how to be abnormal, and I never was *really* a criminal," he says. "I was a stupid wild kid for a short period of time, but not a professional criminal, no." Curiosity led him to see how things had gone wrong and what might be salvageable, so he kept the appointment with the federal agents, who really didn't know who he *was;* they only knew who he *wasn't,* being convinced that J. W. Stevens did not exist. Requesting fingerprints and reading him his rights, the agents informed Dennis that he was free to leave at any time during the interrogation. Where did he get his original passport, they asked. Why was there no birth certificate on file for him? Dennis decided to test the agents' promise that he was free to leave, and did so.

Returning home, he says, "You can imagine the scene I had with DJ. I didn't tell her anything in great detail, just that I was definitely in trouble and the police were gonna come. So I stayed there that night, I probably shouldn't have but I'm really in shock and my whole life is disappearing." The next day was payday, so he returned to his office long enough to draw his check, then went to Well Fargo Bank to cash it and tried to draw out other funds. He had $7500 in a checking account and an IRA containing another $11,000, but the teller balked at handing out so much cold cash, suggesting instead a cashier's check or bank transfer.

Told to return on Monday, Dennis checked into a motel, then was able to get only the $7500 from his checking account in cash and a cashier's check for his IRA. "Leaving wasn't that easy," he recalls. "DJ wanted me to stay one last night at home, so I was going to leave at four o'clock Tuesday morning. I had the car all packed and ready. At ten minutes after four Monday evening, DJ still at work, I go out to the car in bathrobe and flipflops to toss in something and I'm putting the car cover back on and see two police cars ease up and stop across the street in front of my house inside the mobile home park. I knew they were after me." Weaving through mobile homes, Dennis found a place to crouch down and hide. After an hour, a cold San Francisco December hour, he checked, saw no police cars but noticed DJ was home. He went in to dress. "And that was the last I saw of her for nearly a year," he laments.

"And pretty soon," Dennis remembers, "here comes Special Agent Brad Smith. Meanwhile, it was dark and I had never turned the lights on. I'm peeping out, and they're walking around shining their flashlights into the windows to see if they could see me. They kept that up until ten o'clock that night; they even called on the phone and left a message on the answering machine: 'This is officer So-and-So of the Sunnyvale Police Department, we know you're in there and you've got three minutes to come out before we kick in the door.' I'm crouched down, feeling sorry for myself, terrible situation to be in but it was all on me, stupidity."

Finally, the police officers, who had only an arrest warrant, left to get a search warrant. Sure the exit to the trailer park would be under surveillance, Dennis left on foot, jumping over the fence at eleven o'clock at night, working his way through a residential area to the railroad tracks. With plenty of money in his pockets, he planned to try to make it to Santa Clara and catch a train out to San Francisco, where he could hop a bus.

DJ, meanwhile, had endured a week of unexplained strange behavior by Dennis, including noctural disappearances and obvious distraction, prior to December 19, the night the officers appeared at the door. "I came home that night and his car was in the driveway, the cover was on it," she remembers, "and I said 'well, whatever had been wrong probably is right now, because he's back.' And I went into the house and he just really started lighting in on me and I got angry and walked out." Trying to collect her wits in a back parking lot of the trailer park, DJ noticed suspicious characters in business suits loitering near an empty mobile home and reported them to the park manager. DJ turned out to be the object of their interest, as well.

"I just got terribly frightened," she recalls, "because I had no idea what was going on. I told them exactly the circumstances of our meeting and all. I didn't know what to make of any of it. The police came back again the next day, and police cars were going by consistently. What they wanted to do was go through the house, and I said not until I got some advice from somebody on what to do. Nobody had told me what was going on; everybody was just threatening me." DJ was threatened, she says, with prison, and was given shocking (and erroneous) information that Dennis had murdered three people and kidnapped a fourth. "I just flat-out told them 'I don't believe you,' and it's *still* two separate people to me." Not until the end of February or beginning of March did the agents finally accept that DJ had had no prior knowledge of Dennis' situation. "I told them that one of the things I've always admired in this country is that you're innocent until proven guilty, and they said they had to find that out for themselves, but they knew it now," she says.

Dennis, meanwhile, was struggling to get out of Sunnyvale, running along the train tracks through the darkness. Trying to catch a little sleep on some cardboard at the unsheltered Santa Clara railroad platform, Dennis was rousted by a vigilant female police officer. "She was expecting a drifter, derelict, wino, so that's what I gave her. It wasn't difficult to do, 'cause that's how I felt. She says 'What's your name?' Oh boy, I couldn't say J. W. Stevens. I'm trying to remember my back-up name, Larry Hunt, and I forgot the middle name. Her partner's punching it all into the computer in the police car, and she's threatening to take me in if I don't give her a name that works."

Finally verifying a Hunt at the address given by Dennis, with no outstanding warrants, the officer mentioned police were looking for a suspect of similar description named Stevens. She then gave Dennis a ride to a shelter for the homeless, where he spent the remainder of the night before bussing to Los Angeles. After a few weeks, he took off for Las Vegas, where he planned to stay through New Year's, buying plane tickets and paying his bill at the Riviera Hotel with credit cards, perhaps not the smartest move but he says he felt entitled to "get a little good out of all this." He was charging a $300 ski jacket on American Express when he overheard the store clerk giving the store name and exact location, inexplicably verifying that the cardholder was present. Louisiana State Police Investigator Joe Whitmore, it turned out, was about forty-five minutes behind Dennis at this point.

Dennis jumped on a Greyhound for Phoenix, took Amtrak to New Orleans for a few weeks, then returned to Houston and got a job managing a motel in exchange for room and expenses. There, it was a telephone call, made on June 26, 1989, that did him in. With a whole bag full of quarters, he made a long distance call from a nearby pay phone, talked twenty minutes or so, and was never asked by the operator to deposit additional change. "There was a guy waiting for the phone, so I left. I had a bad feeling about that, because if they can't get paid on the coin end, they put it on the other end, and that's how Whitmore found me. He was watching calls to that number. AT&T got me."

According to Whitmore's personal recollections of the challenging decade-long manhunt, it was indeed the passport lost after Dennis' trip to Guatemala which helped him pick up the trail after years without viable leads. "Dennis went to the post office in Sunnyvale, where he lived," Whitmore relates, "and filled out a lost-or-stolen passport form and a request for a replacement. The passport office in San Francisco, where the passport would be processed, got suspicious and pulled the support documents he'd used to obtain the original passport in San Salvador. The only documents that he had to obtain the passport with were a Louisiana birth certificate and a Louisiana driver's license in the name of James Walter Stevens. The passport officer suspected the birth certificate of being fraudulent, because the numbers in the upper right-hand corner were not numbers Louisiana would have. Different states have different prefixes, like on Social Security cards."

After Dennis eluded officers on foot when they arrived at his Sunnyvale trailer with an arrest warrant, Whitmore explains, a subsequent search of the trailer and seizure of his car yielded fingerprints to be sent to the Bureau of Identification in Louisiana, along with a copy of a California driver's license and the Louisiana birth certificate for Stevens. One of the fingerprint technicians on the receiving end thought she recognized the license photo and called in Whitmore.

From that point on, it was just a matter of time, Whitmore says. Dennis had let his back-up driver's license, in the name Lawrence James Hunt, expire. "When he knew the State Department had become suspicious of him, before he ran, he went and renewed that driver's license under the Hunt name, but he had to leave before the license was mailed to him. As soon as it was mailed, of course we had that one also. The Hunt name he was using in Houston when we apprehended him. And that was a fluke, the way we apprehended him, really," Whitmore says.

When Dennis purchased the jacket in Las Vegas using an American Express card, "we almost had him. We missed by only hours. When he got to New Orleans, he called his contact from a pay phone, and myself and Trooper Fournet were sitting in the office of his contact, interviewing him, at the time that the phone rang. We heard the contact say 'No, I'm not interested in any tickets to the state police ball, the city police ball.' Dennis knew we were there, so he got back on Amtrak and went to Houston."

Investigators knew that, while Dennis had left home with a considerable amount of money, it would be only a matter of time before he ran out and would have to contact DJ in Sunnyvale. "So what we did," Whitmore reveals, "we found out who all her relatives were and where they lived, and we contacted every one. Well, the fiancee had her phone number changed right after he left, and Dennis didn't have that phone number, so he was contacting a relative of hers in Massachussetts to try to find out her phone number. You know when you talk on a pay phone, after three minutes the operator will come on and tell you to deposit so much money. Well, this telephone operator apparently wasn't very attentive, because he talked for over twenty minutes without being asked to deposit more change. Then the operator called the party in Massachussetts and reversed the charges. And we had blanket subpoenas on those phone records." That phone call was made in mid-March, and Whitmore had the record of it by May.

"And I figured I knew Dennis well enough to know that he wouldn't do two things: one, he wouldn't commit a crime, and number two, he wouldn't drive because he didn't have a license and he didn't want to get caught driving without one," says Whitmore. A phone call to a friend in the Houston sheriff's department began a block-by-block search around that particular pay phone, pinpointed in a Kentucky Fried Chicken close to the downtown loop, in a seedy area rife with prostitution and drug abuse. Whitmore had figured Dennis would be within walking distance, and he was; he was spotted a mere half a block away, standing outside the motel. At the time of his escape from Baton Rouge, Dennis had written in his parting letter to Whitmore, who he figured would find him if anybody did, that he would not offer any resistance should he be apprehended, and he did not, even though he was armed when the unknown policeman walked up behind him and put a gun to his head. Dennis was taken to the Harris County Jail and, waiving extradition, was returned to Louisiana by Joe Whitmore.

Looking back, Dennis says that the seven months of hiding after the passport fiasco returned him to the same type of survival mode he'd experienced behind bars, not living but merely trying to survive. "I now understand," he says, "why people who are doing 'life on the installment plan' never seem very concerned about being in prison; their life is the same inside or out. The difference with me was that I was very depressed the whole seven months, very worried about DJ and the loss of our life together. I was in bad shape mentally and emotionally, which goes to explain somewhat why I just hung around until they picked me up. I knew my move was to get on the road. Didn't. Not stupidity. Simply beat down."

In the time it took for Whitmore to track him down, Dennis says DJ went through an even worse time than he, being so totally unprepared and having known nothing about his past until the day he left. "She's a lady and had never had any dealings with the police," he says angrily, "so she was totally defenseless against their basic scare procedures. They didn't lighten up on her at all the whole time. She was sure the phone was tapped, and she suffered a hell of a lot worse than I. I told her they might have scared her but at least she hadn't gone to jail, and there's not a doubt in my mind that if she had known the truth she *would* have gone to jail for aiding and abetting a known fugitive."

DJ reflects, "He says he did it to protect me, that what I didn't know wouldn't hurt me. But I'm not so sure, because what I went through certainly hurt me a great deal, and I'm not so sure it's something I'll ever get over. I've often thought, and I mentioned it to him, that maybe I should have had the opportunity to know and to make my own decision." Besides having to come to grips with Dennis' past, she must also have inevitably had mixed feelings about her own unwitting part in his demise, for had he not met her and wanted to follow her back to this country, the passport issue might not have been so critical, nor would the phone call. "That's one of the things I think about a lot," she reflects, "because if he hadn't fallen in love with me, things would have been different. But it's true that it was *his* decision. I asked him why he had made that phone call to my girlfriend that was traced, and he said he just needed to know that I was OK."

When Dennis was caught June 27, DJ had to leave almost immediately for previously scheduled business in Europe, then called the FBI agent she had dealt with and asked to be allowed to speak with Dennis. "At one of the sessions the agents had told me he'd said he'd never let himself be caught alive, which they totally made up. My attorney had called me the day before I left for Europe to tell me he'd been captured. As soon as I returned, I talked to him about forty-five minutes, and I had a list of questions a mile long, and couldn't ask any of them. I wanted to get as many facts as I could, the background, the history, and I still don't have it all."

Since then, DJ and Dennis have spoken weekly by telephone and in December 1989 she made her first visit to see him in person in the visiting room at Wade Correctional Center in North Louisiana. Her feelings now are mixed, she says. "Very, very mixed.

It's a lot to come to grips with. I'm an extremely emotional person. I feel things much more strongly than most people. If it's pain, or joy, it's to the extreme. So yes, I still need to get to grips with it all. But in the meantime, he was a man who was good to me. He was also a friend. And I don't desert friends. So I will try to do what I can do. I just cannot associate what they told me with the person I knew. I even refuse to acknowledge the name that he has; I've known him as Steve, and Steve he will always be to me. "

"The pertinence of my story?" muses a thoughtful Dennis from behind bars at Wade, awaiting trial on simple escape charges. "I don't know. There's no end, no conclusion. Maybe one could say that the fact that I could make it in society for ten years provides a reasonable hope for any prisoner and a lesson for society that rehabilitation does exist. Though it's not currently in fashion, perhaps because the sociology majors haven't been able to actualize their belief that prisoners can *be* rehabilitated, *self*-rehabilitation certainly exists. With what I had to overcome—locked up twenty-two years, no skills but typing, no support, on escape, etc.—maybe I can provide a graphic example, one of hope, one of 'hey, let's not be so quick to throw away the key on people.'"

Says DJ, "Not only has he shown that he had become a totally different person who could do so well outside, I believe he could do even better now that this load that he has been carrying has been relieved, much better, because now he could really let himself go and be himself, whereas before...it must have been a tremendous burden, to carry something like that around with you and not have anybody to talk to when it builds up inside and just have to live with it for so long. I think we are all human beings, even prisoners, and there is good and bad both inside and out. I think everybody deserves a chance, especially if somebody like Steve can prove it, virtually rehabilitating himself without anybody giving it to him. He's what? fifty-four, three years older than he told me he was, and being in prison would be a terrible way to think of having to spend the rest of your life at fifty-four."

And State Police Investigator Whitmore, whom Dennis calls with grudging admiration "a bloodhound," what does he anticipate being the reaction of the Pardon Board to Dennis' assertion that his ten years of productive free life prove he's a viable candidate for release? "I think they'll buy it," he says. "I don't think they'll have any alternative. All indications are that he led a productive, crime-free life while he was out, and there's no one, including myself, who'll ever tell them any different."

The Warden Comments: Anytime an individual, like Swede Dennis in this chapter, can spend ten long years as a productive citizen in free society without getting so much as a parking ticket, it should certainly be evident that he need no longer remain a ward of the state of Louisiana. It is time he had the sanctioned chance to be a tax-payer rather than a tax-user. Granted, he took some short cuts, but we can never underestimate the strength of the desire for freedom, and this should be utilized productively and in a positive way, rather than circumvented or thwarted as it was here, in rehabilitation programs designed to prepare individuals for eventual return to society.

For statistical purposes in compiling recidivism rates, most correctional systems usually consider anyone who has lived outside in society for a period of five years without problems to have successfully re-integrated himself into society. Here is an individual who is overqualified for release using that criterion.

Douglas Dennis, known to everybody at Angola as Swede, had been in the penitentiary for ten years and six months by the time I arrived as Louisiana State Penitentiary warden in 1968. That was just about the amount of time a life sentence usually translated into at that time, once the governor commuted it upon a warden's recommendation. Of course by then Swede had two life sentences to serve. I quickly became interested in him, feeling that he had a lot of potential. He was a very bright individual who by the time I met him had worked through his youthful problems of temper control, and appeared to me to be an excellent candidate for release. My years at Angola only served to re-inforce my first impressions of Dennis.

He worked closely with the administration in upgrading prison programs, almost singlehandedly developing a well-rounded recreation program for the main prison as well as the outcamps. Prisoners need to be kept productively engaged, either in jobs or in organized leisure activities which help with the release of hostility, and a good recreation program is vital in this respect.

In the early 1970s he also took a leading role in the racial integration of Louisiana State Penitentiary, which upon my arrival had not a single black employee. The prison itself was completely and totally segregated; there were black camps and white camps, black work lines and white work lines. I realized that the prison had to be integrated. Having done the same as warden of the Tennessee State Prison in Nashville, I knew it was necessary to hire some black employees before the inmate population could be effectively mixed, and set about recruiting minorities, which had never been done before, despite a chronic shortage of employees. Angola at that time had the unfortunate image of having a number of overtly racist employees, perhaps even members of the Ku Klux Klan if rumors could be believed. I never saw any evidence of that, but it naturally made local recruiting very difficult. Our first black employee was consequently an army retiree from the New Orleans area, though eventually we were able to hire a number of correctional officers from the local minority communities and soon even recruited some professional staff members who were black.

Knowing it was only a matter of time before the federal courts ordered integration of the prison population, I called a small group of inmate leaders into my office and discussed the problem with them, telling them that we had three choices: I could integrate the prison, I could let the courts do it, or I could let them do it themselves. I told them to think it over and let me have their decision by the next day. My strategy was to integrate first the big yard, which was the medium-security part of the Main Prison where the toughest prisoners among the general population were housed; it's good psychology to take on the bully first, and the rest falls into place pretty easily, usually.

At our scheduled meeting the next day, these inmate-leaders said they felt the integration of the inmate population could be handled as long as we permitted friends and persons of the same background to remain together as much as possible. The administration certainly had no problem with that, and so Swede and other members of the inmate committee proceeded to sell the program to the other prisoners. As a result, within a week the total prison was completely and totally integrated, with absolutely no bloodshed and a minimal amount of confusion.

There were actually more problems with staff than with prisoners, if the truth be known, even though the majority of employees had a positive attitude. In fact, the associate warden for security, Hayden Dees, told me he anticipated a bloodbath when the prison was integrated, and resigned the week before changes were implemented. On the other hand, the positive role played by a few outstanding employees like Deputy Warden Lloyd Hoyle could not be overestimated. Hoyle had good rapport with prisoners and spent a lot of time answering their questions and setting to rest their apprehensions. He and Dees' replacement as associate warden for security, Hilton Butler, would later be instrumental in assuring the effectiveness of disciplinary procedural changes guaranteeing inmates their basic rights in internal court proceedings.

Swede's beneficial influence, his intelligence, his qualities of leadership and his analytical mind all contributed greatly to this project's chances for success. Later he would use many of these same qualities to assist inmates facing disciplinary procedures as an inmate counsel-substitute. He was able to do such an excellent job representing prisoners before the disciplinary committee that his abilities attracted the attention of the Department of Corrections staff and they soon requested that he be allowed to transfer to headquarters. When corrections secretary Elayn Hunt asked my opinion of the transfer, I told her I thought it was a good idea, as Swede knew more about disciplinary procedures than just about anyone else.

Prior to the establishment of a formal disciplinary board, there had been little due process in dealing with inmate infractions of the rules. People were locked up, their cases not reviewed, and punishments were arbitrarily meted out. The administration, with a great deal of inmate input, set up the disciplinary committee in such a way as to guarantee that inmates had the same rights as free individuals under the Constitution. The inmate had the right to face his accuser, the right to counsel, the right to a fair hearing, and the right to appeal to the Department of Corrections. It was in processing inmate appeals that Swede worked while in Baton Rouge.

The state of Tennessee had a number of highly successful work-release centers for inmates, with which I had become familiar before I ever came to Louisiana's state penitentiary, and when I returned to Tennessee as commissioner of correction, I enlarged the program greatly. You're working with problems, so you have to expect a few, but to me work-release is one of the most effective ways I know of preparing prisoners for successful release, provided they meet certain qualifications. Not even someone who has committed murder should be summarily disqualified from consideration for such a program; you have to look at the person, rather than the crime.

Work-release enables a man to actually work his way through prison, paying his own room and board, while at the same time maintaining and maybe improving his work skills, an important factor given the rapid advances made in modern technology. Such a program may also permit him to support his family, removing them from the welfare rolls while allowing him to retain his image as breadwinner. Longtermers also obtain benefits by gradually re-integrating, with supervision and support, into a society which may have changed drastically since their last moments of freedom.

My experience has been that employers generally like work-release employees, because they have little or no absenteeism, but requirements for eligibility for work-release within the Louisiana corrections system have been made so stringent that the program has been greatly reduced in size and effectiveness in the years since I was at Angola. Thus one of the most effective tools for cutting the costs of incarceration has been lost, not to mention the lessening of a potentially beneficial impact on inmates themselves.

The problems with the work-release program at CCRC in Baton Rouge stemmed, I think, from a lack of care in selecting candidates for eligibility. You have to look at individual qualities and abilities and attitudes rather than initial crime. When selection of work-release candidates began to be made from department headquarters in Baton Rouge rather than at Angola, problems ensued, and understandably so. There must be personal evaluations performed by skilled professionals for work-release programs to work; past behavior may often be used as an indication of future behavior, but man does have the capacity to improve, and many inmates leave prison as totally different individuals than they come in. The entire correctional program must be based on the innate worth of man and his ability to change.

Had it not been for District Attorney Ossie Brown, I think Swede would have been released soon after he proved that he could perform so successfully at DOC headquarters, his sentence commuted to time served. For some reason, Mr. Brown singled out Swede to bear the brunt of his animosity toward a program he considered too lenient, coddling criminals at taxpayer expense, as he thought, and he used the newspapers in a very negative way in his campaign to shut it down. I was amazed that a district attorney would object to an inmate getting an education. That was something that I had worked for all of my career, trying to see that each prisoner had the opportunity to develop to his full potential through educational and other self-improvement programs.

When Swede escaped, I remember thinking that he would be very difficult to apprehend. If anybody could successfully make it on escape, he probably would, perhaps never to be heard of again. How did he manage to elude capture so long? For one thing, he was pretty much a loner, a very intelligent and streetwise individual. There have been allegations that perhaps he had covert assistance and may have been recruited to work as an underground operative for one of our intelligence agencies. Smuggling illegal foreign nationals into this country, gun-running in Central America, ties to the Oliver North clandestine operations—all have been mentioned in connection with his year out of the country, but Dennis denies any direct involvement in anything of the sort.

But from all indications, once Swede returned to this country, some nine years before his capture, he took up the life of a normal, upwardly mobile, white-collar businessman, forming a supportive relationship with a young woman about whom he obviously cared a great deal. This was perhaps the closest and longest-lasting tie he had ever formed in his entire life, and may help to explain his well-adjusted lifestyle in Silicon Valley, California. DJ strikes me as being a capable, articulate and intelligent person whose support has and will continue to mean a great deal to Swede.

Inmates like Swede can be found in every prison system in the country, people who have worked their problems through and should be given an opportunity to prove their worth as productive members of society. Our societal desire to punish has led to America having the highest prison population in the western world. It is time to re-evaluate and seek new methods of rehabilitating and releasing prisoners. Certainly not everyone is going to be rehabilitated, for this must essentially come from within. A changed man with a great deal to offer society, Swede Dennis has already shown, for nearly ten years, that he can do it.

2009 Update:

Douglas Dennis returned to Angola and wrote perceptive legal analyses for *The Angolite* for a number of years. After undergoing open-heart bypass surgery and being confined to a wheelchair, in 2009 at age 73 his application to the state pardon board was denied despite unconditional support from former Angola Warden John Whitley, former FBI agent Jerry Webb and former Department of Corrections attorney Richard Crane. He remains in Angola.

VI

How Much Is Enough?

STATE OF LOUISIANA VS. NO. 50,584, WILBERT RIDEAU

14TH JUDICIAL DISTRICT COURT, STATE OF LOUISIANA, PARISH OF CALCASIEU

Statement of the District Attorney, as required by R. S. 15:566:1.

It was judicially determined that the defendant, Wilbert Rideau, was born on the 13th day of February, 1942.

On the 2nd day of March, 1961, the defendant entered a plea of not guilty to the crime of Murder, in violation of R. S. 14:30.

On the 17th day of April, 1961, the defendant was convicted of the crime of murder by a jury of twelve returning a verdict of "guilty as charged," in violation of R. S. 14:30 Section One.

The Court on the 20th day of April, 1961, sentenced him to be executed by electrocution in accordance with law as listed below:

No. 50,584 - MURDER - To be executed by electrocution- in accordance with the laws of the State of Louisiana, in all such cases made and provided; that is, by causing to pass through the body of the said Wilbert Rideau a current of electricity of sufficient intensity to cause death and the application and continuance of such current through the body of the said Wilbert Rideau until said Wilbert Rideau is dead. Such execution is to take place at the Louisiana State Penitentiary at Angola, Louisiana, within a room entirely cut off from view of all, except those permitted by law to be in said room, and between the hours of 12:00 o'clock midnight and 3:00 o'clock a.m. upon a date to be set by the Governor of the State of Louisiana.

The facts in this, one of Louisiana's best-known contemporary criminal cases, are not disputed. There are discrepancies, to be sure, in the different accounts, but inmate Wilbert Rideau refuses to discuss them, considering them minor diversions distracting attention

Wilbert Rideau

from the main issue at stake. So the account of the crime as reported in the *Lake Charles American Press* and in the official statement of then-District Attorney Frank T. Salter, Jr., will be given here, with only one major exception noted between that version and Rideau's confession.

It would be that very confession, a scared black teenager interrogated live on local television news shows by Calcasieu Sheriff Henry A. Reid, which would help declare invalid the first of Rideau's three court convictions. Shown on TV three nights running while local passions were understandably high, that confession combined with sensational front-page accounts in the town newspaper, complete with entire pages full of crime-scene photos, to create an atmosphere in which a fair and equitable trial for the defendant was subsequently ruled by the court to have been an impossibility.

"A slightly built Negro teenager sits dressed in drab loose-fitting coveralls in a Calcasieu Parish jail cell today," went the front-page account in the *Lake Charles American Press* on February 17, 1961, "perhaps pondering the few minutes last night when he was rich and powerful. He had $14,079 in a cheap suitcase in a stolen car and he was powerful enough to kill one woman by shooting and stabbing her, wound another woman and a man. It lasted less than an hour and a half. Then Wilbert N. Rideau, nineteen, of 1820 Brick St., found himself branded a kidnapper, a murderer and a bank robber. His prospects now are the cold steel cell and the prison coveralls."

On Wednesday, February 15, 1961, two days after his nineteenth birthday and the day before the crime, Wilbert Rideau had gone into a pawn shop and purchased a .22-caliber Omega revolver, blue steel with a white handle, and a large hunting knife with a five-inch blade. On Thursday, February 16, 1961, just before seven p.m. closing time, he went to the back door of the Gulf National Bank branch in Southgate shopping center on Ryan Street in Lake Charles, near the fabric store where he worked as a stock clerk, and demanded money of bank manager Jay H. Hickman, fifty-five, the mayor's uncle, and two female employees, Dora McCain, age thirty, and Julia Ferguson, age forty-six.

At gunpoint, the bank employees were ordered to fill with currency the gray plastic suitcase Rideau furnished. Newspaper accounts report the amount of cash taken as $14,079, while the district attorney's statement adds $2 to that total; at any rate, when deputies first reached the scene after the robbery, they would find teller's cages open, drawers gaping, currency scattered all over the floor and some $30,000 in cash overlooked in the robbery and left behind in the bank.

After filling Rideau's suitcase with bills, the bank employees were forced into Mrs. Ferguson's black and white English-made Vauxhall automobile. With Mrs. Ferguson driving, the group first travelled downtown, then proceeded along US 171 and Opelousas St. toward an uninhabited area northeast of Lake Charles.

It was on the bridge over English Bayou that the shooting started. Rideau's confession states that as the car slowed, Dora McCain jumped from the front seat and began to run. Rideau jumped out of the car and shot at her, at which point the other two hostages also tried to flee, he said, drawing fire as well. The district attorney's statement conflicts with this account, charging that Rideau ordered the three hostages from the car, lined them up and shot them.

In all, six shots were fired. The .22-caliber bullet which hit Dora McCain in the back of her neck was deflected by her backbone and lodged close to the jugular vein; Mrs. McCain fell to the shoulder on the west side of the parish roadway directly in front of Rideau and "played dead." Hickman was struck in the right arm and fell backward, disappearing from sight in water over his head in a marsh.

Julia Ferguson, with one bullet wound behind the left arm at shoulder height and another at the central base of her neck, fell to the ground near Dora McCain but struggled to rise, at which point she was stabbed with the hunting knife. According to newspaper accounts and later trial testimony on the autopsy performed by Calcasieu Parish Coroner Dr. Harry S. Snatic, powder burns on Mrs. Ferguson's skin indicated that only the neck wound had been inflicted at very close range, but death came from the knife wound in the chest, which pierced a rib and the heart.

As Rideau drove off, Dora McCain made her way through the darkness to a nearby farmhouse and was rushed to Memorial Hospital in Lake Charles, where surgery was performed to remove a bullet from her neck. Jay Hickman stumbled through the marsh to the offices of an oilfield servicing firm, B-J Service Inc., where an ambulance was called to take him to the hospital for removal of the bullet in his arm. The first sheriff's deputies to arrive at the murder scene thought they detected a barely discernible heartbeat in Mrs. Julia Ferguson, but she was declared dead on arrival at Memorial Hospital.

Meanwhile, seventy-five bankers and auditors from across southwestern Louisiana and southeastern Texas were meeting at the Pelican Motel Grill in nearby Sulphur, the feature for Bank Night being a panel discussion on destruction of bank records. It would be missing bank money which would command their attention, however, when the auditor for Gulf National Bank, one of the scheduled speakers, rushed from the meeting upon receiving word of the robbery in Lake Charles.

Driving north on US 165 in Julia Ferguson's black and white Vauxhall with red interior, the gray plastic suitcase of money on the back seat, Wilbert Rideau was stopped by state police near the small community of Iowa, where troopers took his identification and car license number but released him because the description of the get-away car had been broadcast as a Volkswagen. The suspicions of the two troopers, Joseph I. "Sonny" Dupin and George Byon of State Police Troop D, were aroused, however, and they followed Rideau, overtaking him again at Woodlawn near Fenton and pulling him over for a closer inspection. It was then that the Calcasieu Parish Sheriff's Department verified that Rideau and the Vauxhall were indeed the object of the search. Rideau was apprehended a mere hour and twenty minutes after the robbery was reported.

Three decades later, Wilbert Rideau remains incarcerated in the Louisiana State Penitentiary at Angola, thrice convicted of murder by all-white, all-male juries, saved from the electric chair by a 1972 Supreme Court decision outlawing Louisiana's death penalty, four times recommended by state pardon boards for clemency, only to have the governor deny it. Everyone on Death Row when Rideau arrived has long since been released, and he says he has now served more time than 99.9 percent of all prisoners in the history of the Louisiana penal system. His continued incarceration, especially in light of recent pardons-for-sale scandals, gives the state the unfortunate national image that "it has a clemency system which permits murderers to buy mercy but not to earn it," in the words of Professor Ted Quant, leader of Loyola University's Institute of Human Relations.

Self-educated and with a high level of intelligence, a self-taught writer of great promise, a respected journalist who has turned Angola's bimonthly prison newsmagazine into an award-winning publication fighting effectively for penal reform and who has (as his unpaid "gift to the state") co-edited books to be used in college-level correctional curricula, Wilbert Rideau has been called the most rehabilitated man in American prisons today, a stabilizing force in volatile penitentiary politics who has earned the respect of inmates and corrections officials alike.

An articulate spokesman on corrections and the judicial system, he has appeared on national panels and programs, and regularly shares his hard-won knowledge with juvenile offenders and students across the state, accompanied on these community-service trips by only an unarmed guard. He has concrete job offers awaiting him upon release, promises of publishing contracts, writing assignments capitalizing on his unique insights and experiences in ways helpful to society. He is so far removed from the scared teenager who committed a criminal act of desperation in those early sixties pre-Civil Rights days that he unconsciously refers to the perpetrator in the third person when forced to discuss the crime.

Why, then, is Wilbert Rideau still in prison? That question was examined at length in a segment of ABC television's *20-20*, which host Hugh Downs introduced by asking, "Are there cases where admitted and convicted murderers should be released from prison? And if you say *yes*, how does such a person prove that he deserves this second chance?" Co-host Barbara Walters continued, emphasizing that the case of Wilbert Rideau "brings into focus one of the most basic questions about our judicial system: Do we really want to see criminals rehabilitated, or do we simply want to punish them?"

The TV show concluded that "politics, a promise and perhaps his very prominence" had kept Rideau incarcerated so long after hundreds of other convicted "lifers" had been released from the same prison system, where a life sentence usually boils down to eight or ten years actually served, perhaps as many as twelve years, but rarely more. Rideau attorney Julian Murray offered the conclusion that these other released prisoners came and went without making waves, making no valid contributions but at least staying quiet, while Wilbert Rideau excited sufficient interest in his case that he became a fullblown political issue, an "event."

It became politically expedient, Murray insisted, for former Louisiana governor Edwin W. Edwards to keep Rideau in jail, satisfying prevailing sentiment in predominantly white Lake Charles where the governor enjoyed a great deal of support. This speculation was supported by Edwards' own former secretary of corrections C. Paul Phelps, who verified on *20-20* that Edwards told him that early in his gubernatorial campaign he had made a personal commitment to one of Rideau's victims that he would not pardon him (prisoners sentenced to life terms are eligible for release only upon official pardon by the governor, being ineligible for parole).

Murray commented on television about Edwards' promise: "No system of justice worthy of the name allows the victim or the victim's family to determine the punishment. We don't set up our system that way.... We set up a system of laws, not of men. We set up a clemency system, a pardon board system. And Wilbert went through all of the steps. We ask for rehabilitation. We demand a certain amount of time. Wilbert Rideau has done all of those things. Then if he's going to be treated equally, then he should be let out."

Commented Rideau, learning on camera of Edwards' commitment to Dora McCain, "I'm believing in a system, and I'm having faith in a system to be fair with me and all the time the system doesn't even exist for me because of his promise. If you can make a promise to one victim, what's the difference between that and just go 'head on and let them lynch me? I mean I don't see much difference." Noting that he had already served far more time than the country's most notorious outlaws and gangsters, Rideau continued, "I understand I did something awful, and I'm sorry for it. But I just don't understand. I don't know what's required of me. I'm confused. How much more time do I have to do?"

Former governor Edwards admitted on *20-20*, as he admits today, that he *did* feel an obligation toward crime victim Dora McCain, in what television reporter Stone Phillips called the first public admission of the promise. He continues to feel that way even now, insisting in a recent interview that he gave Dora McCain only "the same commitment that I make to the victims of any crime, that before I take any definitive action which would result in the release of a prisoner, I would give them the opportunity to consult with me and express their concerns. In her instance, at the time I talked to her about it, she said she had nightmares every night about the possibility of him being out and coming back to finish the job he started, and that if he were released, at the very least she would want a commitment from somebody that he was going to leave the state or not come back to Lake Charles. So I left the conversation by simply saying that if and when it ever came up, I'd be glad to consult with her before making a final decision, as I have done with many, many people on both sides.

"I've gone to the penitentiary to visit with inmates sentenced to death, to try to find some reason for stopping the execution. I have been consulted by priests and nuns and preachers and parents and sisters and brothers of inmates who were asking for some kind of counsel, and I have been consulted both ways by victims, some saying they didn't mind the inmate getting out or they didn't *want* him out but it didn't matter, and others taking a very hard unyielding attitude that he's a menace to society and they don't want him out. I would say that fifty times to one I have listened to pleas *for* inmates by comparison to pleas *against* inmates, because most of the time the victims are gone or don't care anymore or have lost interest in the case, but the mother and the father and the brothers and the sisters and the preachers and the priests of the inmates, they *never* lose interest."

Normally noted as socially compassionate, during his three terms in office Governor Edwards did release more than two thousand convicts, including several hundred murderers, a continuation of traditional gubernatorial largesse which would ironically return to haunt him. Louisiana political writer-observer John Maginnis has called the pardon power the power of kings, the last of the great life-or-death choices still bestowed upon executives in a democracy, the most impressive of any Louisiana governor's grand arsenal of prerogatives. It was also a powerful political issue which would be used against Edwards in his victorious campaign against conservative one-term governor Dave Treen, who made much of his record of a mere thirty-four pardons granted as contrasted with Edwards' thousands.

In *The Last Hayride,* Maginnis quotes master orator Edwards as telling an appreciative audience on the campaign trail, "Dave Treen makes it sound like I go to the penitentiary every few days with the keys and say, 'Here, you go rape someone,' and 'Here, you go murder someone.' But that's not the way it works.... There may have been some pardons I didn't sign that I should have and some I signed that I shouldn't have, but let me tell you something. The greatest man who ever lived died on the cross to pardon us for all our sins."

Edwards as governor tried unsuccessfully to amend the state constitution to remove the governor from the clemency and pardon business, which he said placed too heavy a burden on one individual not part of the criminal justice system. He succeeded only in having death warrants signed by the courts rather than the governor, and still does not take lightly the awesome responsibility resting in the gubernatorial office, commenting today, "I think the only difference between me and [current Louisiana] Governor Roemer is that I am willing to take time to speak to victims as well as relatives and friends of the inmates. I don't know if it's a good practice. Maybe a governor would be better off if he remained insulated from that, because it is wrenching to talk to mothers or fathers or children or siblings of inmates and listen to their pleas for clemency. But that has to be balanced with the needs of society. If there is an injustice in fact occurring here, then my view is that Rideau should have to bear the injustice rather than society, which should not be required to live with the possibility of him doing that again. To some people that makes no sense at all; others don't even think about it, they just want him out; and still others don't even think about it but they want him left in forever. I at least thought about it. Many, many times."

Edwards continues, "Wilbert Rideau is a different person now for a lot of reasons. Number one, he's twice the age he was at the time. Number two, he's become self-educated and has devoted himself to better policies. To the extent that you can say that based on physical and subjective evidence, he is rehabilitated. My fear is that I don't know what's happening in his mind. What bothers me is that the kind of mind that can snap one time in a lifetime and do what he did without sense or reason twenty-five years ago may snap again. And then where would the blame be? In Rideau's case, I think if it were not for the fact that he is intelligent, self-made, a publisher and had been able to promote himself, and I don't use that in a derogatory manner, then nobody would be paying any attention to him. But he has been able to enlist the support of a number of journalists and publishers and others in his behalf, some of the same people, incidentally, who heavily criticized me for being too liberal in other cases. In my judgment, I think he has effectively forever barred any possibility for clemency because of his own self-generated press. That's unfortunate, because that should not be a consideration."

Edwards insists, "It is wrong to suggest that I told Dora McCain that I would let her make the final decision. But it is certainly right and proper to suggest that I told her I would consider her views. And even if I made an ironclad promise to her never to let him out, that would not be binding on Governor Roemer."

The same *20-20* program featured a short interview with present Louisiana governor Buddy Roemer, who responded to the report of his very own handpicked pardon board first recommending Rideau's release by saying, in his inimitable manner of speaking, "I can't let this man go. Can I ever? I don't know. Am I willing to listen? You bet. Am I willing to learn? You've got it. Can he do some things to talk about the damage he did and what he can do to restore confidence? Certainly. Got more work to do, though. His only chance to overcome what he did is what he might propose he *could* do so that those kinds of crimes would happen less in the future, not more. Only he can address that.... He's done part of that. But he's not satisfied this skinny governor yet." The governor declined to respond to requests for more up-to-date comments on the case, though his comments following the pardon board's April 1990 second clemency recommendation were quoted as being, incredibly, that "the crime has to fit the action afterwards. So far, this crime is worse than what happened to Wilbert Rideau. He's still alive."

How much, then, is enough? When a troubled inarticulate teen works through his feelings of rage and frustration and becomes an educated, articulate and insightful adult capable of not just expressing but deeply feeling great regret and shame for any past crime, is that not enough? When an admitted criminal takes responsibility for his wrongful act and reaches out into the community, speaking and sharing and writing, to save others from the same sorrow, to keep others from making the same mistake, is that not enough? When three entire decades of a lifetime are devoted to rebuilding and rehabilitating and rededicating, do they not take precedence over a long-past moment of passion, wrong though it was, and is that not enough?

Even in the company of these learned lawyers and eloquent television commentators and oratorical governors, one voice rings clearest in articulating the plea that the answer to that question must be a resounding YES, if we believe in the concept of man's potential and in the possibilities of rehabilitation, if we believe in the very fabric of our criminal justice system and the promise of equality of life in America. That voice belongs to Wilbert Rideau at age forty-eight and still in the Louisiana State Penitentiary at Angola. Hear him now:

"I was born about seven miles outside Opelousas and during my early years, my father was in the service, so we moved around quite a bit. When I was six I guess my parents made a decision to settle in Lake Charles, Louisiana, so I could go to school. I went to Second Ward Elementary, not too far away from home, just a run across the field, and then I switched over to W. O. Boston High. There were four children, and I can say we didn't have very much and there were times we had to do without, but a lot of other people did, too. My daddy was always working, hustling.

"When I was in elementary school, I was an honor student, straight A's. After awhile I just lost interest and started hanging around with the wrong crowd, in my mother's opinion, and shooting hooky from school. That's not to say there wasn't an effort to try to rescue me, because the school principal and some of my teachers used to always be after me to get me to stay in school and quit messing around. Perhaps they saw something in me that was worth saving, I don't know. I was good at math and I really liked science. English was my worst subject; I hated it, but I used to write a lot of poetry. It wasn't required, it was just something I liked doing, plus the girls liked it.

"What I really wanted, and back then they hadn't even coined the term *astronaut,* was to be a spaceman. I used to love those movies about Flash Gordon and all that. Somewhere in my mind I always believed there was something out there and I wanted to see it; I figured it was possible. These weren't concrete, fixed thoughts, just general ones like most kids approach life with, an incurable optimism about life. And if I couldn't be a spaceman, I wanted to be a scientist and invent things. That was part of my problem. At some point in time, I had to come to terms with the conflict between the reality and what I was taught in school, what I imagined, what I hoped for. I guess in relation to me and my circumstances at that particular point in time, it was sort of fantasies as opposed to reality. In Civics class, they would teach you that you could do anything you wanted and be anything you wanted. It didn't work that way. I guess it was in the eighth grade when I realized that I was different, that I didn't quite fit, that the world wasn't what I expected or what I wanted it to be or what I was told.

"You begin to see the lies, not so much *lies* as reality. And that's when I began to realize that I lived in a world that was sharply divided by race and that, in a lot of ways, a lot of what I had dreamed about wasn't possible. That was my own conclusion; that was just me. A lot of my friends and relatives used to tell me, when I'd go to talking about things, 'Boy, you'd better get your head out of the clouds and come back down to earth.' That was their attitude. I guess they saw the reality and knew the reality, and they figured I was crazy dreaming about wanting to do things and talking like I didn't know the reality of the situation.

"Most people accepted the situation. But that's life, anywhere you go, whether it's in Russia or here or Vietnam. People generally accept situations, because most people want to be able to pursue their life with a minimum of fuss and to be left alone. They don't want no hassle, they don't want trouble, they don't want cops knocking on their door, they don't want soldiers storming. That's life. And they'll make a hell of a lot of compromises to be able to do that.

"So it wasn't a sitting down and consciously thinking about this, sorting it out in my mind. It wasn't political, because I wasn't even aware of politics. For lack of a better description, I guess you'd call it a sort of instinctual rebellion. Different people rebel in different ways. I mean, you've got some kids who commit suicide because of that same thing, confusing signals, conflicting signals about what life is all about. I don't know why they do it. I just wonder at a society that expresses a whole lot of concern about these kids committing suicide and then never stops to realize that's not the only way people who despair of their situation can express it. The other way is crime. The other way, you've got people in prison.

"But they don't look at that, because people like things clearly defined. Crime is *criminals* and that's considered different from law-abiding citizens who do other things. Like you had a lot of law-abiding blacks who went on and beat their wives every Saturday night and drank themselves into a stupor and died early. That was their way of handling it; I'm not saying it was wrong, but my way was another way. They were law-abiding citizens, and some of them, I suspect, probably decided to commit suicide. You could say that's one way; I think it was all the same thing, though. There's no law handed down from on high that says everybody's got to react the same way to the same circumstances. Some of my schoolmates went on to become politically powerful, wealthy; I ended up in prison; some of my other friends are in the ground right now. That's life. We're all different.

"I suspect with Wilbert Rideau it wasn't no clear thing; it was a gnawing gradual thing, not liking what I'm seeing, not liking what was affecting me. And nobody did understand. I guess I was about thirteen or fourteen by then, and all the other kids, even the bad crowd I was with, they didn't like the situation but it was just part of the natural fabric of their life. It didn't bother them. It bothered *me*. I suspect what happened is that it was a gradual accumulation of frustration, despair, rage. I guess I was one of those people who wouldn't kill themselves; somebody else gotta do it. I mean, I've been in prison all this time, and there've been a lot of times that I've experienced despair worse than any other point in my life, but I haven't rebelled or whatever. I guess for some people it takes a shock to get you together.

"I just reached a point where I didn't care. I didn't *care*. You look at it as crime, but it was more than crime. It was an act of suicide, too. I surrendered to an hour of rage and rebellion. It was a crime, yes, but it was as much an act of suicide. Because I didn't care what happened to me. I didn't care whether I lived, died or nothing. It didn't make a difference. I mean, when the judge sentenced me to die in the electric chair, Wilbert just stood passively as if it didn't mean nothing. It *didn't*. It didn't mean a thing. It wasn't a big deal. And the problem with this is that when you don't care about what happens to you, you have absolutely no hold on life, no grip, nothing. You're dangerous, especially to people you might come to perceive as enemy, and at that particular point in time, I'm not gonna lie to you, I thought white people were enemies.

"So I guess that's what made it possible for me to commit the crime I committed, because it didn't matter. I didn't relate to the texture or humanity of what I perceived as the enemy, but then you have to look at the flipside of it too, I didn't even relate to my own. I'm just a floating bomb out there. I wish there was some kind of way somebody could have seen it coming. People did see that I had a problem, and some tried to help me and talk to me, but they didn't perceive the problem. You have to understand that this was pre-Civil Rights before anyone thought politically about race; this was just one individual in a situation where most people, while they might not have *liked* the situation, at least accepted it and went along with it. So from that state of mind, how many people would perceive what the problem was? They just saw me as another kid shooting hooky, drinking and running the streets.

"In 1959 my little brother and some neighborhood kids committed a burglary and he had this money and wanted to buy some things. Remember we didn't have much, and he wanted an excuse for my mom, because where in the world would he come up with money? I didn't need money, I was working, so he wanted to say Wilbert gave him the money, because that was the only logical place he could have gotten money without causing my mother to wonder what the hell's going on here. He told me what had happened. Well, I don't know nothing about laws. My instincts tell me I know this is wrong, but I'm not gonna tell nobody what my brother done or turn him in to the police. So when they busted him, at that time I was stupid enough to tell them, 'Yeah, I covered up for him.' I never imagined that was a crime. And they sent me to Louisiana Training Institute along with him.

"I was very, very angry about that, because I didn't know until a counselor explained it to me that being an accessory was against the law. I had never heard of it before. You have to understand I'm still in the formative years, I think I was about sixteen, still being made into what Wilbert Rideau is going to become. When the cops came, I told them 'I ain't done nothing, I ain't stole nothing, I didn't go no place.' And they never explained nothing, they never explained a *thing* to me. Nobody ever told me what I was locked up for. They just told me I was being locked up for burglary, and I was furious, because I was innocent. They kept me a few months in LTI and that really impacted me, because I felt I had been given a royal screwing. I didn't see nothing wrong with what I did; I didn't steal nobody's stuff. Way later on a counselor explained to me that when you do what I did, the law says you're just as guilty as the other person. Well, I understood it on an intellectual level, but that didn't change my emotions none, and keep in mind Wilbert's already got this bigger problem with not liking the way things go.

"I guess other people went through the same thing and handled it better. But I don't see myself as having been that different as far as my world. *Inside*, yes. Sometimes being stupid ain't such a bad idea; it makes some of those ruts acceptable, maybe not so much acceptable as endurable. We weren't promised, as the saying goes, a rose garden, I realize that now, but keep in mind you're talking to a different person now than thirty years ago. Life doesn't promise we'll all be wealthy and successful and fruitful and have love and happiness. In fact, I think that's not the way life works. Prisoners especially learn tricks to deal with that. You learn to isolate and deal with a certain amount at a time. If you tried to deal with the collective whole of your experience at any given time, I guess you'd get upstairs and jump off the roof.

"Let me point out that I've always worked. I've never had a problem with working. I've always been ambitious and I can't imagine myself not doing anything. I like to work, and even when I was out in the streets when I was young, I was able to find a job here or there. When I was thirteen or fourteen I started working at the supermarket, and I got paid less than the rest because I was the youngest. That was an acceptable way of thinking back then, not to pay a kid the same as an adult, but I didn't relate to it that way. And when I wanted to work fulltime, the owner said there was a law that you couldn't quit school to work under age sixteen unless you had permission in writing from the school board, and I couldn't get that because my mom didn't know I was shooting hooky from school. I thought I had talked the man into looking the other way, but there was a cost to that, that I wasn't gonna get paid as much as everyone else. I learned that's the way life works, that when you want to do something that's not quite legal, there's a price to it, because the person who's willing to let you do it is doing it for his own reasons and benefit. But I went on and worked, and I went through a lot of stuff like that.

"I was promoted to ninth grade, and I just lost interest. I don't know if I went one week or one month or what, but I just never went. I don't mean to be vague. You have to understand, I don't think much about this. I'm like most people in life; if you've got something you don't like, you shove it in the closet and keep it away from company. That's life. There's no percentage in wallowing in the past. Because the past is gone, it's over with. There are times when I might idly wish that things could have been different, but all the wishing and all the thinking and all the praying, that don't change nothing. It's etched forever, irrevocably. So you just do like everybody else in life; you just pick up your little suitcase and keep moving from day to day. All that's left is tomorrow. And nobody on earth has so much time that they can afford to just lay back there in the past.

"Anyway, I had just reached a point when I saw life in terms of *us* and *them*. Sort of like the feelings some people get in prison. Somewhere along the way, I had concluded that *"they"* had everything, that this was the way it worked. Well, I wasn't gonna accept it on those terms. By whatever means, it didn't make any difference. I suspect, in a general kind of way, what I was doing was just trying to change my overall life, get away, go someplace, leave all of this behind. I had been thinking, in a non-thinking kind of way, of change. The situation was intolerable, unacceptable. I wanted change. I was thinking in terms of taking off and going to California someplace; it was that general in thinking, because if you had asked me where I was going, I couldn't have told you, I didn't know, I didn't know nobody in California. I just wanted change; I wanted something better than this. I wanted *out,* I guess much the same as that person who'll go sit in the car and pipe the fumes in.

"And wanting out was at a desperate enough level that even when I was standing before the judge and being sentenced to death, it didn't mean nothing. I had just reached that level of despair, desperation, whatever. There has been a steady resistance in the Louisiana penal system to understanding and accepting the force of hopelessness, individual hopelessness and despair. The governor don't recognize it; the federal courts don't recognize it; a lot of authorities don't. They've told me, former warden Ross Maggio, interim warden Larry Smith and all, that they don't believe that's the reason guys do things; they say everything is caused by drugs and mismanagement. Well hell, I don't know anybody who'd commit suicide because of drugs or mismanagement; we didn't even know what drugs were back then in Lake Charles, Louisiana.

"Because of my own experience, perhaps, I realize the power, the force of individual hopelessness and despair; I have a healthy respect for it. I *know* it affected Wilbert Rideau. But Wilbert Rideau ain't unique. When I look around, I see it's the reason why a lot of other guys are here in prison. You can blame it on coming up in a bad neighborhood, but things didn't start off that way. You've got some mothers who don't care what happens to their kids, but most mothers, even the bad ones, they want their kids to grow up to be somebody they can point to with pride, even if it's on a subconsious level, even in the projects. It starts off right. My mom always taught me right. So what happens? At some point in time, something causes them to despair of the socially circumscribed pattern of behavior and way of attaining things in life, making them more receptive to another way; they despair of this one and go with the other. It plays with all of us all through life. I'm very mindful of it because of my own experience, which is why I've come to be able to control it so well.

"I haven't thought about the details of the day of the crime for a long time. I don't know if I knew what I wanted to use the gun for; I just don't know. You ask me to reach back from today, thirty years later, into a mind that thought differently and that today is a total stranger to me. Just go with whatever the records say. What you've got is prosecutors saying what was in my mind, and they weren't there. You also have to understand that nobody *cared* about what was in my mind until way later on, after Wilbert Rideau started making news as an award-winning editor or whatever; then people wanted to know what I was thinking, why I did what I did.

"That's a tragic aspect of our justice system. Nobody cared. Nobody ever asked me *nothing*. All they wanted to know was did I know what I was doing, did I do it. That's all they wanted to know. That's the way the system works in Louisiana. Once they're assured of the fact that you did it, as far as they're concerned that's the end of it. Next thing is, 'Let's go to court and let's put this guy in the chair or bury him under concrete.' They do not try to learn from mistakes. Hell, what the system deals with is the mistakes of a whole bunch of individuals, wreckages piling onto the shore, and they don't even try to learn. That's something that always amazes me. They don't even try to take all those old broken lives and try to figure out what went wrong and if we could learn something to apply to other people and prevent this from happening again. The system doesn't work like that.

"The only people who ever asked me something like that, was way a quarter of a century later. And I'm supposed to sit back and think about it, something that normally I try not to think about. Because you have to understand that that is a point in my life that I happen to be particularly ashamed of. I don't *like* it. When I say I'm ashamed of it, I'm not talking about ashamed of it before the public; I've learned to live with that. Once you've lived as long as I have in a prison like this, you tend to be a little less dependent on public opinion and what people think of you. The reason I say I'm ashamed of it is not because it looks bad to the public, but to my own self. I should not have done it. That's not the kind of person I am or want to be, and even in my own solitude, even if you took everybody else off the face of the earth, I would still be ashamed of what I did for Wilbert's sake, because it changed me to know that I did something like that.

"It's a personal thing, and that's the reason that, to the extent that I can, I try to avoid thinking about it. What individual goes around in life looking into their past and picking at the scab over every little sore spot? People aren't like that, prisoners aren't like that neither, and I'm no different. It's just that everybody insists on me being different, thinking about it. I've adjusted to it. I've learned this is part of the price you pay, that you're never going to forget it, you're never going to be able to put it behind you, because the world isn't going to let you. Ten years from now, if I became president of the United States, it would be 'President Wilbert Rideau who early in life robbed a bank and killed somebody.' You're always defined like that, for the rest of your life. You never escape it. That's the price you pay, and you live like that for the rest of your life. It might not seem like much to the average thinking person, but it is. It's a hell of a thing to walk around for the rest of your life with that yoke around your neck. Of course I put it there, and I recognize that. So you deal with it; that's life. We've all got yokes. We've all got burdens to carry in life. It's just that mine is one of those that I carry around on display.

"When I do talk about it, I go mostly off my own memory, not the reports, which I haven't read in years. My memory is deliberately vague so that I can live with it, not to confuse nobody. In the process of mentally pushing away all those years, it becomes vague. You don't have the attention to detail. I've never disputed any of the details in the different accounts. I didn't do it then, and I don't do it now, because it changes the issue. I'm not innocent, oh no, I'm not saying that. Everything didn't happen the way they say, but I accept responsibility for what I did. The problem is that when you commit sins against other people in life, they have the right to define or describe it, however they want to; you relinquish that right, because you shouldn't have done it to begin with. If I say something different from the record, it is a diversion that detracts from what right now is a clean-cut issue of *how much is enough*. So I don't argue with nothing. Whatever is, I accept it.

"I've been in court so many times, God, I don't know how many. There were all the appeals all the way up to the United States Supreme Court on the first conviction, and the Supreme Court threw it out, calling it a hollow formality of a trial, a kangaroo court. That's the way they described it, and they also asked District Attorney Frank Salter and the people there representing Louisiana whose idea it was to put Rideau on TV, because they weren't gonna make the court believe Rideau *asked* to be on TV. And the officials dodged it. There were also sheriff's deputies on my jury, so if it hadn't been thrown out for one thing, it would have been another. Experts in the law told me the Supreme Court wasn't doing it so much for me as to deliver a national message. Remember, they had the Civil Rights movement going on and the way they deliver a message is in cases where they're not going to lose nothing; they knew all that would happen is I would be taken back and re-tried and I wasn't going anywhere.

"After that, there was the debate over whether or not they could even try me again. My trial judge ruled a judicial impasse, saying the state no longer had the authority to try me. State law said you could not take a person from his parish and move him further than the adjoining judicial district, and yet they wanted to take me all the way to East

Baton Rouge Parish. Louisiana isn't like other states; they don't turn prisoners loose as a solution to a problem. The DA appealed the trial judge's decision, arguing that I hadn't committed a crime against the parish but against the state, and so they should have the right to try me anywhere they wanted. 'Course this had never been done before in the history of the state.

"And during one recess in Baton Rouge I overheard the judge saying he thought it was illegal, what they were doing. Judge Elmo Lear was the first judge to try me in Baton Rouge at my second trial, then the appeals process from that went through state, federal and Supreme Court appeals, then back to Federal Judge E. Gordon West, who had the reputation for being the most conservative, toughest law-and-order federal judge in the country. And he threw it out, which sent me back to the state courts again. A new trial was granted on a technicality, something about conscientious objectors to the death penalty on the jury of a capital punishment case, when what we really wanted the federal court to address was the issue of them moving me from Lake Charles to Baton Rouge. Even the Constitution says you're supposed to be tried in a district previously ascertained by law, but the DA asked for a change of venue; I was quite satisfied with my trial judge's ruling, which was that the state no longer had the authority to prosecute me, but the state appealed.

"So the one thing that I still think is illegal is the one that no court has ever addressed, and now it's so far down the line. Unfortunately for me I believed that this clemency system would work the way it had traditionally worked and the way they say it's supposed to work. I guess it was a case of misplaced faith. I should have never had faith about anything in Louisiana. Individuals, yes; have faith in individuals. Have faith in the basic decency of people, yes. The system? Oh my God, that's a mistake. And even politicians and officials, because they run things in Louisiana with no real morality; there's no real morality governing the operations of things. In other places you read that they're trying for at least the *appearance* of morality. I mean, common sense tells us that there's a whole lot of things going on behind the scenes, but publicly they at least try to uphold some appearance. In Louisiana, the governor can say and do things and get away with them, while in other states they'd call for his resignation. Not wait for voters to vote him out; he'd have to resign right there on the spot. The state government of Louisiana is not too different from Angola, but even prisoners at Angola try to maintain a positive image.

"Four pardon boards under different administrations have recommended me for release. I've realized since then that that ain't the real problem. That ain't my problem. I don't have a problem with the pardon board. The problem is political, and it's with the governor, and it's with the reality that requires a governor to have some degree of moral courage. And unfortunately Louisiana has never been noted for that, except for Huey Long; he had moral courage, but it was laced with a substantial amount of insanity.

"Don't ask me why Louisiana does things the way it does. Like the pardon board, they consider recommendations. Nobody in prison can appear personally before the pardon board; a lawyer represents them. Anybody that's being judged, I'd want to look him in the eye; he may con me, may show me one thing and be another, but I want to *look* at him. Parole boards do that, but not pardon boards. They go by records,

Wilbert Rideau (right) with James "Black Mattie" Robertson. Robertson holds the record for the longest confinement in the Louisiana Penal System.
(Photo courtesy *The Angolite*.)

recommendations, files, everything on paper. And they are forced by law to notify the DA and any victims or other interested officials who might want to oppose clemency, so they can appear in person. The deck is stacked against you, the way it is.

"As far as the history of Lake Charles goes, I'm the only person the district attorney has ever opposed before the pardon board. Frank Salter and Dora McCain are always at the pardon board hearings to oppose me and tell them if I get out, the walls of Jericho will come tumbling down. But you know what? When *20-20* was researching their story on me, they wanted to get a grasp on the feelings in Lake Charles and they talked to local newspaper editors and some of the powers that be, and they were told that people there thought it was tragic that a handful could create a national image of the entire community as being bloodthirsty against my release, though maybe it used to be so; they said today if Wilbert Rideau were released, only a handful of people would be real upset and you could count them all on one hand, and you could lead the pack with Frank Salter and Dora McCain.

"Why Frank Salter still? He's a good politician, and I make good copy. If you know how the criminal justice system works, you know that in most cases, the selection of who the DA asks the death penalty for has a lot to do with what kind of newspaper copy that defendant makes. District Attorney Frank Salter is a very influential, very powerful lawyer. He represents the unions, and that's been the base of his power for the longest. He started actively opposing me in 1976, when he was embroiled in controversy over labor violence at the Jupiter Chemical Company construction site in Lake Charles. Some people got killed and injured, and it was implied he had something to do with it; later on he was recused from the case because the higher courts felt he had let the guilty parties off the hook or something.

"The U.S. Congress was investigating him on allegations of intimidating witnesses at a federal grand jury hearing in 1981, with Senator Orrin Hatch of the Senate Labor and Human Resources Committee on union corruption calling the Lake Charles area a mess. Besides, the *Reader's Digest* had come out with a story on Frank Salter and the Lake Charles union troubles, implying that local law enforcement agencies refused help during labor violence unless kickbacks and payoffs were made and union featherbedding was allowed and pre-approved firms like Salter's own construction company were hired. So down there where his power base was, the DA needed some diversion to show he was an all-right guy fighting for law and order.

"It was during this period when he was catching so much flak that he started actively opposing me. I mean, he went to the pardon board hearing with cameras; they had never allowed that before in the history of the pardon board. That had always been against the rules, but he was able to kick the rules over. But then you have to understand that he was a big supporter of Edwin Edwards, and this was Edwards' administration and the pardon board knew it. So today you get cameras in the pardon board compliments of Frank Salter, who needed a diversion.

"It was *20-20* which discovered that during his last campaign Edwin Edwards had made a commitment to the victim. At least they *say* to the victim. You have to understand that the victim's attorney, in any dealings with Wilbert Rideau, is Frank Salter, who was the district attorney prosecuting Wilbert Rideau in 1961. Frank Salter is a very powerful attorney who has close ties with Edwin Edwards. So who did Edwin Edwards really make the commitment to, the victim or Frank Salter? Naturally, being a lawyer, Frank Salter wouldn't claim credit for it. You're talking about subverting the system, so what lawyer is going to claim credit for that? What they're doing is saying conveniently that the governor made a commitment not to free me to the victim, because that sounds better. Of course, after it came out, Edwards said he hadn't promised he wouldn't turn me loose, he'd just promised he would take her sentiments into consideration.

"You're not supposed to do that in America. You don't make promises behind closed doors in America. America don't promise you happiness, it don't promise you wealth. There's only one promise that America makes to everybody, to every citizen, and that's that you will be treated fairly and equitably to the extent possible by the government and its agencies. That's all. That's the only promise America makes, to treat everybody fairly. And what they did runs counter to everything. How would you feel if you had an accident and filed a lawsuit and went to court, and afterwards you found out you had lost the lawsuit because the judge had promised the other side he wasn't gonna let you win no way. It's the same thing, you see. That is not in keeping with what this country's all about.

"Plus, Edwin Edwards clearly did not give that kind of consideration or promise to all the other victims or relatives of victims of criminals he pardoned. He pardoned a whole bunch over objections. It's almost a given, anytime you're talking about reducing a sentence or giving a pardon to a guy who's committed a murder, you're talking about over the opposition of the family. It's a given that they're gonna oppose him, and they always do.

"But for the system to work, you've got to treat everybody the same. If you're going to have any semblance of justice, you've got to strive for basic fairness. Traditionally the system has asked that you demonstrate that you've changed, that you're no longer the same person you used to be. That's always been the traditional official criteria for clemency or parole or whatever. 'Course we know unofficially part of the criteria is influence or money or whatever. That's the way the system works. The system isn't supposed to, but it operates on anonymity, influence, sometimes money, and whim. Just plain whim. Just like Edwin Edwards turned me down and released several hundred murderers, all on the grounds of rehabilitation.

"I'm rehabilitated. All the wardens in this place for the past twenty years have said I'm rehabilitated. I mean, even Governor Edwards said I was rehabilitated. He told a whole news conference, a room full of reporters, that he believed I was rehabilitated and if it was up to him, he'd turn me loose, but he had an obligation to the community. Well, so did Pontius Pilate. That's the way he thought, that's his kind of justice; it's not subscribing to the larger standard of justice. When you talk about community sentiment, really what you're talking about is mob rule. It's the same thing. Rather than do justice, you're gonna just surrender to the mob; that's local sentiment. Well, you get Barrabas, Christ going on the cross. 'Course I'm not Christ. But it's the same principle involved, the same kind of justice. It's *not* justice. And if you're gonna do that in all cases, then you no longer have a system.

"Edwards released over two hundred murderers, and only a couple of them had served more time than me. Whether they did more to show they'd changed than I did, I don't know. Hell, I changed, whether you believe it. Whether you feel I'm conning or whether you feel like it's legit, you have to admit it's day and night. It's that kind of change, day and night, that's the contrast, and if it's a con it's the best one going because it's lasted thirty years through hell or high water, and that's hard to do. Edwards was one of those who said I was one of the most rehabilitated men in America, but he's not gonna tell you that today; the secretary of corrections said it, the pardon board said it, newspaper editorials said it, wardens said it. These wardens here run the system and all of them over the past twenty years said release Rideau. They watch me twenty-four hours a day, they see me when I'm high, they see me when I'm down, they see me when I'm in dangerous situations and how I react to them and how I handle them. And if you can't trust them, who do you trust? If you can't trust these experts' opinions of who's safe to let out and who's not, then you just as well go 'head on and pour concrete over the system, because if it doesn't work for me, it doesn't work for nobody else, neither.

"Justice in America ideally, I know it's idealistic, it's not supposed to have anything to do with race or creed or color or social status or political influence. It's not supposed to have anything to do with that. But we do know that rich people don't get executed; we do know that rich people don't go to prison. We ain't got none in here, so you have to conclude that either they're all saints out there on the streets never doing wrong or else the system works for their good and there are some inequities someplace. But that's the nature of life. I'm not complaining. The world was here long before I got here, and it'll be here long after I'm gone, and it'll be the same world. I mean, the world I grew up in I understand is not that much different from the world today. It's just that a long time ago I felt it intensely. 'Course I didn't have a grip on reality; now I understand that's life.

"If there weren't problems and the society wasn't divided by race, it would be divided by religion; look at Beirut and the Mideast, Ireland. We find reasons to mess over people. I guess if you removed all the other reasons, it would come down to shoe size, big-feet people against little-feet people. That's life. It's wrong, but if you look all over the world, it's a natural part of the fabric of human existence, whether you're talking about the untouchables in India or wherever. What can you do? You're one little bitty person. You may not like it, but this has existed since the beginning of man, and it's gonna exist until the end of man. You can't save the world, but you can save that little area around you. That's all anybody can do. This is the basic nature of the world, of life as we know it. And you got to accept it, well not so much *accept* it as adjust to it.

"You accept it, depending on what your moral fabric is, what you think is right or wrong, but you don't let it beat you out of shape and turn you into one of the animals too, simply because you got other animals roaming the jungle. Right here in the penitentiary, it was bloody down there and you had animals roaming around, but I wasn't gonna let myself become one too. I mean, I had been one once; that's enough. That was too much in one lifetime. I wasn't gonna let this place dictate to me who I'm going to be, what I'm going to be, how I'm going to live, no. I wanted to be a writer, so I'd sit over there in the cellblock shower after everybody took a shower; I'd sit over there on the bench and go to typing.

"Whatever you want to do, you've got to stick to your dreams of right and wrong and what you believe, otherwise you're nothing. I mean, some of these guys in prison say if you don't get out there with a knife, you're not a man. But that's not my way. If you're not true to yourself and what you feel is your purpose and mission in life, and I *do* have a mission, then what's the sense of it all? I mean, why bother going through all this mess, why not go ahead on and jump out the window? Whether it's for me or for you, it's the same thing. It's just like Martin Luther King said, if you don't have something you believe in enough to fight for and maybe even die for, then you have no reason for living, what are you living for?

"Things ain't been working out for some time in here, and I've been holding onto that, even though this is probably the worst place in the world to try to hold onto dreams. I've held onto it for thirty years; I don't see any change. It's like the concrete you walk on; it's *me*. It's not something like a notion or an idea I got. It's so woven into my personality and my psychology after all these years until I ain't got no choice. I gotta be the me that's talking to you right now, whether it's here in Angola, whether it's in New York City, regardless, because it's me. That's the real me. If I'd been anything else, I wouldn't have survived this long. You don't survive on ideas; you survive on *you*, what makes you tick. You survive drowning because you know how to swim. Swimming is not an idea. You either know how to do it or you don't, one of the two. That's just the way it is.

"I think things will work out, and if they don't, I mean if you cut it off sharp right now right this minute, if Wilbert have heart seizure right here in front of you, I haven't done what I wanted to do, my life hasn't been the way I wanted it to be in all the ways that are important to me, what I consider important in life in terms of family and love and normality, in all those ways I guess I'm a failure because I'm in prison and I don't have those things. I mean, I'll never know grandchildren, that's dead, even if they let me out of here right now I wouldn't have any because I'm not gonna live that long. In all those ways I'm a failure. But on another level I can be satisfied with my life so far, with one regret. I can be satisfied with what I've been able to do with my life, proud of the way I've lived it for the past twenty-eight years. I don't have anything to look back in shame on other than my crime. I've been the best person I'm capable of being. I know that, even if the rest of the world doesn't, and in the final analysis you're happy not because other people think you're a great person but because you think so.

"I know I've done well, even if I don't have a bank account. Let's see, what I got here?...$26.32 in my account. Even if I don't have riches, even if I don't have the ability to party all night and all those other measures of success, I don't have a Mercedes and in fact I just got me a pair of Brogans the other day, that doesn't have anything to do with it. You can't take one of those things with you to the grave anyway. You learn what is important in life and what is meaningful, and what isn't. And if success in life on a different level is taking what God gave you and expressing your appreciation for the gift of life by using it and living it and showing you appreciate it, I did that. I mean, what life really boils down to is one long continuous test, testing you and seeing what you do with it. I passed the test. I know I've done well. If it's a race, I've run well, maybe didn't come out the winner but wasn't the loser neither. I came out good. I'm satisfied. I feel good about myself because I know I've made a difference. That's what I set out to do and I know I did it.

"I'd like for there to be more. But if there ain't, I'm satisfied. I realize that things may not necessarily pan out the way planned. Life rarely works out that way for anybody, because life is a whole series of compromises for the best of us. I may not become a successful bestselling author out there; I may just become an old mediocre author. I'm not gonna be a *starving* one because I'm practical; I'll get a job first. But that's OK. The way I look at life is I've done all this, I was given a bad period here and I did good, and even if I have nothing but a nine-to-five job out there paying mediocre wages, to me it balances out nicely. I mean, for the first time in my life, I'll be able to really enjoy what I've yearned for more than anything else in my life, and that's normality. To the average individual, it's sort of taken for granted, because it's natural to you, you've been knowing it all your life. I've *not* known it. To me it would be a joy. It would be like waking up in paradise. It doesn't necessarily mean that all the flowers bloom or that the air is fresh; it could be polluted. It don't matter; it's still a paradise to Wilbert.

"At a point in time when most people are kind of dull on life and taking things for granted and tired, this will be all fresh to me, a new adventure. It may be old hat to somebody out there my age; they've lived life and they're probably bored with a lot of it. Not Wilbert. Wilbert is just getting started and he loves it. I don't have any kids, what would I leave money to, so why pursue the almighty dollar? I think the more important thing is living life in a way you can be proud of. I've got one thing, only one, and I think in a way I'm ahead of most people in that, I've only got one thing I'm ashamed of. I tried to do good; I gave it my best shot. And that's what I'm gonna do with my books and everything else, give it my best shot and take it as I get it and be thankful.

"I speak to a lot of groups and kids involved in a criminal court program in New Orleans and different places. A lot of people along the way have helped me, and I feel an obligation to help other people. Maybe that's what they mean by good always comes around. If I get half a chance, as long as it won't hurt nothing, if a guy walks through that door with an idea or a problem or whatever, I'm gonna help him. Sometimes they burn you. Sometimes they run games on you. Administrators aren't the only ones get con games run on them; they run con games on me, and sometimes they embarrass me. But the only thing I ask is that if I help you and it turns out well, you help somebody else. Keep the circle going.

"The governor is aware that I have job offers; some of the people have personally talked to him about it. I'd like to become a writer, and have just finished co-editing a University of Southwestern Louisiana textbook on corrections. But part of the price of being a convict is people don't like the idea of you going out there and doing too well. There's a publisher who wants me to work in his organization, another who wants me to help him create a new publication in New York, and I've got offers to write books. I've been getting movie offers since 1979 and have so far as of today not signed any piece of paper; I have consistently refused them in the past. I'm dealing with a public short of understanding, and I'm mindful of what they'll think about it. I'll just be another hardworking person out there on the street, except that I have an immense amount of hard-earned knowledge and experience that I can put to use in books and whatnot to benefit society in the long run and help other people.

"On *20-20* they showed a nonfiction book I wrote on Death Row on the mind of the criminal. That was gonna be my legacy, what I was gonna leave after they shot the juice to me, to let them know that they weren't *wrong* but I wasn't exactly everything they thought I was either, that there was a little more to Wilbert Rideau than the crime indicated. I wrote two novels, too. That's what I really want to do, write fiction. When I got off Death Row, I got into journalism and got to liking it, realized the power that goes with it and the opportunity to make a difference. Very few people in prison have the opportunity to really make a difference, so I just put my all into journalism and put everything else on the shelf. And I'm satisfied with what I did.

" If I died tomorrow and never saw freedom, I'm satisfied not with my whole life but with what I did with the latter part of it. It was in the ditch. My starting point was as low as anybody's gonna get in society. In a situation where society wants to kill you, everybody's against you, that's as low as you can get. I've managed to move away from that and to some extent redeem myself and also make a difference. *The Angolite* has done a lot of individual stories that have helped, but the biggest thing is that this magazine has withstood all the changes in corrections directors, wardens, supervisors, security officials and all, and it's still chugging right along without being adversely affected by any of it. That says a lot about the strength of it. Usually changes of that magnitude affect everything.

"The shortest story I ever did that had impact was way back in 1976 or '77, a little paragraph on this blind white guy out at the hospital, and the pardon board turned him loose. 'Course next time we did something about a blind dude, we had to spend about 30 pages telling about it, and it took about a year before they turned him loose. Things have changed; a paragraph don't turn people on now. We did the "House of the Dying" article about terminal cases in the hospital, and half of them are gone that were in the story. We ran "The Longtermers" about forgotten men with terribly long sentences, and a lot of them are gone. And I'm gonna tell you something else, a secret that's not a secret, a substantial number of the bigger corrections stories you read in the newspapers across the state come out of right here.

"Even before I went to *The Angolite* and was doing some other writing, Warden Henderson told me I could write for any publication I wanted, he didn't care; he said if a company out there on the street was foolish enough to want to enter a contract with an inmate, a contract they could not enforce, then that was their business. I asked him if I had to submit anything for approval first, and he said no, that was between me and the company, whatever I wrote. What he was doing was making me the first censorship-free inmate in the country. I didn't have to submit nothing to nobody; I'd write for the *Shreveport Journal* or *Penthouse*, drop the article in the mail and send it to them and they'd send me my check. That was a unique situation, which I don't believe existed anywhere else.

"By the time I started editing *The Angolite* in 1975, the earlier Wilbert Rideau and the new Wilbert Rideau were two totally different things. I no longer saw any enemies in life other than Wilbert Rideau. I mean, I recognized that I've only ever got one real enemy in life, like most people have in life though we rarely realize it; our own worst enemy is always ourself. The thing that did that was when I was sitting on Death Row. See, as long as I was in jail, I was the same old me, but when they brought me up there, when I was in that cell, the thirteenth man on Death Row, I never in my life reached a point of despair like I did there. I don't know what it was; it was like a lifetime of everything just sunk in right there. It was just like everything was reduced to ashes, like nothing, just like jelly. That's where the rebuilding started. I realized the gravity of the situation, and it all sunk in, not like just snapping my fingers because it was more than just a minute. There wasn't no flash of light or nothing like that. It was just a period, beginning with when I sat on that bunk in that cell, just started thinking, started realizing.

"This was a period of revelation for me, because keep in mind I saw things in black and white to begin with. White was the enemy, black was us, and it was us against them. There was a period when it began dawning on me that white people may have done a lot of things to me, and a white world may have, but they were also the ones trying to save my life, too. You expect your enemy to try to kill you, and you expect your family and people of like identity to stick with you, and then you realize it don't work that way. People are individuals, and it ain't got nothing to do with color. I had this clear image, the way I saw life and people, and it just went to smithereens. That's life, and you've got to judge people individually. I guess I really was born right there on Death Row.

"See my ring? That's an Angola rock mounted in there. I could be president of the United States and that ring would still be on my finger so I would never forget where I come from. I don't ever want to forget where I come from. Most people do. I *don't* want to forget, because I was born here, I was raised here, and whatever I am to do and whatever I'm gonna be in the future, it's because of this. I happen to be one of those people who've benefited from being in prison. When I say benefited, I'm not talking about that it's been easy, that I walked in and it's all been ice cream and peaches, because it ain't. I suffered. I *still* suffer. Life is miserable. But while a lot of people are crushed by adversity, some people are strengthened by it, some people may define themselves by it, some people thrive in it because of the challenge to overcome it. I guess I'm one of those people.

"I couldn't do anything about the past; I couldn't do anything about the fact that I didn't handle my life right in the past, but that's over and done with. All I've got left is the future. I can handle that. Ever since I was born, which was back in 1962 on Death Row, I had another shot at it. I was always trying to educate myself on Death Row, and everyone would say, 'Man, you don't need no education for the electric chair.' That's true. But for whatever it was worth, I was gonna be the best Wilbert that Wilbert could be, corny as it sounds, regardless of whether I was gonna die in the electric chair. It didn't make any difference. I was gonna be the best me I could, for my sake and because I owe a lot of people. I got a big obligation, one that I feel.

"And once I got a shot, when they commuted my sentence and let me off Death Row, most of the guys around here will tell you they rarely see me angry or flustered or messed up. The reason is that I have an advantage over everybody else in the world, because no matter how bad things get, I can always say, 'It ain't that bad, Wilbert, remember you wasn't even supposed to be here to be experiencing this.' A problem? Great, I get to experience it. I wasn't even supposed to be here to experience it. I don't believe the Lord created a problem he didn't give us a solution to; you just have to hunt for it, that's all, and too many of us don't know how to hunt.

"It wasn't that I was helped by any specific programs or methods. I got help along the way in terms of people who cared, people who were generous, people who would smuggle books to me in jail, I'm talking about *deputies*. Remember, this is the enemy; back then it was all white deputies, you didn't have blacks working on the forces. Same thing at the penitentiary. The people I expected, given my perception when I was a kid, to dump on me and hurt me, some of them *did* do it, believe me some of them did it and made my life miserable, but the flip side of the coin is that a lot of them tried to help me. Some of them saw things in me that Wilbert hadn't even seen yet. And I guess whatever I am today is attributable not to some collective effort but to a whole bunch of individuals who happened to be at the right place at the right time when I needed them the most and were willing or cared enough to help me out in whatever way I needed at that particular point in time. They were just individuals. That's the reason, when I go to colleges and am talking to kids and they ask what difference one person can make, I tell them you *can* make a difference. It made a difference with me, starting when I hit bottom on Death Row.

"It was a reversal of roles. I was in the same position, perversely enough, that my victim was in. For the first time in my life, maybe not the *first* time but the first time in awhile, I was feeling everything. Everything was opening up. You realize how you feel, and you're haunted by your victim, knowing that however bad you feel, she must have felt worse. And that does something to you. And everything else, knowing who you let down. My mom, hey, she was a victim too; I let her down. And over a period of time, sitting there, I also thought about suicide, but I realized that it wouldn't accomplish anything. What I needed to do more than anything was to redeem myself. Because I'd just let too many people down, including Wilbert Rideau. Suicide is just throwing a towel in, that accomplishes nothing.

"I'm a fighter; I'm gonna try to make it right. If I do something wrong, I'll try to make it right, because that's just the way I am. That don't mean I could ever *do* it, but hey, at least I want the credit for trying. Part of my faith is that I believe that if you subscribe to a hereafter or whatever, to a judge greater than you or anything on earth, a lot of people believe that the sheet gotta be white or black, gotta be clean or antiseptic, and you're gonna be judged on how many times you went to church and how many times you dropped nickels in the collection box and all that; well, I believe differently. I believe we are created imperfect. We are so imperfect that our creator, He's not looking for us to be perfect, He just wants to see if we're gonna try. I think that's what we're all gonna be judged on, if we *try*. Yeah, He knows we're gonna fall on our faces in the mud, but He's gonna give us credit just for trying. That's my hope and my salvation; if I ain't got that, I'm in trouble. And when we stand in that big courthouse at the end of the line and everybody's walking up there for judgment, I can't walk up there with a clean sheet or nothing like that, but I want Him to at least be able to look at me and smile and say, 'I understand, Wilbert, at least you *tried.*' That's all I want."

If anybody has ever tried, Wilbert Rideau has, for nearly three decades. If anybody has ever had the right to ask "How much is enough?" Wilbert Rideau has that right.

In his eloquent plea for clemency presented in 1978 before the pardon board, Wilbert Rideau wrote, "Who remains unchanged by Experience as he journeys through life? What adult can compare the person he is now with the person he was as a teenager and honestly say that he has not changed, that he has remained the same, unaffected by the passage of Time, Crisis, Experience and Education? My survival of this experience—indeed, my ability to transcend the pain of it—my growth and my accomplishments, stand as a monument to my self-discipline, my spirit, my desire and determination to improve myself and do something meaningful with my life, my triumph over doubt, hate and the forces of despair and madness. I have been tested to the breaking point as few men ever are and have never been found wanting. Indeed, I have emerged from a cauldron of pain an improved individual for the experience. What more is asked of me? To move mountains? Separate seas? Conquer unconquerable worlds? Am I to be a god? Or merely a man? Have I not suffered enough? How many tears? How much pain? How much sorrow is demanded to balance an hour of rage and rebellion? I come before you, having spent half of my life being punished, suffering. Yesterday is lost to me forever and today is insufferable. I ask you gentlemen to give me Tomorrow."

In an addendum to that original clemency plea, presented before yet another pardon board in 1984, Wilbert Rideau clarified his hopes and goals still further. "My only hope for sanity and salvation," he wrote, "lay in my transcending it all, refusing to become embittered, and striving to make something of my life in spite of it all. It has become important to me to make a success of my life. It is a kind of atonement for my crime, part-payment on a debt that can never be paid, and the only avenue of social redemption afforded me by society. And I owe the best that I can give of myself, not only to the community of Man but also to my victims so that their pain and loss will not have been for nothing. I deeply regret what I did, but no words of apology are adequate and there are no avenues to express the sincerity of my feelings except through deeds—what I do with my life...Having been punished all of my adult life for the crime of my youth, I now seek a second chance at living in the community of free men, an opportunity to do something productive and meaningful with the remainder of my life that will enable me to earn forgiveness from society, favor with God, and peace with myself."

How much *is* enough?

The Warden Comments: The long, long case of Wilbert Rideau points out the absolutely vital necessity of removing politics from prison policies and establishing a reasonable minimum-time framework after which deserving inmates no longer judged a danger to society must be considered for release by a professional board of parole or pardon, thereby giving inmates hope and an incentive to change by taking advantage of beneficial institutional programs.

This is especially needed in the state of Louisiana, which these days is handing down inordinately long sentences. "Life" in this state means a full lifetime behind bars, whereas even in other conservative Southern states like Mississippi, "lifers" can be considered for parole after serving less than ten years. In Iowa, sentences are handed down for "not more than five years," or "not more than ten years," with a professional parole board dispensing early releases only to those inmates who have earned them by good behavior and demonstrated rehabilitation.

In most states, in fact, an individual on a life sentence can be considered for parole after an established minimum number of years served, which does not mean that he will necessarily *be* paroled, but only that his case will be reviewed and his release based on merit and self-improvement, with politics playing no part in this process. Even in cases where there has been a lot of notoriety and objection from the community where the crime was committed, we should still consider release and appropriate placement outside that particular area or even outside the state.

The governor is a political animal, especially in this state, and no one ever won any votes releasing inmates from the penitentiary. Therefore it isn't fair to the governor or to the inmates for the burden of release for those not eligible for parole to be placed on the gubernatorial office, but in Louisiana any deviation from the prescribed sentence set by the court must be initiated by the governor. Any commutation, any pardon, even any restoration of citizenship is an executive function. In some states the restoration of citizenship is routinely awarded inmates leaving prison; in other states, it is a local judicial function entailing the mere completion of an application form. The granting of pardons has an unfortunate propensity for becoming a political issue in Louisiana, though many of the pardons here are given to those long since released from prison, solely for the restoration of citizenship and the right to vote or bear arms.

Everybody is against crime, even prison inmates; they do not want anybody stealing from them, they do not want anybody raping their wives, they do not want anybody molesting their children. The general public is certainly sensitive to the fear that has been generated from many quarters, and politicians find no more effective platform upon which to run than "get-tough-on-crime." Unfortunately this has had the result of lengthy sentences absolutely out of proportion to the crime and prison populations without hope of release. And a prison population without hope is a time-bomb waiting to go off.

Nothing has a longer history of failure than the field of corrections, and indeed, the corrections system seems to have become more punitive than ever during the last three decades. Sentences have become longer, yet perversely are less effective, with prisons serving primarily as what Ramsey Clark calls "Factories of Crime." Perhaps, as the late Dr. Karl Menninger has suggested, we of the general public *need* criminals to vicariously relieve our own guilt feelings, serving as scapegoats upon whom we can self-righteously displace our own submerged hatreds, hostilities and fantasized crimes.

Louisiana's imprisoned population has risen 124 percent in the last decade, leading to problems with overcrowding, staff shortages, inadequate facilities and insufficient funds. What are we doing about this? Building more prisons. Instead, we should be looking at ways to cut crime, keep first offenders from turning "pro" and rehabilitate those already in the prison system who prove themselves deserving and desirous of rebuilding their lives in more productive ways. Society is best protected, really, if an individual is released from prison equipped to become a productive self-supporting, tax-paying citizen.

How can we do this? In-prison educational programs are one way, though most effective of all would be to reach potential offenders before they enter the prison system at all. Louisiana District Judge Robert Downing, who finds that most juvenile offenders appearing in his court read only at a third-grade level, cites statistics on state penitentiary recidivism, showing that as high as sixty-nine percent of inmates released within the last decade subsequently re-entered the prison system. Those inmates benefiting from vocational educational programs in prison, however, had a greatly reduced recidivism rate of fourteen percent, and of that latter group, those eased back into society through a half-way house or similar supervised program had only a four percent rate of recidivism, an impressive indication of success.

But instead of exploring and enhancing his potential, our prison system keeps the man who has made a mistake at his worst, not only in Lousiana but across the country. Virtually unlimited power over prisoners has tended to corrupt those who serve as keepers, while inadequacies in training programs and other beneficial influences inside limit inmate participation to those with shorter sentences, generally. In spite of this, and even without adequate professional guidance, time itself does solve a lot of problems, permitting perceptive prisoners to work through problems on their own toward more constructive attitudes. This is certainly true in the case of Wilbert Rideau, who seems to have rehabilitated himself with very little help from the system itself. Rehabilitation, after all, must ultimately come from within, as has been the case here.

Wilbert Rideau obviously had a thirst for knowledge coupled with a good mind and a determination to change. The first time I met him, he was on Death Row requesting something to read. There was no library at Louisiana State Penitentiary when I became warden; in the past, inmates condemned to death had traditionally been permitted to have only religious books such as the Bible in their possession. With the help of the State

Library system, we were able to establish a fine facility with a trained librarian, who could then make rounds on Death Row and among the outcamps, permitting inmates access to requested books. Wilbert read everything he could get his hands on, learning from each book; a ninth-grade dropout, he now tests at college level or above, largely due to his own efforts at self-improvement.

There were also only a few "on-paper" academic and vocational programs when I arrived at Angola, serving little useful purpose and with no accredited instructors; during my tenure, with assistance from the Department of Education, these programs were greatly expanded under qualified teachers, reaching many inmates. In a prison population where so many incoming inmates were functionally illiterate, designing academic and vocational programs to serve their needs was difficult, but not impossible. Our academic program was designed on two levels, one to remediate illiterate inmates and one on a higher level leading to GED high-school equivalency diplomas. In addition, we were able to develop an affiliation with LSU wherein prisoners were allowed access to correspondence courses at the university level, providing some challenge even to inmates like Wilbert Rideau.

Does rehabilitation work? My answer is a resounding YES. Common sense will tell you that to do anything constructive with a population that is ninety percent unskilled, sixty-four percent functionally illiterate, and another large percentage with mental problems, an intensive academic, vocational and counselling program is an absolute necessity. Personally I don't believe that rehabilitation in the real sense has ever been tried in this country, perhaps because the requisite public support has never been generated, though there have been some shortlived creative programs which have been shown to be effective. We are too concerned with retribution and punishment rather than rehabilitation; often we continue to punish even after release from prison. There are a number of professions and trades which are not open to released inmates with felony convictions, barber college being one example.

I have yet to see an individual, all things being equal, who did not have an interest in *something* if time was taken to determine through good testing programs his aptitudes, his interests and his needs. That is ostensibly what our prison classification system is supposed to do. In actuality, however, institutional needs usually come first, before we consider the needs of the prisoner. Ideally, we should develop a classification system capable of determining the appropriate setting to meet each individual inmate's needs while protecting other prisoners and the rest of society at the same time. It is my personal feeling, for example, that no correctional facility should be built housing more than four hundred prisoners.

Many times we hear the criticism that prisoners are "shooting angles," participating in programs only to enhance their records in hopes of gaining release. My feeling is that some of the beneficial aspects of the programs will rub off even on these reluctant participants, who should be allowed to work their way out. One cannot attend meetings of Alcoholics Anonymous or Narcotics Anonymous, for example, without absorbing at least some of the helpful messages of these beneficial programs.

At the same time, you cannot isolate an individual with the worst segment of society and expect him to automatically assume new and more socially acceptable values; he may conversely learn instead new skills to become an even better criminal. A mere hot-check writer may leave prison knowing how to crack safes, for example. Prisons should be used as a last resort, after trying other creative alternatives like victim restitution, supervised parole by trained professionals (it is cheaper to hire somebody to watch the perpetrator than to keep him in prison), halfway houses, work-release programs in which prisoners actually work their ways through prison, house arrest and other such programs. It would be interesting, from an economic standpoint, to compare the costs of housing one prisoner in the penitentiary for thirty years while his family draws public welfare support and other state benefits, as compared to allowing him supervised work-release in his community, where he can have access to local support services and contribute financially toward not only his own upkeep but that of his family as well.

When I first met Wilbert Rideau, I was impressed with his intelligence, though at that time he still had some hostility to work through. When the Supreme Court declared the death penalty unconstitutional and he was released from Death Row to the general prison population, Wilbert was assigned to the canning factory as a clerk but wrote me a note saying he had not been allowed to function as such, because of what he perceived as racial discrimination. Since he had been writing the whole time he was on Death Row and wanted to work on the prison magazine, *The Angolite*, before long I made arrangements for Wilbert to help there part-time and later was able to assign him full time.

Wilbert performed admirably in all his prison jobs, including work in the canteen and classification systems, but it has been as a prison journalist that he has left his mark, making meaningful contributions which have in some instances altered and improved the entire penal system of this country. He began his own *Lifers* magazine, contributed features to regional publications as perhaps the country's first inmate columnist, became the first prisoner to receive a Robert F. Kennedy Journalism Award as well as the prestigious George Polk Award, and turned *The Angolite* into a hardhitting professional magazine respected across the nation. As one of the administrators of the National Council on Crime and Delinquency commented, "From behind bars, Wilbert Rideau is contributing to the fields of criminal justice research and reform more than many eminent criminologists who are free to tap the ideas and information of dozens of colleagues."

During his tenure guiding *The Angolite* as its first black editor, the publication has garnered top honors from annual American Penal Press contests, been recognized more than once by the American Bar Association for outstanding public service in contributing to increased public understanding of the American system of law and justice, and been a final-five finalist for the prestigious National Magazine Award in competition with such big-time publications as *Scientific American*, marking the first time in history that a prison magazine had ever been nominated for this recognition and eliciting from the 9200-member American Society of Magazine Editors the comment that it was hoped Wilbert Rideau's "achievement will be recognized within the prison system as it is by his peers in the outside journalistic arena."

Rideau and Loren Ghiglione, at the time president of the American Society of Newspaper Editors.

Although I have been gone from the penitentiary for several years, I have remained in contact with Wilbert Rideau and have retained an interest in the outcome of his case. I have found him to be capable of great growth, both educationally and emotionally. At this time, he is a mature, eloquent and responsible spokesman for inarticulate inmates less capable of speaking up for themselves or their causes.

Mindful of his responsibilities to both inmates and administration, Wilbert has observed highly ethical journalistic standards, sometimes at no small personal danger, for as he has said, his readers are not the type to merely write letters to the editor in times of controversy, generally preferring a more immediate and physical response. Yet Wilbert has never exhibited any violent tendencies in his twenty-eight years in prison. As former Angola chief of security Walter Pence, no bleeding-heart liberal by his own description, has said, "Behaving in a responsible manner and doing what's right is not easy for a man living in the criminal and sometimes violent world of prison. The easiest thing for a prisoner is to simply be criminal. To be and do *right* requires considerable effort, courage and even sacrifice on the part of the inmate. Yet during all the years I've known Wilbert, he's always strived to do the right thing, and he did it in such a manner as to earn the respect of both prisoners and personnel."

Former classification director Kelly Ward agreed, describing Wilbert even a decade ago as "a model prisoner by anybody's standards. Rather than be defeated by his prison experience like so many others, he has turned it to his advantage, emerging from it a better man for the experience. His triumph over his personal problems and his experience in pain and misery is a study in the power of determination and says much for Wilbert's inner strength, self-discipline, intelligence and desire for something better in life. He has matured with the passage of time, and has obviously learned better and more effective means of pursuing his goals in life, which automatically enhances his ability to effect a productive and meaningful life for himself in a socially desirable manner."

It is my own considered professional opinion that Wilbert Rideau should have been released from the Louisiana State Penitentiary years ago. Until there is a change in correctional legislation, any governor of the state of Louisiana must of necessity find the courage to risk releasing deserving prisoners; unfortunately, not one of the administrations under which Wilbert has been imprisoned found that courage in his case. No one is being protected by his continued incarceration, and in fact the public is being victimized by having to pay unnecessarily for his keep. Society is also being deprived of the beneficial contributions which I feel sure he will make upon release.

2009 Update:

Wilbert Rideau's conviction was thrown out in 2000 by the US Fifth Circuit Court of Appeals on the grounds that blacks were excluded from the 1961 grand jury that indicted him. In 2005 he was retried and found guilty not of murder but of manslaughter, which carries a maximum penalty of 21 years. Having already served 44 years, he was instantly freed. His pro bono defense team consisted of attorneys Julian Murray of New Orleans, George Kendall of New York, Ron Ware of Lake Charles and (until he became too ill to continue) the late Johnnie Cochran.

Conclusion

C. Murray Henderson's work in military government with the German judicial system during the demanding period immediately following World War II left him with an abiding interest in corrections and a strong desire to make an impact in an area so rife with abuses. In 1979 as a guest of the Dutch government he had an opportunity to tour all correctional institutions in The Netherlands. There he found a unique criminal justice system different even from other European systems, providing a jury of judges rather than peers, a preventive certainty of punishment rather than inordinately long sentences, and a tradition of relocating released inmates to begin life anew in different locales free from the negative influences of the past.

Henderson was especially impressed that time spent in prison in The Netherlands was devoted to intensive counselling, vocational training, substance abuse programs or rehabilitative efforts tailored to meet each offender's individual needs. As the minister of justice there remarked to him, "We Dutch have always gone our own way; when the rest of Europe was burning witches, we developed a system at Gouda where one could be weighed and obtain a certificate certifying that person was not a witch." Since witches were characteristically weightless, the act of official weighing precluded many executions of witches in The Netherlands.

One day while Henderson was in The Hague, he witnessed the trial of certain members of an ethnic minority group from former Dutch colonies charged with dynamiting a train, resulting in loss of life. The sentence for this crime was seven years, surprisingly short by American standards. "I assumed that Parliament would rise up in indignation about the short sentence," he says, "but there was no objection. One after another member of Parliament rose to declare that more police protection was needed, however. The high concentration of police you see on the streets in compact European cities certainly has a benenficial impact in lowering crime.

"We could learn a lot from European criminal justice systems," Henderson continues. "We continue to incarcerate people by the thousands, our prison populations grow—it's the one real growth industry in this country—and our sentences are inflexible and interminable, when actually there are other sanctions which can be equally effective and less expensive in the long run. Required restitution to victims, for example, has a therapeutic effect on the perpetrator as well. Carefully screened work-release programs not only assist in gradually reintegrating low-risk offenders back into society, but prove effective in reducing the burden on the taxpayer compared to extended institutionalization. Prison industrial and employment programs can also lower costs while providing skills and work experience to enhance employability upon release. Cost-effective new technology can be used in supervised parole, house arrest and general administration of the overall process.

"The important thing, though, is to get to the *cause* of crime. Approximately sixty percent of those entering prison are functionally illiterate, though some may have somehow obtained a high school diploma without being able to read or write. Thomas Jefferson said, 'Man cannot be free and ignorant at the same time,' which applies doubly to prisoners, for if we release them from custody as uneducated and untrained as they entered prison, they will soon be back. Approximately ninety percent of prison inmates are unskilled. Some studies indicate that as many as fifteen percent of any prison population is actually psychotic, with another thirty percent manifesting psychiatric problems to the point of needing professional help. Depending on whose study you want to believe, as high as eighty percent of all crime is drug or alcohol-related.

"If any part of the above statistics is true, then common sense would dictate that at least part of the answer must start with decent educational programs tailored to meet the individual student's needs. Too often we hear teachers say a problem student "doesn't adjust to school." But what have the educators done to change a dull unchallenging curriculum to adjust to the student's needs? By what criteria do we assume that every child must learn trigonometry or Shakespeare? In this country it is time to develop a two-track school system on the European scale capable of enabling each student to develop to his fullest individual potential. School teachers must really become school *teachers* instead of school keepers who merely watch children seven hours a day. This is not to say that teachers must compensate for the deficiencies of the home, but the teacher may very well be the only positive role model in the life of a young student from a dysfunctional family or otherwise deprived background.

"I think for too long we've assumed that every young student was bound for college, and most of our education has been directed in the area. Really, the best time to start teaching trades is in technical high schools. This is only one example of the sort of preventive measures we need to pursue. If we really worked at meeting a child's individual needs beginning in kindergarten, perhaps one day corrections would be out of business.

"It is imperative that programs be developed that will enhance the individual inmate's self-image in a positive way while improving his literacy and vocational skills, significant factors in lowering prison populations. The results of such programs may be seen in states like Iowa, where the percentage of the population considered illiterate is extremely low and where the length of indeterminate prison sentences depends upon the inmates' verifiable efforts toward rehabilitation. Compare that with Southern states like Louisiana, where illiteracy rates are skyhigh and upwards of 368 persons for every 100,000 in the general population are incarcerated for inflexible lengthy prison sentences at state expense (it costs $25,000 a year to maintain each inmate in Angola), compared to a national average of 224 incarcerated per hundred thousand in this country, the United Kingdom average of 40 per 100,000, and a Swedish average of only 16 per 100,000. Here we hand down the longest sentences in the world, yet at the same time have the highest percentage of our population in prison of any country.

"In the United States we live in an open-class system, which within itself may create some problems and cause unnecessary anxiety. Through high-pressure advertising, children are bombarded with the message that they are deprived if their families don't own two television sets, two cars and other luxuries. What we are doing is creating an unrealistic desire for material things without furnishing the means to fulfill this desire. The disparity between what people want and what they can reasonably expect is one cause of widespread discontent and unhappiness which can precipitate delinquent behavior.

"Large consolidated school systems, now the norm, allow students to exist in near-anonymity, lacking the supportive personal interaction between student and educator which used to be so significant in smaller districts. Increasingly mobile populations and the decline of the family unit remove further support systems and can result in children failing to forge the all-important positive bonds of friendship with peers who may soon be left behind.

"Successful parenting is not necessarily a skill which comes easily to everyone, nor is it a skill for which training is readily available, unfortunately. Training in parenting skills, perhaps as a high school course, might help immeasurably in ending the seemingly endless cycles of child abuse or neglect. Recent studies indicate that child abuse can play a major part in the development of criminal behavior, along with deprivation, inadequate education, lack of training, poor self-images, substance abuse and other factors. Though there are undeniably some people who simply make conscious decisions to become criminals regardless of background or environment, prisons for the most part are for poor people, and eighty percent of most prison populations have at some period of their lives been known to the welfare department.

"Obviously, our prisons haven't been doing their jobs. We need to attract career workers to the field of corrections who are open to new approaches and are willing to search for workable answers. We must create an atmosphere where innovative new ideas are encouraged and will thrive; you can't be hidebound by tradition and expect to accomplish much. Nor can our goals be accomplished without public involvement and support; the general population tends by choice to remain insulated from the world of corrections, yet surely would not tolerate what goes on in our isolated prisons if they only knew.

"In the late 1700s the Quakers established what they called a penitentiary on Walnut Street in Philadelphia. Actually this was a treatment-oriented program, an attempt to change behavior. By all reports, it was quite successful, with an extremely low rate of recidivism. Inmates were not allowed to associate with other prisoners, so they did not learn additional tricks of the trade, and all they had to read was the ***Bible***. This drastic treatment might not have met with everybody's approval, but at least they were doing something.

"In actuality, there have been few improvements made in the system since then. Nothing has had a longer history of failure than the American correctional system, not because of any shortage of knowledge in the field, but rather a reluctance to apply it. Potentially beneficial programs are often postponed or scrapped altogether because of budgetary constrictions or fear of failure. Certainly what we have done in the past has not met with conspicuous success, yet we continue to rely on these same tired and ineffective approaches.

"We must find the courage to seek out new methods, maintaining a therapeutic attitude, trusting in man's ability to change, and above all recalling the humanity of those individuals whose lives we have the responsibility to salvage and improve for the protection of society and the ultimate benefit of us all. "

Anne Butler

2009 Update:

Former warden C. Murray Henderson, ironically, would himself be convicted of attempting to murder his estranged wife Anne Butler in 1997. She survived; he died in prison.

Bibliography

INTERVIEWS

8-3-89 Wallace McDonald, Louisiana State Penitentiary at Angola (present: Anne Butler, C. Murray Henderson, unidentified guard)

8-9-89 Mary Margaret Daugherty Charouleau, Idlewood Nursing Center (present: Anne Butler and C. Murray Henderson)

8- -89 Two interviews with former 23-year Angola inmate Bob Colley (present: C. Murray Henderson)

8-22-89 WC & Adele Percy, telephone, St. Francisville, LA (Anne Butler)

8-22-89 Patsy Welch Dreher, telephone, St. Francisville, LA (Anne Butler)

8-23-89 Capt. C. C. Dixon, his home just outside the front gates of LSP at Angola (present: Anne Butler and C. Murray Henderson)

8-23-89 Hallie and Hazel Walters, their home/barroom, Tunica (present: Anne Butler, C. Murray Henderson, Hal Walters Jr.)

8-24-89 JoAn Spillman Oubre, her home, Morganza (present: Anne Butler, C. Murray Henderson)

8-30-89 Sheriff John C. Durio, his office, courthouse, Allen Parish (Oberlin, LA), (present: Anne Butler, C. Murray Henderson)

8-30-89 Robert L. Thomas, Clerk of Court, courthouse, Allen Parish, Oberlin (present: Anne Butler, C. Murray Henderson)

8-30-89 Harold Hudgins, The *Oakdale Journal* (former photographer for Oakdale Beacon, 1962), Journal Office, Oakdale, LA (present: Anne Butler, C. Murray Henderson)

9-4-89 Capt. C. C. Dixon, his home at the gates of LSP, Angola, and his son Bert Dixon at the free store on Angola, regarding photo identifications (present: Anne Butler, C. Murray Henderson, Mrs. C. C. Dixon)

9-6-89 Nola Faye Cole, her home, Kinder, LA (present: her boyfriend, Anne Butler, C. Murray Henderson)

9-6-89 John Navarre, attorney for Abel Ortego, his office, Oakdale, LA (present: Anne Butler, C. Murray Henderson)

9-6-89 Mamie Reed, mother of Gerald Fontenot, Kinder Apts., Kinder, LA (present: her daughter, Anne Butler, C. Murray Henderson, assorted children in and out)

9-6-89 Judge Ed Mouser, attorney for Anita Ortego, his home, Oberlin, LA (present: his wife Anne, Anne Butler, C. Murray Henderson)—off the record

9-7-89 Dallas Bertrand, retired state trooper, his office, City Hall, Oberlin, LA (present: Anne Butler, C. Murray Henderson)

9-8-89 Warden Hilton Butler, Angola, by phone (C. Murray Henderson)

9-9-89 Russell Sonnier, brother of Gerald Fontenot, his home, Melville, LA (present: Anne Butler, C. Murray Henderson, Russell Sonnier's wife)

9-9-89 Claude Gunnells, Angola security chief, his home, Melville, LA (present: Anne Butler, C. Murray Henderson)

9-24-89 Ponder Favor, Tommy Favor, Jane Favor, Atchafalaya Inn restaurant and Sheraton CentrePark Hotel, Arlington, Texas (present: Anne Butler, C. Murray Henderson)

9-25-89 James Bynum, City Hall and his home, Maypearl, Texas (present Anne Butler, C. Murray Henderson, city hall clerk, his wife Anne Bynum at home)

9-25-89 Mitzi Lucas Riley, by telephone, Arlington, Texas (Anne Butler)

9-25-89 Frances "Flaxie" Fletcher, by telephone, Arlington/Dallas, Texas (Anne Butler)

9-25-89 Ponder Favor, Janice Favor Kitterman, Italian restaurant and Sheraton CentrePark Hotel, Arlington, Texas (present: Anne Butler, C. Murray Henderson, Janice's boyfriend)

9-25-89 Dan Coats, by telephone, Arlington, Texas (Anne Butler)

9-26-89 Garlene Parris, Sheraton CentrePark Hotel, Arlington, Texas (present: Anne Butler, C. Murray Henderson)

9-29-89 Ron Wikberg, The *Angolite* office, Louisiana State Penitentiary, Angola, LA (present: Anne Butler, C. Murray Henderson, Wilbert Rideau)

10-4-89 Bossier Parish District Attorney Henry N. Brown, DA's office, Bossier Parish Courthouse, Benton, LA (present: Anne Butler, C. Murray Henderson)

10-4-89 Vol Dooley, retired Bossier Parish sheriff, telephone, Bossier City, LA (C. Murray Henderson)

10-4-89 Mac Richardson, Bossier Parish Sheriff's Office, Benton, LA (C. Murray Henderson)

10-18-89 Wilbert Rideau, The *Angolite* office, Louisiana State Penitentiary, Angola, LA (present: Anne Butler, C. Murray Henderson, Ron Wikberg)

10-24-89 former Louisiana governor Edwin W. Edwards, his office, Baton Rouge, LA (present: Anne Butler, C. Murray Henderson)

11-13-89 Douglas "Swede" Dennis, Wade Correctional Institute, Homer, LA (present: Anne Butler, C. Murray Henderson)

11-27-89 Joe Whitmore, LA State Police, Greenwood Plantation, St. Francisville, LA (present: Anne Butler, C. Murray Henderson)

12-28-89 "DJ," Holiday Inn Financial Center, Shreveport, LA (present: Anne Butler, C. Murray Henderson)

1-29-90 Douglas "Swede" Dennis, by telephone from Wade Correctional Institute, Homer, LA (Anne Butler)

BOOKS

Carleton, Mark T. *Politics and Punishment: The History of the Louisiana State Penal System.* Baton Rouge: Louisiana State University Press, 1980.

Maginnis, John. *The Last Hayride.* Baton Rouge: Gris Gris Press, 1984.

Menninger, Karl. *The Crime of Punishment.* New York: Viking Press, 1966.

Moody, William B. *In Jack's Favor.* Stephensville, Texas: Stephensville Printing Co., Inc., 1979.

Petersen, David M., and Charles W. Thomas. *Corrections: Problems and Prospects.* Englewood Cliffs, N. J.: Prentice-Hall, Inc., 1975.

Tattersall, Peter D. *Conviction.* Montclair, N. J.: The Pegasus Rex Press, Inc., 1980.

MAGAZINES

The Angolite, August 1971, September/October 1988, November/December 1988, January/February 1989, March/April 1989, May/June 1989.

Boulard, Garry. "Governor Won't Commute Sentence of Prison Journalist," *Editor and Publisher,* October 4, 1986.

Delaney, Joseph. "Prison Editor Proves Pen Is Mightier Than Sword," *NABJ Journal,* October 11, 1989.

Franklin, Karen. "Wilbert Rideau's Prison Prose," *Washington Journalism Review,* June 1989.

Graham, John, loaned by Dallas Bertrand, "Case of the Jealous Dr. Jekyll-Mr. Hyde—Louisiana, Many Moments of Pleasure, Hours of Horror," *True Police Cases,* December 1962.

Harrison, Stanley, loaned by Dallas Bertrand, "Woman Without Mercy," *Inside Detective,* October 1962.

"Inmate Journalist Gets His First State Award," *The Louisiana Weekly*, January 28, 1989.

"New Year, New Home for Jack Favor," *The Christian Ranchman*, January 1989.

Norwood, Joseph. "Rideau 1989," *Chainlink Chronicle, A Prison Magazine*, September 1989.

Potter, Joan. "A Louisiana Inmate Leads His Magazine Into the Big Leagues of Journalism," *Corrections Magazine*, March 1979.

Tomlinson, Kenneth Y. "Murder at Jupiter," *Readers Digest*, July 1977.

NEWSPAPER ARTICLES

BATON ROUGE *MORNING ADVOCATE*

10-20-48 "Distinctive Beauty Marks Large Afton Villa Tea Honoring Mrs. Earl Long"

10-21-48 "Search Still Pressed For Slayer of Wife of State Prison Officer"

10-22-48 "Posse Continues Big Manhunt For Prison Houseboy"

10-23-48"Search for Trusty Moves Into EBR"

10-24-48 "Reward of $500 Offered For Arrest Of Trusty"

10-26-48 "Posse Disbanded in Trusty Hunt, Search Continues"

10-31-48 "Body of Trusty Found in River at Morganza"

2-6-49 "Behind the Big Gates" by Margaret Dixon

4-7-78 "'Angolite' Contest Finalist"

4-12-78 "Angolite Is Finalist In Contest"

7-17-79 "Angola Inmate Cited by ABA"

4-1-86 "Most Murderers Serve Less Than 7 Years, Survey Says"

6-18-86 "Rideau to Continue Quest" by Douglas Demmons

3-2-88 "Editor of 'The Angolite' on Larry King Show" by AP

3-11-88 "Edwards Steps up Pardon Approvals" by Marsha Shuler

2-16-88 "EWE Reduces Shreveport Doctor's Sentence" by Marsha Shuler

4-29-89 "Roemer Should Release Rideau" by Kathy Morales, letter to the editor

7-19-89 "Convicted Killer Lived on the Lam Nearly a Decade" by John Semien

10-22-89 "USL Class Gets Look at Angola" by James Minton

4-20-90 "Roemer Won't Stop Prejean Execution" by Marsha Shuler

BATON ROUGE *STATE-TIMES*
10-20-48 "Angola Wife Slain; Hunt Pen Trusty"
3-7-51
4-3-51 "Angola Nurse Resigns Post"
7-4-51

NEW ORLEANS *TIMES-PICAYUNE*
5-29-36 "Youth Slain by Error, Two Accidentally Shot in Convict Chase"
2-26-51 "Angola Officials Deny Brutalities—Inmates Cut Heel Tendons As Accusations Fly" by E. M. Clinton
2-27-51 "Angola Inmates Cut Other Heels—'Heel String Boogie' Goes Into Second Verse"
2-28-51 "Long Invites 27 To Probe Angola—'We Have Nothing To Hide' Says Governor"
"More Convicts Slash Heels As Angola Troubles Spread"
3-9-51 "Prison Nurse Calls A 'Sewer Of Degradation'—Penitentiary In Dark Ages, Probers Told," by E. M. Clinton
4-20-51 "Prison Reform Steps Proposed—Citizens Group Agrees On 20 Recommendations," AP
3-1-84 "Senator Calls For Indictments in Lake Charles" from wire reports
12-19-84 "Prison Editor Considered For Clemency" by Jason DeParle
5-10-86 "A Rare Exception" editorial
1-26-89 "La. Clergy Reaffirm Efforts to Aid Poor" by Sheila Grissett
3-30-89 "Prison Journalist Lectures Students on the Real Thing" by Keith Woods

ST. FRANCISVILLE (LA.) *DEMOCRAT*
10-22-48 "Mrs. Spillman Killed"
1-28-88 "Angolite Wins First Place in Nation"

THE OAKDALE (LA.) *JOURNAL*
June 1962 through May 1963 issues

SHREVEPORT TIMES
April 18, 1964 "Bossier Bait Stand Owner, Wife Slain"
April 25, 1967 "Seven Jurors Picked For Favor Trial"

April 26, 1967 "Jury Picked In Murder Case"

April 27, 1967 "Murder Trial Witness Given Severe Grilling By Defense Lawyer"

April 28, 1967 "Jack Favor Denies Any Connection in Murders, 2 Hours on Witness Stand"

April 29, 1967 "Favor's Fate Still Hangs in Balance"

April 30, 1967 "Ex-Texas Rodeo Star Convicted in Dual Murder, Sentencing Set"

May 22, 1967 "Favor May File Motion For Retrial"

May 23, 1967 "Motion Asks Retrial of Jack Favor"

June 6, 1967 "Jack Favor Files Plea for Retrial"

April 11, 1974 "Two Testify in Trial of Favor"

April 12, 1974 "Favor Trial Hears Four State Witnesses"

April 13, 1974 "Deputy Says Favor Implicated By Cumbey in Richey Murder"

April 14, 1974 "Dooley Testifies for State in Re-trial of Jack Favor"

April 16, 1974 "Cumbey Testifies in Favor's Trial, Says He Was Lookout"

April 17, 1974 "New Line Voiced At Favor's Trial, Pointing To Cumbey"

April 18, 1974 "State Rests Its Case Against Jack Favor, 1964 Double Murder"

April 19, 1974 "Favor Defense May Rest Today"

April 20, 1974 "Jack Favor Acquitted," "Jack Favor Is Acquitted in Death of Mrs. Richey"

SHREVEPORT JOURNAL

12-29-77 "Inmate Newspaper at Angola Wins National Press Award" by James Burns

12-29-77 "Lifer Is Editor of Angola's Prize-Winning Newspaper"

2-1-85 "Edwards A Year Later: Paroles and Pardons Difficult" by Stanley R. Tiner

7-25-86 "Edwards Weighs Opinions on Prisoners"

8-14-87 "Wilbert Rideau, Free Mind, Imprisoned Body," by Matthew J. Jacobs

3-14-88 "Rideau's Case Shows Mercy in LA is Only For Sale," letter to editor from Ted Quant, Institute of Human Relations, Loyola University, New Orleans

6-15-88 "Wilbert Rideau—Still in Prison, Still Writing, Still Waiting" by Matthew J. Jacobs

12-9-88 "Inconsistent Justice—Why Does Wilbert Rideau Remain in a Louisiana Prison?," editorial

SHREVEPORT SUN

1-31-80 "The Eleventh Hour: An Account of a Black Man's 20-Year Fight For Freedom" by Andrew Harris, editor

5-15-86 "Edwin Edwards and Political: The Rideau Case is Re-Opened" editorial

7-10-86 "Justice By Popularity Poll" editorial

12-15-89 "Institute Blasts Roemer For Failure to Release Rideau" by Andrew Harris, editor

HOUSTON CHRONICLE
5-22-88 "Jack Favor: bloodied but unbowed"

DALLAS MORNING NEWS
10-8-89 "Inmate Journalists Put Prisons To The Test" by Todd J. Gillman

LAKE CHARLES AMERICAN PRESS
2-17-61 "Bank Robber Faces Charges"
2-17-61 "Crime Story Recounted By Rideau"
2-17-61 "Youth Captured After Murder, Bank Robbery"
2-17-61 "Car Make Error Delays Capture"
2-17-61 "Two of Three Bank Hostages Alive After Fate Takes Role"
2-17-61 "Story Unfolds On Two Survivors"
2-17-61 "Final Rites For Mrs. Ferguson Set Saturday"
2-17-61 "Bank Robbery News Enlivens Bankers Meet"
12-22-84 "Edwards Says 'No' To Rideau"

THE DAILY REVEILLE, Louisiana State University
11-14-86 "The Politics of Murder" by H. Clay Ward

LEGAL REFERENCE BOOKS

FEDERAL SUPPLEMENT, LSU Law School Library, 348 F Supp 423, rev. 472 F2nd, 1382; Jack G. Favor PMB 65386 v. C. Murray Henderson, Warden, LA State Pen., Civ. A. No. 17628, US District Court, WD La., Shreveport Division, May 16, 1972, Supplemental Opinion 6-2-72, Order Directing Supplementation of Records 8-11-72

COURT RECORDS, CORRESPONDENCE AND OTHER REFERENCES

Bossier Parish Courthouse, Benton, LA, transcripts of Jack Favor's two trials 1968 and 1974.

Fact Sheet, Institute of Human Relations, Loyola University, New Orleans, on Wilbert Rideau , 5-88.

Support Letter for Wilbert Rideau, Institute of Human Relations, June 1988.

Wilbert Rideau's Clemency Plea to Board of Pardons, June 10, 1978.

Wilbert Rideau's Clemency Plea to Board of Pardons, December 12, 1984.

North Mississippi Rural Legal Services Notes, "Dateline: Prison!" by Joseph Delaney, 9-10-88.

Black Radio Exclusive, "KLSP-FM: The Incarceration Station" by Bill Quinn, Hollywood, CA, 5-27-88.

Support Letter for Wilbert Rideau to Pardon Board, Walter Pence, 12-7-84.

Louisiana State Penitentiary Classification Profile, Subject Wilbert Rideau #75546, 10-27-75.

Support Letter for Wilbert Rideau, American Society of Magazine Editors, 5-10-78.

Support Letter for Wilbert Rideau, National Council on Crime and Delinquency, 6-19-81.

Index

www.ingramcontent.com/pod-product-compliance
Lightning Source LLC
LaVergne TN
LVHW082333200926
848481LV00012B/3335
* 9 7 8 1 9 3 5 7 5 4 5 5 8 *